In the First Country of Places

SUNY Series in Environmental
and Architectural Phenomenology
David Seamon, Editor

In the First Country of Places

Nature, Poetry, and Childhood Memory

Louise Chawla

STATE UNIVERSITY OF NEW YORK PRESS

Published by
State University of New York Press, Albany

© 1994 State University of New York

For information, address State University of New York
Press, State University Plaza, Albany, N.Y., 12246

Production by E. Moore
Marketing by Nancy Farrell

Library of Congress Cataloging-in-Publication Data

Chawla, Louise.
    In the first country of places : nature, poetry, and childhood
memory / Louise Chawla.
        p.   cm. — (SUNY series in environmental and architectural
phenomenology)
    Includes index.
    ISBN 0-7914-2073-6 (HC: acid-free). — ISBN 0-7914-2074-4 (PB :
acid-free)
    1. American poetry—20th century—History and criticism.
2. Children in literature. 3. Psychoanalysis and literature.
4. Psychology in literature. 5. Memory in literature. 6. Nature in
literature.   I. Title.   II. Series.
PS310.C5C43 1994
811'.5409—dc20   93-41811
                                                                          CIP

10 9 8 7 6 5 4 3 2 1

16595

Contents

Preface

This book is about poetry, memory, and relationships to nature. As a developmental and environmental psychologist, most of my research involves the development of environmental attachments, environmental concern, and the characteristics of places that best serve children's needs. In this book, I have stepped back from this pragmatic involvement in children's issues to ask a life-span question: "When people grow up, what personal significance do childhood memories of the natural world retain?" The research reported here has raised this question with five contemporary American poets: William Bronk, David Ignatow, Audre Lorde, Marie Ponsot, and Henry Weinfield. It examines these poets' different uses and evaluations of childhood memories depending upon their philosophies of nature and forms of writing.

Why, as a psychologist, have I gone to poets with this question? There are a number of compelling reasons. For one, the largest body of literature that casts light upon this question is in literature itself. It is the work of poets and novelists. Psychologists have been assiduously studying the mechanics of memory for many years. The mechanics of a thing, however, have little to do with its personal meaning or significance. The long-range significance of experience has been the concern of psychoanalysis; but this field has concentrated upon exploring unconscious significance. In relating childhood to adulthood, it is fair to argue tacit connections; but a limitation of any argument of this kind is that findings must be phrased in the theoretical vocabulary of the theory maker, as the meaning of experience is assumed to be opaque to the people described. For ourselves, the significance of our past is what we know. Its personal significance must be personally defined. No matter how many ways our past may affect us, for us its meaningfulness derives from conscious experience, as we interpret it in our own terms. Therefore the question adopted here has been: "Consciously, what significance do people attribute to memories of nature? How do they value them, in their own words?"

To anyone familiar with the field of phenomenological psychology, it is evident that this question falls within its domain. Phenomenology seeks to understand the everyday world of lived experience in the words in which people present themselves. Therefore this book can be described as a phenomenology of environmental memory.

Personal words of feeling and meaning have always been the language of literature. Long before Edmund Husserl originated phenomenology at the beginning of the twentieth century, imaginative literature had been observing, analyzing, and describing the meaning of human experience, including the autobiographical significance of places. From the time of Romanticism, childhood and a child's encounter with the physical world have been important literary themes. Therefore the largest treasury of records of environmental memory exists here.

There is a second critical reason for my having brought my questions to poets. When environmental professionals speculate regarding the lived meaning of environmental experience, they often cite poets, or other professionals who have derived ideas from poets. Their references, however, often omit the tradition of beliefs and the historical experience that poetry reflects. To evaluate the ideas, it is necessary to understand this context.

One of the most widely cited examples of this rule is Edith Cobb, a philanthropist and social worker who was encouraged and aided in her research and writing by her close friend Margaret Mead. This book was prompted by Cobb's observations. Emphasizing the importance of encounters with the world during middle childhood, Cobb summarized the results of a lifetime of autobiographical research in a suggestive statement:

> In my collection of some three hundred volumes of autobiographical recollections of their own childhood by creative thinkers from many cultures and eras, ranging from the sixteenth century to the present, it is principally to this middle-age range in their early life that these writers say they return in memory in order to renew the power and impulse to create at its very source, a source which they describe as the experience of emerging not only into the light of consciousness but into a living sense of a dynamic relationship with the outer world. In these memories the child appears to experience both a sense of

> discontinuity, an awareness of his own unique separateness and identity, and also a continuity, a renewal of relationship with nature as process.[1]

This connection between creativity and childhood experience has been cited within anthropology, human ecology, geography, landscape design, natural science, education, and poetry itself as evidence that environmental experiences in childhood make lasting contributions to adult creativity.[2]

This claim has intriguing implications. If it is correct, it traces a line of influence in which the nature of the places that creative thinkers encounter as children, and the nature of their encounter, profoundly affect the course of their thought as adults. Their thought, in turn, affects the course of our culture. For these reasons, I have repeatedly returned to reconsider this statement.

My own attempts to reexamine this theory have suggested that it must be broadly qualified. Sometimes it seems to hold. Sometimes it does not. The qualifications that I have found form an engrossing story in themselves.

Cobb advanced her theory as a universal rule: that it is the experience of all children, and that all creative thinkers draw upon it. When I began to investigate the origins of her thought, her own creative sources began to appear more particular than universal. Her book *The Ecology of Imagination in Childhood* quotes Wordsworth.[3] Her collection of autobiographies, which she deeded to Columbia University Teacher's College, predominantly record nineteenth-century British childhoods. Although Cobb drew upon many streams of thought, if the dominant tradition behind her review of memory must be assessed in one word, that word would be "Wordsworthian."

To reexamine Cobb's claim, I did a content analysis of thirty-eight autobiographies by twentieth-century men and women from diverse backgrounds, who made their way in the world in diverse fields.[4] This review disclosed that ecstatic memories of "a living sense of a dynamic relationship with the outer world" were described only by autobiographers who were either artists themselves or amateurs of the arts, who encountered places characterized by a multilayered sense of freedom. These people were privileged to have known an open beckoning world, whether they ranged city streets, forests, or fields; a world they could appropriate as their own; where they felt comfortable; where they could explore at will free from supervision or constraint. This finding comes at a time when writers about children's environments habitually lament the loss of just such places.[5] Rural open spaces, undeveloped lots, and streets that are moveable feasts of people are being built up or taken over by traffic and other dangers. Between the environmental conditions of children of the past and most children today, there is a great distance.

Since Cobb advanced her claim within the poetic tradition of Wordsworth, I have reopened its assessment within this tradition. The people who appear in this book are poets, like Wordsworth, but the world around them has changed. For twentieth-century American poets, there is no valley of Grasmere, such as he had, either to grow up in or to retire to. Within a changed landscape, at a different time in history, writing a different poetry, what significance do childhood perceptions of the world retain?

If the essential concern that has motivated this book must be compressed into one sentence, it would be, "Today, does citing Wordsworth work?" With five contemporary American poets, the following study explores the question of whether childhood environmental memories continue to be creatively drawn upon, and how they are.

This preface is like most in that, although it comes first, it was in fact written last. It is forethought recollected in afterthought. An earlier preface draft was written, but by the time research for this book as a whole was completed, it had to be discarded. This original version assumed that the major determinant of memories' significance would be the qualities of remembered places themselves: whether they were beautiful or bleak, welcoming or fearful, expansive or confined, and free or circumscribed. It assumed, further, that reading and interviewing the five poets studied here would primarily gather what my discipline has called "environmental autobiography"—detailed reminiscence of well remembered places. What occupied the interviews instead, in response to the poets' own interests and emphases, was the general role that childhood memories of nature played in their poetry, depending upon their philosophy, literary theory, and style.

This outcome brings up a third good reason for conducting this research with poets. They tend to be well informed regarding our culture's heritage of thought about nature, childhood, and memory, and to be observant of cultural changes. In one way, published American poets are a very specific group who cannot be taken as representative of a vast unpublished population. In another way, however, their personal distinctiveness as intellectuals and writers is balanced by the communicative representativeness that their role assumes. Tuned in to words, they are attentive to meanings that a larger population shares. They pick words up and spread them further, actively contributing to the common pool of signification that all people of their period draw upon. Therefore the discussions of childhood memory presented here may prove a sensitive indicator to representative trends it is now taking.

Through their intellectual reflectiveness, the poets studied here have made a fourth special contribution to the development of this research. In their writing, they define their place within the world and how they see the world; and one of the decisive factors that shapes their perception has been the influence of science. In defining their own perspective, each of these people has found it necessary to evaluate scientific approaches and conclusions regarding human relationships to nature. Therefore as I have worked with them, I have had to become self-aware of my own conduct of social science. By necessity, this work has been more self-critical, more attentive to history, more responsive to the need to reconcile the sciences and humanities, than psychology has traditionally been. Fortunately, it is written at a time when the need for such a transformation is increasingly heard among science's practitioners as well as critics.

In formulating their views on environmental memory, these five poets represent different poetic traditions and different philosophies regarding memory, childhood, and nature. Therefore in addition to being a phenomenology of five individual perspectives of environmental memory, this book serves as a study of the contexts of these perspectives—or a hermeneutics of memory. As much as the pages that follow may be less of an environmental autobiography than I first anticipated, they have become more of an intellectual and cultural history.

Acknowledgments

As a study that crosses the boundaries of disciplines—psychology and literature—this book owes its existence to the encouragement of many people. Although there is currently considerable rhetoric about the value of interdisciplinary research, its practice, I have discovered, faces many hurdles. Therefore I am especially appreciative of the people who showed faith in this project, keeping my own faith in my work alive.

When I first conceived of this study as a graduate student in the environmental psychology program at the City University of New York, I was encouraged from the outset by my advisor, Leanne Rivlin. Other people who gave advice and support at this time were Kathy Christensen, Roger Hart, Joe Glick, and Marvin Magalaner. This project could never have begun successfully, however, without the contribution of Allen Mandelbaum. Poet and translator himself, he gave me introductions to his friends who became participants in this study: David Ignatow and Henry Weinfield, and through his friend Jane Cooper, Marie Ponsot. He also introduced me to Elizabeth Sewell: poet, translator, novelist, and literary historian. It was his recommendation that she review with me literary traditions regarding childhood memory and poetic inspiration. In an afternoon's talk often punctuated by the phrase, "You might take a look at . . . ," she generously filled this role.

Once this research was underway, the five poets who have took part each furthered it, sharing not only their time and thought but also their friendliness. I hope that the following pages adequately reflect the respect that I feel for their thoughtfulness and their work. With the poet Henry Weinfield, the dialogue begun at this time has continued. As one of his fields of scholarship is British Romantic literature, I owe him particular thanks for keeping me on track in this area.

When I began this work, I was warned that it would be difficult to find a press that would take a risk with such interdisciplinary material. In the field of memory research, I was encouraged to persevere by Ulric Neisser and David Rubin. The manuscript also benefited from the reading and helpful advice of Tom Greeves, Kenneth Olwig, and Lynda Schneekloth. Its coming into print, however, is primarily due to David Seamon, who created a refuge for work that bridges the sciences and humanities through the State University of New York Press Series in Environmental and Architectural Phenomenology. David invited this book's inclusion, and provided the combination of direction and freedom that forms an author's editorial ideal.

At the press itself, Carola Sautter and Elizabeth Moore have given reliable support, for which I am grateful. In preparing the manuscript for publication, I am indebted to the Kentucky State University Faculty Research Fund, which provided for the word processing of the original draft, and to Carla Collins, who did this work quickly and accurately. Evalyn Verhey, in the university's graphics department, designed the figure that illustrates the Romantic model of development. Whitney Young College, the university program within which I teach, absorbed many of the miscellaneous expenses incurred in preparing the manuscript for press. The university's computer service staff repeatedly helped me in a field in which I am not literate. Its library staff cheerfully tracked down material to keep me literate in what are—for me—more accessible fields. All of this help has been invaluable.

Research carried out within a setting of home and family traditionally gives thanks to family members for patiently putting up with the researcher's absences and lapses. Now a veteran participant observer of this situation, I can verify that this tradition of gratitude is founded on real life events. Without my husband Devendra, who has encouraged this research and this researcher along, this book would not be. Without my daughter Ambika, its topic—memory of childhood—would not be nearly as meaningful, or as pleasant, to reflect upon. As for my own memories, my uncle and aunt who brought me up, Donald and Marguerite Miles, gave me the sustaining childhood and many beautiful places that motivated me to take up this topic.

Introduction

In this book, environmental psychologist Louise Chawla explores the relationships among poetry, nature, and childhood memory. What meanings, asks Chawla, do people attribute to recollections of the natural world and, especially, do the environmental experiences of childhood contribute in a lasting way to adult understanding and creativity?

Most broadly, Chawla's book can be described as a phenomenology and hermeneutics of environmental memory. Procedurally, this topic might be explored in many different ways—through, for example, self-reflection, interpretation of autobiographical accounts, or in-depth interviews about childhood. Chawla's approach is innovative in that she explores the lives and works of five contemporary American poets—William Bronk, David Ignatow, Marie Ponsot, Henry Weinfield, and the late Audre Lorde—as they speak about childhood, memory, and the natural world. Procedurally, Chawla conducts her examination through a careful reading of each poet's poetry and other written work; through studying critical commentaries on each poet's work; and through interviews and discussions with each poet.

Chawla strikingly demonstrates the great variety of ways in which the five poets understand and experience the natural world, both as children and as adults. William Bronk and Henry Weinfield, for example, see nature as infinitely greater in time and place than human beings, while Audre Lorde and Marie Ponsot believe that human existence assumes an integral connectedness to all things, including the natural world. Yet again, David Ignatow describes a world that, though in continual flux far beyond the control of humankind, offers a supportive resonance between nature and imagination.

In illustrating the diverse ways in which the five poets interpret the meaning of nature and its recollection, Chawla convincingly demonstrates that her work has central relevance for a comprehensive psychology of memory. First, she illustrates how, in various ways, the five poets call into question or provide variations on the still-prevalent Romantic notion, most perceptively articulated by poet William Wordsworth, that children experience a special sense of wholeness with nature and that this wholeness leaves a lasting adult impression. Second, she uses the poets' presentation or recollection to illustrate the reductive conception of memory that current positivist psychology holds. She calls for a radically different developmental theory that would find a fitting place for all the diverse meanings that childhood and adult experience include.

To provide one avenue for this new theory of memory, Chawla draws on the developmental phenomenoloy of Swiss philosopher Jean Gebser, who spoke of five different modes of human consciousness that, suggests Chawla, provide a conceptual means to integrate childhood and adult sensibilities into an existential whole. In using Gebser's phenomenology in this way, she provides the groundwork for a comprehensive model of human experience that ranges from the bodily and instinctive through the emotional and aesthetic to the intellectual, symbolic, and spiritual.

As the third volume in the SUNY series, "Environmental and Architectural Phenomenology," *In the First Country of Places* is important because it indicates the complexity and richness of the relationship between human beings and the worlds in which they find themselves. Especially, Chawla demonstrates how different understandings of nature and memory reflect different experiences of socialization and enculturation.

In the author's interview with Henry Weinfield, he explains that, "There is some way in which art brings us closer to *home*, whatever that is. And therefore to the world. It brings us closer to being." Chawla hopes that the five poets' understandings of memory and nature might provoke each of us to ponder their meanings in our own lives, both past and present, as we remember childhood and face ourselves as adults. In this way, we might strengthen our self-awareness and realize ways to open ourselves and grow.

DAVID SEAMON

Chapter One

Placing the Past

This book is an inquiry into how memory of childhood places and things endures and works its way into poetry. Its purpose is twofold: to attend to memory in poetry; and to hear, through poetry, how memory may work its influence in a multitude of lives.

The subject of environmental memory relates to all the fittings of the physical world that surround us: the natural world of animal, vegetable, and mineral, and the built world of human artifice. Its scope covers three dimensions of perception: individual objects; settings such as home, city, and region; and global moods or feelings for the world. These three dimensions—objects, settings, and moods—may be isolated for study, but in lived experience they are inseparable. Memories of single things evoke their settings. Settings evoke moods. Moods evoke settings and associated things. Remembering places is like scrutinizing a landscape painting. There are foreground, middle ground, and background; but which is which shifts, depending upon our point of focus.

This book explores environmental memory with the specific purpose of considering the influence of childhood experience. What do we remember regarding the world we knew as children, and what do these memories mean to us? How do we assimilate childhood places into our sense of self? In particular, how do we accommodate childhood experiences of the natural world into adult beliefs about our relationship with nature?

To explore these questions, I have turned to poets, because their reflections on this subject have become a cultural legacy. Childhood memory has been an important theme in poetry since the Metaphysical and Romantic literature of the seventeenth and eighteenth centuries. Our modern habits of autobiographical self-scrutiny and our emphasis upon childhood as a time of formative influence date back to this historical period. As poets such as Wordsworth developed the theme of memory, they claimed that children enjoy a special receptive relationship with nature, which leaves lasting endowments in maturity. Edith Cobb's observation, cited in this book's introduction—that autobiographers repeatedly return to childhood memories of nature in order to renew creative power—accords with this claim.[1]

The Romantic theme of childhood memory, however, took form under conditions that no longer exist. The pastures, forests, and farmland dotted by mines and mills, which composed the world of Romantic writers, have given way to massive industrialization and urbanization. By the year 2000, half of the world's population is projected to live in metropolitan areas.[2] Two hundred years after Wordsworth began his Romantic musing, people grow up in a changed world. I began this book after I discovered that Cobb's collection of autobiographies was written mostly by writers, musicians, and other artists who grew up in the nineteenth century and the first decade of the twentieth. Would poets who grew up after the First World War, I wondered, report the same resonant memories of relationship with nature? The central question that this book addresses is what has happened to environmental memory, and in particular memory of nature, under the changed physical and cultural conditions of the twentieth century?

Choosing Five Poets

To pursue this question, I decided to read and speak with contemporary poets who grew up under varied social and geographical conditions far removed from Wordsworth's Lake Country. If poets have been doing what we expect of them, I wondered—if they have been sensitive to their own experience and if they have spoken for many of us who are less articulate—what new stories about childhood have they been telling? Have they given us new words that we can use as we think, feel, and speak for ourselves?

I took these questions to Allen Mandelbaum, poet, translator, National Book Award winner, and teacher at the City University of New York Graduate Center, where I was pursuing a doctorate in environmental psychology. He gave me introductions to advisors and participants for interviews. One introduction was to Elizabeth Sewell, who guided me to sources of the Romantic concept of childhood and nature. Poet, novelist, literary historian, and expert on Samuel Taylor Coleridge and his influence upon Wordsworth, she was eminently qualified for this role. I met her at her home in Greensboro, North Carolina. In the course of the day that we spent together, I discovered that she had been a close personal friend of Edith Cobb and had followed the unfolding of her ideas. Sewell observed that Cobb was not only much indebted to Wordsworth, but deeply impressed by the English countryside—so much so that Sewell believed that whenever Cobb used the word "nature," she had the English landscape in mind.

British and unabashedly Romantic herself, Sewell astonished me—a young psychologist well schooled in contemporary developmental theory and scientific objectivity—when she threw back her head with ringing laughter at modern psychologists' analysis of childhood animism and their presumption that the earth and sky are not alive. She considered the "de-animation" of nature by empiricist science a temporary cultural aberration. Living in a garden apartment in urban Greensboro, Sewell herself had often pondered the significance of childhood in a changed world, and therefore she encouraged my inquiry. When I returned to New York, I read more about the sources of the Romantic tradition that she had outlined, and also investigated the history of contemporary developmental theory. The second chapter of this book comes out of this review.

Given this background, I was prepared to talk with contemporary American poets about their use of their childhood experiences of the natural world. In my choosing whom to work with, one criterion was diversity. I sought people whose residential, social, and cultural backgrounds represent some of our nation's contemporary diversity, and whose styles of writing represent some of the major divisions within modern poetic theory. At this point, Allen Mandelbaum came to my aid again, giving introductions to David Ignatow and Henry Weinfield, and to Jane Cooper, who recommended Marie

Ponsot. Cooper said that she would be happy to contribute herself, but that everything she would say about her rural Florida childhood would duplicate Wordsworth; and therefore, if I wanted a sympathetic but different voice, I should speak with Ponsot, a city poet who grew up in urban Queens, New York, and who still lives in the neighborhood of her childhood home. Weinfield arranged the interview with his friend William Bronk. Audre Lorde accepted an invitation by letter to participate.

These five poets evaluated their childhood memories of nature from five distinct perspectives. William Bronk expresses a Buddhistlike nihilism, a consciousness of the awesome void of nature that annihilates self-identity. David Ignatow describes changing orientations to childhood memory as he moved from youthful Transcendentalist enthusiasms to a stoic existentialism. Audre Lorde, of West Indian descent, reviews childhood according to her African heritage that she reconstructed. Marie Ponsot, a Catholic, works within her spiritual tradition. Henry Weinfield, the most scholarly of the five poets, gives Romanticism the most deliberate personal reappraisal.

In addition to their different philosophical perspectives, these five people represent different human conditions: three are men, two women; one is black, four white; three were raised in secure upper middle-class homes, two in struggling immigrant families; four have children of their own, one does not; one grew up in Harlem in Manhattan, three in quiet boroughs of big cities, one in a rural town. In age, they ranged from Weinfield, who was in his mid-thirties at the time of the first interview, to Ignatow, who was almost seventy. Through their distinctions in age, background, and belief, they express widely shared human circumstances.

In addition to this representative diversity, my other criterion in choosing these five poets was anticipation that I would find repeated reading of their work rewarding. In reflecting upon what made their work intriguing, I found a distinction made by the poet Denise Levertov applicable. In *The Poet in the World*, Levertov distinguishes poetry that is narrowly self-expressive from poetry that expresses, or reveals, the world.[3] The first, which is self-absorbed, tends to be autobiographical. The second may or may not be autobiographical, but it always examines the poet's relationship to the world and the significance of experience. Given that I began with questions about the significance of memory and nature, whether or not childhood explicitly appears in a poet's writing, it follows that I gravitated to poetry of the second kind.

In observing how these poets were chosen, I must note that "choice" is a double-pointed word. These people chose to contribute, finding their use of childhood memory a subject worth their time and reflection. All five extended an unhurried friendliness and courtesy in response to my questions.

Before meeting each poet, I read everything available that he or she had published: poetry, essays, autobiography, reviews of other writers, journals, letters. Where available, I also read interviews by other people and critical reviews of the poet's work. As I read, I formulated questions regarding childhood and beliefs about nature and memory. I formed an initial interpretation of the significance of the poet's childhood experience, which I prepared to test during interviews.

After I had completed reading and reflecting upon each poet's work, we met for tape-recorded interviews. Bronk was the only poet who lived outside the city of New York, so that I traveled to spend an afternoon with him in his upstate New York home. Given Lorde's full schedule of speaking engagements, she made time between trips to share a long lunch at a restaurant in Greenwich Village, a neighborhood she had frequented since adolescence. I met Ignatow and Ponsot for two interviews, he in his office and she in her home. Because Weinfield was in his thirties and his ideas were still in flux, I met him initially for two successive interviews at the City University of New York Graduate Center, and later shared two follow-up conversations.

Chapters 3 through 5 of this book come out of these interviews and my close reading of each poet's work. These chapters present these poets' accounts of the sources of their creative strength and the role of early memories in their life and writing, and they review how each poet has imaginatively shaped memories for use. The presentations are grouped thematically according to the orientation that each poet has described. In chapter 3, Bronk and Weinfield share an essentially common confrontation with nature. Lorde and Ponsot, in chapter 5, share an essentially common connection. Chapter 4 traces how Ignatow has moved from alienation from nature in mid-life to a resigned reconciliation.

By chance, I worked with these poets in the following order: Ignatow, Weinfield, Bronk, Ponsot, and Lorde. I interviewed the three men, followed by the two women. I listened with growing surprise to what the men had to say about childhood and nature. Their views challenge those of Wordsworth, as chapters 3 and 4 show; but I had anticipated these differences. What surprised me was that the relationships to nature and childhood that the men expressed contrasted so much with my own experience that at first I found them difficult to comprehend. My surprise was intensified, because I had never previously recognized these differences as starkly as this research forced me to do. I had grown up among men, gone to school with them, worked with them, and married one, always taking for granted that they experienced nature and childhood in essentially the same way that I did. It was not until I was immersed in the intensive reading and close listening that this research required that I recognized how deeply disparities may run. As this research proceeded, it demonstrated how feelings and beliefs determine the meaning of remembered places more than do physical qualities, important as physical qualities may be.

When I came to the reading and interviews with Ponsot and Lorde, I found myself back in my familiar world again. At the end of their interviews, I was able to talk about the differences I had observed between our self-understanding as women and the men's experience. Both women had raised sons and daughters, and were already sensitive to these differences. Chapter 6 presents my attempt to articulate the distinctions that I discovered and Lorde's and Ponsot's attempts to account for them. Both Lorde and Ponsot find themselves in sympathy with the Romantic image of childhood and nature, but this male tradition contrasts with their experience in some respects. Therefore chapter 6 discusses the women's alternative forms of relationship to nature and childhood at length.

None of these five poets laughed at prevailing psychological theory as Elizabeth Sewell had done; but all of them initially met my introduction as a psychologist with something varying between slight alarm and quizzical reserve, warming to their subject as they found that I was familiar with their work and with poetic tradition in general. All of them, I found, believe that psychology distorts and diminishes human experience by forcing it into the sterile language of jargon. Therefore in working with them I had to reassess the language that I had learned as a psychologist, as well as psychology's explanations of children's relations with places and things. Whereas chapter 2 traces the historical origins of dominant developmental theory in psychology, chapter 7 suggests how theory can change to accommodate the diverse perspectives of childhood and nature that emerged in the course of this research, in a language that enlarges rather than diminishes human experience.

The Language of Memory

In seeking to understand why the subject of environmental memory has been prominently explored in literature but largely neglected in psychology, I concluded that the poets' concerns about language were well founded. The language of contemporary psychology is based upon presuppositions that exclude the full-bodied memory of places of personal significance. Poetry, in contrast, appeals to these memories. This observation may be best explained by the following five examples.

In the following texts about memory, note their use of words and their assumptions about time and place. Three of these passages are by poets, one by a psychologist, and one by a literary critic. They represent the different literatures that I searched for past research and reflection regarding the long-term significance of remembered places; and they suggest why I found little relevant material in the psychology of memory or literarary criticism, but an *embarras de richesses* in poetry. The passages are presented in the historical order in which they were composed.

The origins of Western thinking about memory are oral and mythic. In the eighth century B.C., the Greek poet Hesiod related the myth that memory gave birth to the nine muses who inspire tragedy, comedy, dance, music, sacred song, epic and lyric poetry, history, and even astronomy, the apex of ancient science. According to this myth, memory is a great power, a Titaness, daughter of Gaia and Uranus, earth and sky. She is the source of all civilized arts, enabling us to talk about the present and the future as well as the past. For Hesiod, this myth was local history, for the muses chose for their dwelling place Mount Helicon, famous for its fragrant plants and cool springs, on whose slopes, legend has it, he kept watch as shepherd. Near the beginning of the *Theogony*, Hesiod recorded the muses' story:

> Come thou, let us begin with the Muses who gladden the great spirit of their father Zeus in Olympus with their songs, telling of things that are and that shall be and that were aforetime with harmonious voice. . . . Them in Pieria did Mnemosyne, goddess of Memory, who reigns over the hills of Eleuther, bear of union with the father, the son of Cronos; they bring a forgetting of ills and a rest from sorrow. For nine nights did wise Zeus lie with her, entering her holy bed remote from the immortals. And when a year was passed and the seasons came round as the

months waned, and many days were accomplished, she bare
nine daughters, all of one mind, whose hearts are set upon song
and their spirit free from care, a little way from the topmost
peak of Olympus.[4]

Twenty-five hundred years after this mythic account, in the
early nineteenth century, the German poet Goethe stood up at a
dinner party to protest a toast which had praised memory as a static
image of the past. For Romantic reasons, he reaffirmed a conception
of memory as the mother of creative inspiration, but rather than
making it an external power, he described it as a power integral to
human beings:

> I do not recognize memory in the sense in which you mean it.
> Whatever we encounter that is great, beautiful, significant,
> need not be remembered from outside, need not be hunted up
> and laid hold of, as it were. Rather, from the beginning, it must
> be woven into the fabric of our inmost self, must thus live and
> become a productive force in ourselves. There is no past that
> one is allowed to long for. There is only the eternally new,
> growing from the enlarged elements of the past; and genuine
> longing always must be productive, must create something
> new and better.[5]

In mid-twentieth century, the poet William Carlos Williams
created a modern epic, *Paterson*, out of the material of his time and
place. In the following fragment, he identifies memory with the
falls of the Passaic River, whose banks he tramped as a boy. Between his boyhood in the late nineteenth century and the 1950s, he
watched his native New Jersey landscape suffer cataclysmic change
as it went from pastoral farmland to urban industrial wasteland. In
the waterfall, a constant configuration of movement from his childhood through old age, Williams found a metaphor that reaffirms the
mythic and Romantic tradition that memory can bring renewal.
Like Hesiod, he invested memory in an external power, but like
Goethe, his words suggest that he considered it an integral human
accomplishment:

> The descent beckons
>   as the ascent beckoned
>   Memory is a kind
>   of accomplishment

> a sort of renewal
>
> even
>
> an initiation, since the spaces it opens are new
>
> places[6]

Writing after Williams, in the 1970s, the literary critic Barrett Mandel reworded Goethe's and Williams's rejection of a static past in more radical terms. In his words, memory is no longer a productive force "growing from the enlarged elements of the past," nor a power of renewal. In keeping with late twentieth-century literary criticism's emphasis upon language as the primary human reality, to be constructed and deconstructed, Mandel made memory purely mental, a fictive verbal creation:

> The past . . . never really existed: it has always been an illusion created by the symbolizing activity of the mind.[7]

Also writing in the 1970s, the psychologist Henry Ellis defined memory in another set of mental terms. Behind his definition lies an empiricist tradition that goes back three hundred years. Ellis's image of memory as a data-processing system for encoding, storing, and retrieving information echoes John Locke's seventeenth-century phrase that memory is "the storehouse of our ideas."[8] Ellis describes memory atomistically, as pieces of information—as it has been for research purposes since Ebbinghaus studied the retention of nonsense syllables one hundred years ago. In a popular review text, Ellis defined the main processes that contemporary research has identified:

> Memory refers to storing information and to accessing or retrieving information. *More generally, memory encompasses three basic processes: encoding, storage, and retrieval. . . . Encoding* refers to arranging information so that it can be placed in storage. The process of encoding includes modification of information such as selecting certain features for storage. . . . *Storage* refers to storing information in the memory system. The fact that we can remember information for days, weeks, or years implies that information is stored. *Retrieval* refers to the process of accessing or getting at the stored information. Information may be stored in memory, but storage is no guarantee that we can get at the information. All three processes are part of memory, and thus it follows that a failure in any one of the processes can lead to a failure in memory.[9]

For the purposes of this book, the critical observation regarding these five passages is that they assume different relations to time and place, which implicate different uses of language and memory. These differences illustrate why autobiography and the imaginative literature of poetry and fiction stand almost alone in their examination of the significance of environmental memory.

Placeless Memory

As psychology and literary criticism have usually been practiced, it can be said that they have no place. As chapter 2 reviews, when the foundations of modern science were established, the philosopher René Descartes explicitly boasted that his consciousness had no place. In different ways, the passages by Mandel and Ellis continue this tradition. Both authors employ a language of abstractions, in the literal sense of the Latin root *abstraho*, "draw away." They draw thought away from particular people, places, and things in order to speak in universal generalizations.

Mandel's claim that the past is an illusion created by mental symbols takes the present out of the body and deracinates its connections to physical places and things. In the tradition of the later work of Wittgenstein and the deconstructionism of Derrida, Mandel's position privileges linguistic activity over physical knowledge. Finding meaning a web of words rather than something inherent in embodied experience that words seek to express, this tradition of linguistic and literary criticism does not acknowledge that qualities of places may have intrinsic significance. As Mandel says elsewhere, the present creates the past "by inspiring meaningless data with interpretation, direction, suggestiveness—life."[10] Applied to places, the implication is that, here too, human consciousness gives life, in the sense of order, direction: places do not have "a life of their own."

Later in his essay, Mandel argues that memory becomes organized around a theme, in the sense of a vital principle of character and personality that gives human life narrative structure. I have accepted this argument; and in chapters 3 through 5, I have looked for the autobiographical themes that organize how five poets use memories of nature. Given a focus on words rather than relations with the world, however, Mandel, as well as other critics in his analytic tradition, have nothing to say on the subject of place memory itself.

I also reviewed psychological research on memory, which Ellis summarizes. This work, I found, has a paradoxical relationship to place. It belongs to the empiricist tradition of Hobbes, Locke, and

Hume that privileges sensation as the primary form of knowledge. In this sense, this research emphasizes physical experience, but only as it is measured by the objective quantitative instruments of the laboratory. Applying this standard, psychologists have inventively manipulated different conditions to assess the accuracy and quantity of people's memories vis-à-vis verifiable physical facts. This empiricist standard has been so pervasive that it has influenced literary criticism, which has been predominantly preoccupied with analyzing how autobiography departs from factual verity.

Because sensation occurs in the present, empiricist psychology, as much as linguistic analysis, has been locked into a time scale of isolated successive instants of mental processing. This sensationalist approach, however, is even less equipped than linguistic analysis to explore people's interpretations of memory. Ellis's text, for example, devotes more than fifty pages to a review of laboratory research regarding the mechanics of memory, but includes no line on research into the long-term significance of remembered places and events.

There are a few exceptions to this research pattern. In the 1920s, Frederic Bartlett performed experiments on people's perception and memory of meaningful pictures and stories.[11] He found that, from the outset, people attend to things selectively and that what they notice varies with social background, interest, values, and age. He also observed that once material is encoded into long-term memory, details quickly become stereotyped and organized around a theme that persists indefinitely—a discovery that supports Mandel's claim that each human life has a theme that organizes memory. Other researchers have noted that accessible memories do not become numerous until the age of five or six, after children have acquired language and learned the routines of everyday life.[12] Rubin, Wetzler, and Nebes found, nevertheless, that people recall more events from childhood and young adulthood than from more recent middle age.[13] Comparing autobiographical records by women and men, Herrmann and Neisser observed that women tend to have more memories about childhood and to value them more highly than do men.[14] Despite this useful general information, as I searched the vast psychological literature on memory, I found nothing directly relevant to my questions about the significance of remembered places.

Placeless Language

Psychology has also been predisposed to neglect the meaning of places because it has adhered to the empiricist tradition of word use. As Hobbes noted in 1640, "by the advantage of *names* it is that we are capable of science," but names come in two kinds.[15] Some words, Hobbes noted, are equivocal and inconstant, referring to passions, opinions, sentiment. Others are unequivocal, propositional terms. Hobbes established that science must only use bare denotations of the second kind. In keeping with this rule, Ellis begins his review of memory research by strictly defining his terms. The consequence of this tradition is that psychologists have been interested, for example, in whether people can name from memory items in a room or buildings on a street, but not in the sentiments or passions associated with them.

Bound within the empiricist tradition as it is, contemporary psychology has ignored the personally construed significance of memory. In 1978, the cognitive psychologist Ulric Neisser reviewed the existing literature to satisfy an interest in "real uses of memory in humanly understandable situations." He balefully concluded that, "If X is an interesting or socially significant aspect of memory, then psychologists have hardly ever studied X." In contrast, he suggested:

> What we want to know . . . is how people use their own past experiences in meeting the present and the future. We would like to understand how this happens under natural conditions: the circumstances in which it occurs, the forms it takes, the variables on which it depends, the differences between individuals in their uses of the past.[16]

Partly in response to Neisser's criticism, there is now a thriving study of memory in everyday contexts. The latest edition of Ellis's text includes references to it, and there are several recent review collections.[17] All this work remains preoccupied, however, with what Neisser has termed the verity, or accuracy, of memory. For example, a chapter on "Memory for Places, Objects, and Events," in *Memory in the Real World* by Gillian Cohen, is limited to people's ability to identify objects, recall where they are located, and navigate a route based on map reading or previous familiarity.

This new literature includes a number of studies of "environmental reinstatement effects," or people's recall of events when they return to a former place.[18] Given people's testimonies about how memories assail them when they revisit a childhood place, I expected to find insights into my subject here. I found, however, that this work has limited itself to recording how memories increase in number and accuracy under reinstated conditions, so that laboratory rooms adequately serve its purposes. Therefore even in the new research on memory in everyday contexts, the personal significance of childhood places, and their use in meeting the present and the future, remain unaddressed.

The Poetry of Memory

In contrast to the literary criticism exemplified by Mandel, or the psychological research reviewed by Ellis, the work of Hesiod, Goethe, and Williams *has place* in the sense that it is situated in personally meaningful geographical settings, whether real or imaginary. Whereas the tradition of linguistic analysis has focused on word use, and empiricist psychology on sensations, poetry has explored the complex qualitative interplay between words and sensations. Whereas linguistic philosophy and psychology have pursued general conclusions in abstract language, poetry has explored the universal in the particular, relying upon readers' common experience of a common earth to secure sympathetic participation and understanding. Therefore the qualitative significance of place experience has been one of poetry's subjects since earliest recorded times.

The language and formal structure of poetry invite this focus. Poetic form derives from music and dance, and therefore from body rhythms. The "feet" of prosody were originally dancing feet. The "verses" or turns of poetry were dance turns. Poetry was danced and sung to commemorate the marriages, births, deaths, seasons, and harvests that mark the cycles of nature and human life. As Hesiod observed, by placing human events in this formal order, poetry "brings a forgetting of ills and a rest from sorrow." Drawing upon embodied knowledge deeper than "the symbolizing activity of the mind" and more integrated than discrete pieces of encoded information, poets have traditionally treated memory as a power "woven into the fabric of our inmost self."

Poetry also evokes embodied experience through myth and metaphor. Myth communicates human powers through external things, and metaphor notices likenesses between one thing and another. Elizabeth Sewell has observed that myth and metaphor connect the mind to its physical surroundings.[19] When we say that our memory is like a waterfall, or like a larger-than-life mother who inhabits mountains and couples with the powers of the sky, we know ourselves in relation to the world's sensed qualities. Sewell has also observed that science tends to relate the mind to machines—as in Ellis's comparison of memory to a filing cabinet or a data processing system. In contrast, poetry maintains human relations with nature through its predominant use of natural metaphors.

Whereas empiricist and analytic traditions since Hobbes have emphasized words' denotations, poetry emphasizes connotations. This orientation to language opens it to environmental memory. Rooted in bodily experience, poetry seeks not to simplify words' multivocity but to compound it and to set it in play. Writing on the subject of *Innocence and Memory*, the Italian poet Ungaretti noted that if memory referred only to the past, it would lead to despair.[20] Instead, he called memory a word "charged with presentiments," which opens forwards as well as backwards in time and thereby contains seeds of renewal—echoing the myth of Mnemosyne who gave birth to the muses who tell of what is and what will be as well as what was.

Words have this range, Ungaretti observed, because of the imprecise personal associations that they evoke. What lifts a word from the pages of a dictionary to make it a living force with the potential of approaching truth is not its denotation but its connotations: "this margin of infinite allusions through which imagination and emotion can wander." This margin of connotations derives from experience with particular people, places, and things, and their related words. Through these imprecise associations, Ungaretti argued, words most accurately articulate experience, as their indeterminacy lives actually within ourselves. We ourselves are compounds of error, ambiguity, and possibility which overflow bare denotation. Poetry, said Ungaretti, has always used this allusive quality of memory in order to approximate reality. He welcomed twentieth-century physicists' interest in probability and uncertainty for the reason that science too approaches truth to the degree that it accepts "our inability to know, except in indeterminacy, reality."[21]

As chapter 2 reviews, Wordsworth believed that primary words for primary things are poets' main material, because their allusiveness draws upon the animated perceptions of childhood when these words were first learned. "Water," "fire," "door," "blue," "sweet," "sky": such words, Wordsworth claimed, work upon us because they refer to the basic elements of the natural and built world that we first encounter and name with childhood's strong emotions. Thus primary nouns and adjectives join sensation and emotion to thought, creating a potent vocabulary for poets' use.

In Wordsworth's defense, it can be argued that when it comes to familiarity with the true grit of the earth, as a physical fact, childhood is irreplaceable. For most of us, it is the only time when we get down into mud puddles and up into trees. Unsupervised, childhood play is a variety of contact sport: "bruised, scratched, and mud-caked," as William Carlos Williams described childhood abandon, to a degree that few adults, even in their worst moments, ever manage to recapture.[22] Beyond their lexical definitions, the mountains, rivers, trees, and city walls that cast their presence across poems ancient and modern must have their margin of indeterminacy filled in by personal experience; and by body to body contact with the real thing, childhood prepares for a vivid, well-fleshed symbolic life.

This book's title alludes to an essay of the same name by the poet Howard Nemerov.[23] Its phrase originated in his five-year-old son's assertion that, "In the first country of places, there are no requests." (I have dropped the predicate, or I could have done no interviewing.) In agreement with Wordsworth, Nemerov noted that young children are in a quandary because they combine strong emotion and intense sensory experience with a limited vocabulary: they have more to say than they have words to say it with. Therefore they must use verbal flexibility and ingenuity. When Nemerov was writing down his son's pronouncements, his wife looked over his shoulder and observed that, equipped with a limited vocabulary, young children are forced to use what little language they do have *hard*. Inventive metaphors and overextensions of words result.

Poets, Nemerov noted, despite vaster equipage, find themselves in the same situation as children in that they too must use language "hard." Often no single word captures a complex of insight and feeling. Then, like children, they must extend their language; and the world of objects comes to their aid. Being wordless but fluent with sensual texture and human associations, objects amplify language, lending their names and qualities when standard denotations lag. Through myth, metaphor, symbol, and simile, objects extend meaning. They also tantalize poets to find full expression when simple words like "river" or "flower" fail to adequately convey the sensual fact.

According to Nemerov, the connections that poetry draws between human thought and feeling and the world are real insights, not poetic fancy. Therefore the first country of places combines the animated world of physical discovery in childhood and the allusive world of language, laying a foundation for the discovery of meaning through poetry. How different poets relate these childhood and adult worlds is what this book explores.

The Language of Phenomenology and Hermeneutics

If empiricist psychology were the only means available to study memory, I could not have written this book, which turns to poetry from the discipline of environmental psychology. Its turn to literature has been made possible by the methods of phenomenology and hermeneutics.

Edmund Husserl, the founder of phenomenology, shared the empiricist faith that there is a concrete external world to which we are related. In contrast to the empiricists, however, Husserl rejected the possibility that we can know objective facts about this world through unmediated sensation. All that we can know, said Husserl, is how we constitute our consciousness of the world and, simultaneously, consciousness of ourselves through relations with the world.[24] Building on the work of Franz Brentano, Husserl's fundamental insight was that consciousness is always consciousness *of* something. The consequence is that the world derives its meaning from consciousness, and consciousness derives its meaning from the world.

In *The Phenomenology of Internal Time Consciousness*, Husserl outlined a radically different conception of memory than that of either empiricism or linguistic analysis.[25] In contrast to the position that time consists of recurring mental points of the present in which words are thought or sensations are registered, Husserl observed that time is experienced as an unbroken flow. The present is connected to a sense of the past reaching behind us and to a sense of the future coming to meet us. Like Williams, Husserl described memory as a current in which consciousness of past, present, and future converge. In this way, Husserl prepared phenomenology to describe how people use the past in meeting the present and the future.

Husserl also stressed that consciousness is embodied. Thus he laid a foundation for the study of human relatedness to a physical world that carries the marks of time within itself: a world in which the body changes dimension and ages, shadows move, the seasons cycle, moss grows on trees, and treasured objects and places contain histories. Husserl directed attention to the concreteness of lived experience in the original sense of the Latin verb *concrescere*, to grow together. Our consciousness of the world and the world of which we are conscious coalesce in an intimate, taken-for-granted whole, which he termed the *lifeworld*. For phenomenology, there is all the difference in the world between reinstating a laboratory room or a childhood room.

Husserl also took exception to the empiricist position that memory is a mere representation of past sensation—"decaying sense," in the words of Hobbes.[26] Rather, he argued that memory is an independent activity of consciousness. Therefore it is not to be judged according to its accuracy in terms of objective measures of the external world. It is to be studied in terms of its own functions, which are to constitute the permanence and meaning of objects and people, and the permanence and meaning of individual consciousness through its relations with people and things. Thus this book's questions about how people constitute the meaning of childhood memory are phenomenology's domain.

Living and working as he did during the First World War and the build-up to the Second World War, Husserl dedicated himself to articulating what is universal and unitive in human experience. In writing this book, I have been indebted to his concern with the life-world, with the self- and world-constituting activities of consciousness, with the importance of memory as an activity in its own right rather than a mere representation of sensation, and with qualities of embodied experience that overflow any single expression in words. To examine how people interpret memory differently from different perspectives, however, I have drawn upon the work of Heidegger.

Heidegger, who briefly collaborated with Husserl, was profoundly influenced by his mentor's analysis of the lifeworld and his observation that human experience occurs within horizons of time and place. More than Husserl, Heidegger emphasized that human existence is subject to historical fate. Therefore Heidegger gradually moved away from Husserlian phenomenology to create a philosophical hermeneutics that explored how people interpret the world and their place in it under different historical conditions.[27]

As Heidegger moved away from Husserl's goal of articulating essential universal truths of human experience, he developed an alternative concept of truth as *aletheia*—a pre-Socratic term meaning the "unforgotten" or "unhidden." Truth, Heidegger argued, is not a fixed characteristic to which intellectual assertions conform. It is an occurrence, when a person and something perceived come together in a "clearing" in which the thing (another person, an object, a place) is given freedom to reveal itself. In his later work, Heidegger maintained that we create a clearing and approach the truth of things most closely through the receptive language of poetry.[28]

This book draws upon Heidegger's application of hermeneutics to the interpretation of human understanding as it unfolds

within historical time and place. Without rejecting Husserl's position that there are some human universals, it takes from Heidegger's concept of truth as *aletheia* a belief that truths must be
repeatedly reenacted in time through attentiveness to how things
show themselves and a search for language that reveals rather than
distorts. As Heidegger recommended, it turns to poetry as a revela-
tory expression of experience.

As a social scientist, however, I could not have written this
book without the mediating work of Gadamer, Heidegger's student
and lifelong friend. Heidegger rejected both physical and social science as naive instruments of technological control, which force
things into distorting, exploitive frames of reference.[29] Gadamer
sought to heal this rift between the human sciences and literature by
applying Heidegger's insights to science.

In doing so, Gadamer extended the concept of the hermeneutic
circle, which states that the meaning of a whole can only be known
by reference to its parts, the meaning of a part by reference to the
whole.[30] One consequence of this circle, Gadamer noted, is that every
answer is an answer to a question: a principle that sounds straight-
forward enough, but as Gadamer developed it, it implies that all understanding is historical. The past impels the questions that we frame
in the present, which direct the movement of knowledge into the future. It also follows, Gadamer argued, that the arts, the humanities, the
human sciences, and individual understanding develop like conversations, and that every conversation is a conversation with traditition.

In addition to seeking to clarify how this conversation progresses, Gadamer sought to reanimate the ancient Greek ideal of dialogue, in which a question is taken up and turned about by speakers
for different perspectives of understanding within a society.[31] Truth,
in Gadamer's work, combines the contributions of Husserl and Heidegger. As Husserl sought to freely vary perspectives in order to discover the essence of a phenomenon that remains constant across
variations, Gadamer's dialogic truth explores a subject through the
diverse perspectives of different participants in a conversation.[32]
Similar to Heidegger's *aletheia*, this form of truth requires receptive
openness to what each participant has to say, as well as to the phenomenon under discussion. With an interest all his own in how people seek truth in society, Gadamer illuminated the play of revela-
tions that results as thought circles around a subject with growing
understanding, as people engage in conversation with each other and
with their tradition. Gadamer's model of conversation has been the
model for this book.

A Conversation with Tradition

The different chapters of this book represent different steps in Gadamer's hermeneutic method. This opening chapter describes the boundaries of this book's subject—its circle. Chapter 2 reviews major Western traditions of thought that anyone pondering the significance of childhood memories of nature must negotiate. As this chapter shows, it is a paradoxical, divided tradition that is due for reassessment. In chapters 3 through 5, five contemporary poets engage in conversations with this tradition as they muse upon how well customary conceptions of childhood and nature fit the circumstances of their lives. Each poet presents a distinct perspective, which chapter 6 constitutes into a revised understanding of adult relations to childhood, qualifying existing traditions to reflect how memory works according to gender and philosophy of nature. Because developmental psychology has elaborated a major modern tradition of thought about the meaning of childhood and nature, chapter 7 proposes how its theory can be made more receptive to the diverse meanings of memory that these five poets reveal.

Chapters 3 through 5, which present each poet's life and work in turn, evolved through my personal "conversation" with each poet's writing and the face-to-face conversations of the interviews. At the same time, these chapters are clearings in the Heideggerian sense, as I concentrated on hearing each poet's position as openly and accurately as possible, and the poets in turn shared their experiences and thoughts. In the course of these exchanges, I vividly felt the principles of the hermeneutic circle apply. Approaching each poet's books with questions, I formed provisional "answers" or interpretations. These "answers" determined the questions that I brought to the interviews. In each question-and-answer sequence, the poet's responses called my thinking up to that point into question, enlarging or revising it and lifting my succeeding question to a new level of understanding. As Gadamer has observed, when the dialectic of knowledge is effective, the expanding dimensions of the hermeneutic circle are most accurately described as a spiral.[33]

Following the reading and interviews, I shared a written synthesis of each poet's position for his or her review. All five poets confirmed my interpretation of their life and work as valid, and some observed that it gave them new insight into themselves. Incorporating any corrections or clarifications that they suggested, I composed the final interpretations presented here.

As each poet's words follow in turn in this book, I hope that readers will hear these five people in conversation with each other as they concur or take exception to each other's position, and that through this dialogue in which the subject of environmental memory is viewed through multiple persectives, readers will find some of their own processes of self-understanding challenged or clarified.

The positions that these poets have taken are not theirs alone. In other studies, I have interviewed a broad spectrum of people regarding their relations with nature: lawyers, engineers, biologists, architects, teachers, farmers, local officials, citizen activists, people with advanced degrees and people who never advanced beyond grade school.[34] Sensitized to the relations to tradition and personal experience that these poets describe, I have often heard their words echoed by more "prosaic" people. The different traditions regarding childhood and nature that these poets confront are not just artifacts of the written word, analyzable by scholars and known to men and women of letters, but otherwise separate from human experience. They form persisting, conflicting ways of understanding human relations with nature.

It was the insight of Husserl that, for the most part, people go about life immersed in the natural attitude of pregiven assumptions, including the assumptions that we have a self, that nature has order, and that we are related to nature: what self, what order, and what relationship we usually do not bother to ask.[35] It was the observation of Heidegger that poets are distinguished from most people precisely because they think long and hard about such issues. In every human life, however, there are times when pregiven assumptions break down, when the quandaries of life press upon us and we are forced to think for ourselves.[36] At these times, it can be expected, memory no longer floats through our lives as an unexamined element, but becomes a necessary instrument in confronting issues that this book has raised. The poets chosen here are exemplary because they have combined the uncommon activity of poetry with this common activity of trying to make sense of life, whatever that life may be.

Chapter Two

Childhood and Nature

In the seventeenth century, at the same time as the philosophical foundations of modern empirical science were laid, it became popular among philosophers, scientists, and poets alike to compare children to poets through the medium of a special relationship with nature. As science gained influence, and scientific standards of validity became popular standards of truth, to know something in reality came to mean to know it scientifically. In this climate of scientism, poets' and children's ways of knowing nature came to be classified together. It became general wisdom that the knowledge of children and poets is fanciful and subjective, in contrast to objective, reasoned, scientific modes of perception. It became correspondingly commonplace to say that poets retain a childlike vision of the world and that children see the world like poets, and to hear poets assert that early memories of the world glow within them like inextinguishable embers.

Consistent with this tradition, when Edith Cobb reviewed her collection of autobiographies that are predominantly by poets and

other artists, she reported that authors repeatedly returned to childhood experiences of nature in memory "in order to renew the power
and impulse to create at its very source."[1] This chapter reviews the
development of these associations among children, poets, and nature,
first through scientists' versions, and then through poets' rejoinders.

Although conflicting accounts of childhood and nature were articulated in the seventeenth century, the roots of the conflict extend
to the origins of Western culture. The figure of the redeeming child,
of the little child that shall lead us, appears in Isaiah and the Gospels.
In contrast, the Apostle Paul (I Corinthians 13:11) admonished the
faithful to reason like a man and to give up childish ways. In Plato
and throughout Platonism, there is internal division between affirmation of the created world as an ensouled organism of divine
beauty, whose forms can be intuited through poetic possession and
childhood anamnesis, and rejection of the mutable natural world in
favor of the purer beauty of mature reason and intellectual creation.

In the summary that follows, these two sides of Western tradition have been described as "the science of childhood" and "the poetry of childhood." They form the hermeneutic context of this
book's exploration of the meaning of childhood memory. When five
contemporary poets reflect upon their own experience in chapters 3
through 5, they have oriented themselves within this context. Perhaps its internal conflict has persisted ever since the beginning of
Western culture, because it represents essential human ambivalence
regarding the contradictory characteristics of nature and childhood:
pain and pleasure, vexation and attraction, wildness and innocence.

THE SCIENCE OF CHILDHOOD

A convenient date to begin the scientific account of childhood
is 1637, the year of the publication of René Descartes' *Discourse on
Method*, which epitomizes one version of childhood and nature,
and the birth year of Thomas Traherne, one of the first poets to
elaborate the second. In writing the *Discourse*, settled in his chair
at his table within the shelter of his room, Descartes moved pen
across paper with hand of flesh and bone to record that he understood himself to be:

> a substance the whole essence or nature of which it is to think,
> and that for its existence there is no need of any place, nor does
> it depend on any material thing; so that this "me," that is to

say, the soul by which I am what I am, is entirely distinct from the body, and is even more easy to know than the latter.[2]

Descartes' boast reiterated the dominant doctrine of Platonic philosophy and Christian theology, which separated the soul from the body, even as he extended this separation to provide a point of certainty for the grounding of modern science. According to Descartes, the one indubitable principle of pure knowledge is our own pure consciousness, whose whole essence it is to think. He further proposed that it is the nature of our consciousness to think according to the analytic, deductive rules of logical syllogisms. We can attain certain knowledge in this way because the world beyond our minds—all the beasts, plants, and objects in it, including our own bodies—form one great mechanism, established according to parallel logical, deterministic laws by the great Lawmaker. Therefore to the degree that we formulate our knowledge of the world in the language of logical propositions and mathematical equations, we approach truth and certainty. This pure consciousness, Descartes added, is associated with our soul. In contrast, the entire world of sense perceptions is a soulless material mechanism. To the extent that we identify ourselves with it, we err.

Childish Ways

By such a standard, it is patent that children and poets are prone to err. Both groups animate the world and describe it imaginatively and metaphorically. Thus John Locke, in his popular seventeenth-century guidebook, *Some Thoughts Concerning Education*, counseled that if a child should show a poetic vein, "the parents should labour to have it stifled and suppressed as much as may be."[3] If the world is a mechanism to be known and manipulated by objectively recording cause and effect sequences of sensations, then imaginative perception and language dangerously distort truth. Pragmatic, Locke also noted that "it is very seldom seen that any one discovers mines of gold or silver in Parnassus." Mathematics, logic, and the laws of natural science were the studies needed to invest capital judiciously and to keep accounts. Locke relegated the function of poetry to, at best, light entertainment.

As social science emerged in the eighteenth century, it assimilated this empiricist ideal of truth and method. As eighteenth-century conceptions of a general social science branched into nineteenth-century departments of sociology, anthropology, and psychology, each discipline internalized this rationalist model of thought and action as its highest ideal of human achievement. As life became increasingly secular, both the physical and social sciences added a simple modification: Cartesian dualism was transformed into the monist assumption that the mind can be explained as a product of the body.

Empiricist philosophy had some liberating implications. Locke's concept that the mind is a blank slate at birth, on which experience leaves impressions that are joined by association into increasingly complex ideas, lightened the stain of original sin and gave aristocrat and commoner an equal innate status.[4] In this sense, Locke is the guiding genius behind the Declaration of Independence.

Nineteenth-century philosophers and scientists, however, were quick to redefine new categories of intellectual castes. In the 1820s, the positivist philosopher Auguste Comte condensed Enlightenment theories of social progress into a three-part evaluative scale that remains entrenched in the theory and practice of developmental psychology, ingeniously varied as it has been. Every society, Comte said, must progress through three stages. In its infant theological stage, it believes all phenomena to be created and sustained by the action of supernatural beings, or one Supreme Being. In its second, metaphysical stage, these supernatural agents become replaced by abstract forces, such as humors, influences, and Nature itself, which are believed to engender and explain all phenomena. In the final positive stage, people have the wisdom to abandon their search for the origin and destiny of the universe in order to devote themselves to explaining phenomena through empirical laws. Each individual, Comte added, must also progress through these three stages. "Now does not each one of us," he asked, "when he looks at his own history, recall that he was successively a *theologian* in childhood, for his most important ideas, a *metaphysician* in his youth, and a *physicist* in his maturity?"[5] Comte called the highest stage of maturation "positive" because it held science in positive regard as the authoritative source of knowledge.

As Stephen Jay Gould demonstrates in his book *Ontogeny and Phylogeny*, this general scheme of social evolution became a ruling theme of nineteenth-century biology, sociology, and psychology. Its hierarchy set white Western middle and upper-class men with scientific educations apart from women, children, poets, artists, the lower classes, the criminal, the insane, colonized peoples, savages, and, some even said, the Irish.[6] Some of the claims are brazen. Consider, for example, Schopenhauer:

Women are directly fitted for acting as the nurses and teachers of our early childhood by the fact that they are themselves childish, frivolous and short-sighted; in a word, they are big children all their life long—a kind of intermediate stage between the child and the full-grown man, who is man in the strict sense of the word.[7]

Or consider Herbert Spencer on children:

As the child's features—flat nose, forward-opening nostrils, large lips, wide-apart eyes, absent frontal sinus etc.—resemble for a time those of the savage, so, too, do his instincts. Hence the tendencies to cruelty, to thieving, to lying, so general among children.[8]

In the twentieth century, this intellectual hierarchy has taken a more subtle, qualified form, but it persists. As the review of memory research in the preceding chapter indicates, for example, a "good" memory is judged by how accurately and in what quantity it conforms to original sense data, which is a "positive" skill for science. A profoundly influential version of this evolutionary scheme has also marked sociology and developmental psychology.

Refining ideas of the nineteenth century anthropologist Edward Tylor, the sociologist Lucien Lévy-Bruhl published successive books in the 1920s in which he concluded that the operation of primitive minds is "mystic" and "prelogical," in contrast to the objective logical mental operations that characterize mature Western minds. The distinguishing trait of the primitive mind is that thought and perception form a synthetic whole:

Their mental activity is too little differentiated for it to be able to regard the ideas or images of objects by themselves, apart from the sentiments, emotions, and passions which evoke them, or are evoked by them.[9]

The result is that the external world appears animated by thought and feeling:

We may say that to the primitive the surrounding world is the language of spirits speaking to a spirit. It is a language which the mind does not remember ever having learnt, but which the preconnections of its collective representations make quite a *natural* one.[10]

Central to Lévy-Bruhl's analysis of primitive mentality was his concept of "collective representations." He defined them as representations that transcend the individual: they are common to all members of a society; they are transmitted from generation to generation; they awaken sentiments such as respect, fear, and adoration; and they impress themselves upon the individual as articles of faith rather than products of reason. He compared the collective representations of primitive minds to the way that words fuse sound with meaning; yet he sharply distinguished the mental processes of "primitives" from those of "men of our type."[11]

As Lévy-Bruhl's books came out, they were read by the Swiss epistemologist Jean Piaget. Engaged in the study of cognitive development, he was patiently observing and listening to infants and children. He concluded that children up to the age of eleven or twelve showed many traits comparable to Lévy-Bruhl's savages. The same exotic beliefs that anthropologists had culled from old travel journals and fieldwork in distant jungles and deserts could be collected in the nearest schoolyard. Like primitives, he found, children's thought is characterized by *realism*, or an inability to separate internal mental processes from the external world. As a result they give names, dreams, and feelings an independent existence, as if they are aspects of the world rather than aspects of the mind. Other evidence of the child's inability to firmly bound the self and the world is *artificialism*, or the assumption that human beings, or an anthropomorphic God, created nature. In addition, the world of children, like the aboriginal world, is permeated by *animism*. Even inert things are perceived to be living, conscious, and purposeful.[12]

Piaget observed that the eccentricities of children are comparable not only to primitive mentalities, but to past stages in the development of Western science. Realism is "anthropocentric illusion . . . in short, all those illusions which teem in the history of science." Artificialism, he noted, is analogous to Aristotle's belief that nature exhibits internal creative, teleological dynamics. The term *animism* derives from the Pythagorean and Platonic conception of a world soul, *anima mundi*, which was believed to be immaterial but inseparable from matter, giving matter its form and movement.[13] Piaget measured scientific as well as individual advance by the degree to which these forms of thought are recognized to be illusions. Like his predecessors, he defined the highest level of intellectual achievement to be logicomathematical thinking. Piaget's theories are currently under active revision, but most of this reevaluation challenges his description of the stage development of logicomathematical thought, not his hierarchy.[14]

Consequences of Comtean Hierarchies

Since the seventeenth century, as modern science has defined its methods, purposes, and identity, it has categorized alternate frames of mind on the basis of their utility for empiricist science. Children, poets, primitives, women, and some of the most advanced minds of classical, medieval, and Renaissance civilization have been diagnosed to see the world in similar ways. Their forms of knowledge have been set in contrast to an objective ideal, which asserts that the truth of the world and people's place within it is to be discovered through impersonal observation and mathematical analysis.

As a measure of how deeply this system of categories has become engrained in what Edmund Husserl has called the "natural attitude" of popular beliefs, it is instructive to observe what has happened to these theories. Comte, late in his life, regretted that positivism had been narrowly construed to represent the rule of the intellect alone, whereas its true goal was to direct the intellect to the service of the heart and the social affections. "If," he warned, "instead of being content with this honorable post," the intellect "aspires to become supreme, its ambitious aims . . . result in the most deplorable disorder."[15] Lévy-Bruhl, as he proceeded in his research, retracted his concept of prelogic and recorded in his notebooks that "there is a mystical mentality which is more marked and more easily observable among 'primitive peoples' than in our own societies, but it is present in every human mind."[16] Piaget qualified his stage descriptions by observing that even educated adults show childish or primitive thinking under conditions of emotion or inexperience. Nevertheless, these reservations are known to few but specialists, whereas Comte's three stages, Lévy-Bruhl's prelogic, and Piaget's terminus of logicomathematical thinking remain generally disseminated catchwords of their work.

These authors' choice of descriptors perpetuate this bias. The one mode of perception is described as "lower," "less developed," "prescientific," "prelogical," or "primitive." The other is described as "higher," "developed," "scientific," "advanced," or "civilized." The connotations of these words are more memorable than any disclaimers by any author that the terms are not intended to be evaluative.

What these theories share is that each posits a continuum from childhood to adulthood, from primitive conditions to advanced civilization, in which the beginning and end of the sequence are treated as two opposed, disparate modes of perception. The more carefully that gradations along this continuum of phylogenetic or ontogenetic progress are distinguished, the more they accumulate to demonstrate, in effect, a radical break between primitive and advanced, artistic and scientific, or child and adult states of mind.

Propagated through theories of this kind, the prevailing scientific model of the world has promoted two concurrent yet conflicting visions of the relationship between childhood and adulthood. These evolutionary theories have declared that the adult progressively emerges from the child, just as advanced civilization emerges from primitive society. In this sense, science has related childhood to adulthood. The final positive state achieved, however, is seen to be so distinct from its beginnings that it amounts to a cleavage of childhood from adulthood. Adult logic appears as remote from childish prelogic as is modern Western civilization from the primitive societies that it colonized.

The Psychoanalysis of Childhood and Nature

The preceding scientific analysis of childhood has been extended, in ambivalent new forms, by the psychoanalytic theory of Sigmund Freud. As a medical student and researcher, Freud assimilated the evolutionary, monist principles that dominated university thought in the late nineteenth century: that all physiological functions can be reduced to laws of physics and chemistry; and that these laws determine mental as well as other organic phenomena. Therefore the ultimate goal of science is to explain everything in terms of physicochemical reactions of elementary particles. By 1898, however, Freud conceded that he would have to relinguish this aspiration in the face of the limits of existing knowledge:

> I have no desire at all to leave the psychology hanging in the air with no organic basis. But, beyond the feeling of conviction (that there must be such a basis), I have nothing, either theoretic or therapeutic, to work on, and so I must behave as if I were confronted by psychological factors only.[17]

Despite his monism and his medical degree, when Freud turned to psychological factors alone he found a model for their operation in Platonic dualism. He compared his vision for psychoanalysis to Plato's metaphor in the *Phaedrus* in which the charioteer of the soul is charged with giving the lead to the winged horse of reason and reining in the wild horse of the body and the passions, if spiritual destruction is to be forestalled.[18] Like Plato, Freud believed that this goal is to be secured through the exercise of *logos*, or deliberative speech. But whereas Plato counseled the study of mathematics, physical science, and philosophy to strengthen the reign of reason, Freud proposed the momentous turnaround that reason must concentrate upon naming and understanding the wild horse in its charge. To identify and pacify it, he concluded, reason must attend to the connotative, associative language of madness, myth, dreams, everyday speech, poetry, and childhood.

Freud intensified the paradox of nineteenth-century science that related adulthood to childhood and yet encouraged discontinuity. He created an artistic science, or scientific art, that analyzed myth and memory. At the base, he found childhood. "In our innermost soul we are children," he concluded, "and remain so for the rest of our lives."[19] Thus he rebound childhood to adulthood after the two had been authoritatively distinguished.

In pursuing this discovery, Freud came to the further paradox that this redemptive descent into the past, which is necessary if reason is to control passion, is perilously like a descent into hell. The childhood that Freud discovered would probably have taken Spencer by surprise. It was not only primitively sensuous and undisciplined, but perversely sexual. He concluded that adulthood is permeable to childhood because as children we are never innocent of adult lusts. Childhood loves, hates, and fears anticipate adult dilemmas because sexual arousal and competition already agitate early life. Therefore mature reason can rule only by negotiating a truce with the forces of memory and desire.

Freud determined that environmental symbols conveniently serve to mask these sexual tensions. Through the method of free association, he evolved a new use of reminiscence in which conscious memories mark entrances to the warren of the unconscious: half signals, half screens. Thus he concluded that sharply recalled childhood scenes are screens for repressed traumas and conflicts associated with the remembered moment.[20]

Like screen memories, physical objects fuse the stated and the implied. Superseding the metaphysical and magical codes of the Middle Ages and the Renaissance, Freud developed a new symbology in which external places and things substitute for the true objects of human desire. In his analysis of symbols in *The Interpretation of Dreams* and *A General Introduction to Psychoanalysis*, environmental objects and scenes predominate. For example, he found houses to be regularly recurring representations of the human body as a whole, and of woman's body in particular, as they share the property that he called "the essential thing in woman," that she encloses a space. Landscapes of woods and water, gardens and flowers represent female sexual organs: things that are upright in form or that have the property of penetrating, the male.[21]

According to Freud, this double reading of objects and landscape is not just a trick of memory that begins to mask our true intent in adulthood. According to his analysis of a young child, this covert use of places and things begins at the outset of life as a strategy for neutralizing psychic threats.[22] By this means, environmental memories become symbols saturated with the body's secrets.

Nature was not only a safe symbol, but one of the great protagonists in Freud's thought. He considered the basic motive behind civilization to be to raise defenses against nature, to extract wealth from it, to dominate and control it. The great tragedy of human existence, he believed, is that however much civilization may alter our relations with nature, it cannot free us from ultimate subjection to it. Through earthquakes, floods, storms, disease, and death, "nature rises up against us, majestic, cruel, inexorable; she brings to our mind once more our weakness and helplessness, which we thought to escape through the work of civilization." This condition is not without precedence. "Once before one has found oneself in a similar state of helplessness: as a small child, in relation to one's parents."[23] Down through time, he concluded, religion has seized upon this parallel by personifying nature as God the Father or the Great Mother. By this means, societies comfort themselves with the delusion that they can supplicate and serve that which is in fact blind to them.

Freud noted that as natural symbols tend to symbolize woman, so nature is often personified as a woman. He himself often used the pronoun "she" for it. He believed that this parallel represents a real connection. To an infant, his mother seems like a giantess before whom he is utterly helpless and vulnerable. As a male comes into consciousness of nature in manhood, he finds himself in the same abject position. As a delusional protection against these subjections, Freud proposed, man fantasizes in the place of the Terrible Mother, the Goddess of Death, her opposite, the Goddess of Love, or other young women. In his essay "The Theme of the Three Caskets," for example, he interpreted Psyche and other young heroines of literature and myth to enfold "the three forms taken on by the figure of the mother as life proceeds: the mother herself, the beloved who is chosen after her pattern, and finally the Mother Earth who receives him in the end."[24]

In sum, at the source of men's feelings for the world, Freud identified a correspondence between their experience of nature and their infant experience of their mother. He expected this correspondence to be most direct and active in children themselves, but he believed that it persists in adulthood—in some individuals, with childlike intensity. In this case, Freud equated these feelings with religious emotion.

In response to a correspondence with Romain Rolland in which this Western admirer of the Hindu mystic Ramakrishna claimed that the deepest source of religious energy is a sensation of "eternity," of "limitlessness and of a bond with the universe," Freud countered that this "oceanic" feeling is an artifact of an infant's sense of oneness with the breast. As a neonate, carried about, cradled, and nursed, the infant knows only one undifferentiated, unified flow of sensations. Freud estimated the religious feeling that his friend described to be a continuation of this primal "feeling which embraced the universe and expressed an inseparable connection of the ego with the surrounding world." A mystical sense "of an indissoluble bond, of being one with the external world," he declared to be the survival of an infant's experience in its mother's arms. The root of religious feeling, he concluded, is our body's memory of oneness with our mother.[25]

The lure of art, Freud believed, is like religion. It conjures up illusions of satisfaction and thus buffers us against nature's and civilization's rigors. Through the artist's or poet's sleight of hand, repressed desires are dressed out in acceptable diversions, so that we may indulge ourselves without shame.[26]

Consequences of Freudian Theory

When these different aspects of Freudian theory are added together, they present deep paradoxes for the meaning and use of childhood memory, and in particular memory of nature. The basic nineteenth-century paradox—that science simultaneously related childhood and adulthood, yet estranged them—took refined twentieth-century forms.

Freud not only directed that reason should study unreason, as nineteenth-century sociology and psychology had studied the child, madness, and primitive society, but he asserted that renewal and psychic health are found through this means. Yet the path to renewal that he described presented such a frightening aspect that a person could despair at the character of unconverted human nature. The path to renewal that Freud prescribed required looking at the Medusa of innate impulses through the mirror of scientific understanding, and returning, disenchanted but wiser, to the world of moral restraint. In this way he reinforced the traditional division between "men of our type" and the psyches of women, children, poets, and primitives. At the same time, Freud revealed that these deviances are not, as Comte proposed, a first stage that can be overpassed, but a persisting force through the agency of the child in everyone's "innermost soul." Therefore the temptations of childhood ways of thinking and feeling require heroic control.

Freud encouraged one of the distinguishing features of the modern world: a preoccupation with self-understanding that shows itself in self-analysis, the reconstruction of personal and social history, and the taxonomy of different states of mind. Like his predecessors and contemporaries in science, he demonstrated a fascination with understanding the sources of mental life, and a dedication to a final stage of civilized maturity. In tracing the line of individual development, he testified, as others did, that children find the world animated, intentional, responsive (but with what animations and intentions!). He set maturity in opposition to this origin. Thus he magnified the paradox that Comte, Lévy-Bruhl, and Piaget share: that they encouraged remembrance of forms of thought that they instructed readers to abandon.

Another paradox that is particularly relevant to this book is that Freud attached special significance to the memory of places and things, but only on his own terms. He encouraged the detailed reconstruction of places and things in memories and dreams, with all their sensory qualities, but for the sake of hidden meanings rather than for their intrinsic value. Although he resurrected the evocative power of environmental memory, he did so in order to direct it to predefined rational ends.

Another difficulty is that Freud, like his predecessors and contemporaries, proposed to chart a general psychology, yet he took "men of our type" as his standard and focused upon men's relationship to women and the world. Therefore, for women, Freud created the special paradox that he offered a guide through memory that had been plotted in a man's world.

Finally, Freud manifested the general philosophical paradox of modern science as it has attempted to construct a materialist explanation of mental functioning. He assumed that purely physiological factors orchestrate psychological life. Beginning with this faith in physical factors, he found no ultimate human identity apart from the physical world. For Freud, the unavoidable human tragedy is that we are one with nature. Believing in final futility, he directed his followers to reconstruct their self-identity in a world that provided the self no permanent basis for identity. The obverse of this monism is that when he turned his attention to psychological factors, he found no objective world apart from subjectivity. All intuitions of an animated interactive world became the projection of inner frustrations, desires, and fears. He fostered the painstaking recollection of childhood, at the same time that he presented new reasons to judge the world remembered vain and illusory.

Despite these paradoxes, the meanings that Freud assigned to memory cannot be lightly evaded—in part, because these paradoxes reflect general perplexities of our century. Freud's beginning position that everything will ultimately be explained as the product of physicochemical reactions epitomizes the modern secular spirit. Therefore his interpretations of remembered relations with the world were quickly assimilated by intellectuals, leaving a legacy that all educated people of this century must continue to negotiate. Freudian theory has given writers and readers new reasons to plumb early memories, and new expectations regarding what they will find there. To writers as well as analysts, it has suggested that reminiscence veils elusive and allusive complexes of meaning, some of which carry us far back in time. It has become a general wisdom of our age that we never lose the child within us—that we are so profoundly formed by early experience that it exceeds our conscious knowing and telling. We have also come to assume that reconciliation between reason and unreason, or the conscious and unconscious, requires a reconciliation between childhood and adulthood.

There is another side to this story of memory and the meaning of childhood places and things. Coincident with this scientific account and in self-defense against it, poets and other artists developed an alternative version of the meaning of nature and childhood. Drawing upon other strands of the same Platonic and Christian sources, they took up possibilities that scientific culture rejected to weave radically different interpretations.

THE POETRY OF CHILDHOOD

In the seventeenth century, at the same time as the methods and scope of empirical science were being defined, a new interest in childhood manifested itself in poetry. Some historians have suggested that nostalgia over the beginning of the loss of the agrarian preindustrial world was projected onto the figure of the child. Others have attributed new attention to the child to the growing influence and domesticity of the middle class.[27] Whatever its sources, as this new theme of childhood developed, some of its principles were written in deliberate opposition to the scientific account described above. First articulated in Metaphysical poetry, this interest was taken up and magnified by Romantic art and philosophy. In France, Rousseau identified childhood with the pure state of nature that social artifice corrupts. In Germany, Goethe described childhood's receptivity to the supernatural. In England, Wordsworth honored childhood as a wellspring of inspiration. In the New World, the Transcendentalists took up this theme.

This section traces the classical and Christian elements that Romanticism reworked into a more secular fabric of thought. It emphasizes their combination by Wordsworth, who became a principal advocate for the Romantic vision of nature and childhood, and who was admired and imitated by the American Transcendentalists. He continues to be cited when people claim that children have a special bond with nature. Therefore for the purposes of this book, Wordsworth will be taken as the primary voice of tradition against which contemporary changes will be measured.

The Romantic theme differed from the preceding scientific account on three fundamental issues: the function of memory, the quality of nature, and the character of childhood. The dogma of Descartes, Locke, and other philosophers of the New Science was a mechanical theism—that the universe is God's creation, but a mechanism from which God exists apart. It follows that an adult mind is required to master nature's operations. This New Science secularized the Platonic and Christian dualism that separated the world of pure ideas and pure spirit from the world of matter. The Romantics, in contrast, emphasized the converse side of Platonic and Christian tradition that described the universe as an ensouled organism, in continuous living relationship with its creator. As Coleridge defined the Romantic alternative, the universe by itself is not God, but the divine spirit forms and pervades all parts of the universe and shows self-consciousness in mind and memory.[28] Therefore the world's truth can be receptively intuited at any age.

This Romantic position is a legacy of the Renaissance, when classical scholarship flowered, Plato was rediscovered, and Neoplatonic ideas were revivified. It is equally a product of the Reformation, which taught the soul's individual relationship with God and which counseled close study of the Bible, where the devout read Christ's appraisal of childhood for themselves. Romanticism combined a Platonic conception of nature and memory with a gospel conception of childhood, during a period of religious and philosophical pluralism that encouraged self-assessment.[29]

Platonic Memory

In a letter of 1815, Coleridge reminded Wordsworth of their common understanding that his friend's primary mission as a poet was to create a philosophy that would replace the dualism of Locke and the "Mechanic Dogmatists," to effect a "Reconciliation from this Enmity with Nature."[30] During their formative years of friendship, Wordsworth drew upon Coleridge's Neoplatonic scholarship to advance this goal.

Plato's *Timaeus*, like the book of Genesis, describes how the universe was divinely created as a good and beautiful whole; but it goes further than Genesis by making the universe itself a living creature through which one great soul—*anima mundi*—breathes. In Plato's *Symposium*, Socrates assigns the office of coordinating and sustaining relations between God and the creation to Eros, or love, who manifests his influence in everything from the amours of beasts to the raptures of philosophers. Although love takes higher and lower forms of expression, on the whole it affirms that the world is not a fallen place where all but the most penitent proceed to damnation. The pulse of love ensures that birds, beasts, and all the elements of the earth move in harmony, orchestrated by the divine plan, and that nothing in the universe is wholly dead, as everything respires divine aspiration.

In Neoplatonic symbolism, these principles are represented by a circle. A circle signifies the sustaining current of Eros, which flows ceaselessly out of God down through all levels of creation, to attract all things back to God. Because no part of the circle can be distinguished from any other part, it shows that the force of divine love is present at every point. It also expresses the infinite ongoing revolutions of the universe in time, and the timelessness of God's eternal presence.[31]

In the *Meno*, Plato related the divine nature of the universe to memory. According to his theory of anamnesis, the souls of all creatures pass through a series of earthly bodies. Between earthly visits, they partake of the paradisal rewards or purgatorial punishments that they have merited. During their period of disembodiment, they recognize their divine origin and true condition. Returning to corporeal constrictions, they retain this wisdom, like an ember of Being buried beneath the ashes of worldly distractions. Earthly progress, therefore, is not a learning but a recollecting.

In the *Phaedrus*, Plato related anamnesis to the classical art of rhetoric, which taught speakers to remember their topics—or *topoi*, places—by elaborating landscapes in the mind, and by locating ob-

jects that would remind them of their arguments' sequence along a
path that they could later mentally retrace.[32] Of what use is excel-
lence in this art of rhetoric, Plato asked, if it does not awaken memory of true Being, of the Good? Well applied, rhetoric must remind
listeners of the truths their souls once knew. In keeping with this
theme, the dialogue unfolds in a pleasant grove beside a sacred
stream, suggesting at once a *topos* for sacred recollection and the Platonic doctrine of Ideas, according to which beautiful embodied
things inspire the perceiver to crave the divine forms of which sen-
sible objects are reflections.

Christian Platonism

Wordsworth's "Ode on Intimations of Immortality from Recollections of Early Childhood" suggests that children are especially
receptive to Platonic anamnesis. To cover himself, in a preface to
the ode, Wordsworth assured readers that he never intended this
suggestion of preexistence to give pain to pious Christians. He
could plead honestly. In the fifth century, the rhetorician St. Augustine converted a Platonic sense of memory into Christian doctrine.
Instead of the Good, what beaconed at the base of memory, Augustine reasoned, was God. He set up a logical proposition: since a
happy and blessed life is universally desired, it must be known
through memory; and the source of happiness and blessedness is
God. Therefore God, container of memory, must be retrievable
within it.[33]

In the thirteenth century, St. Bonaventure, a Franciscan friar
well read in Platonism and St. Augustine, wrote *The Mind's Journey
to God*, a spiritual manual that promoted three guidebooks for
the recovery of the memory of God.[34] The Book of Scripture leads
a person to a correct reading of the Book of Nature. Versed in
the Bible, people can find traces of God, correspondences to higher
truths, everywhere in external nature. With eyes opened to the
work of God in nature, they can turn within and read a similar im-
print in the Book of the Soul. In the Middle Ages and the
Renaissance, this theology sanctioned poetic license to find the
physical world a storehouse of symbols—mnemonics for spiritual memory.

Embedded in all these teachings was the principle that the
physical world itself cooperates to preserve memory. That places and
things recall something else beyond themselves was the rule
of rhetoric, the doctrine of Platonic Ideas, and the counsel of

St. Bonaventure. These traditions made memory a vital force with powers of spiritual protection. They suggested that pressing backwards in memory fosters spiritual advance.

Between childhood source and adult salvation, however, stood the Christian doctrine of original sin. Helping to create this orthodoxy, Augustine, in his *Confessions*, remembered his willful youth with contrition. "The weakness of infant limbs, not its will," he observed, "is its innocence."[35]

Childhood was not honored as a period of innocence and divine intuition until the seventeenth century, when this association appeared in the work of the Metaphysical poets Henry Vaughan and Thomas Traherne. Wordsworth may not have known of Traherne, whose writing remained in manuscript form until the twentieth century, but a copy of Vaughan's *Silex Scintillans* found its way into his personal collection.[36] Whether Wordsworth synthesized his ideas independently or with Vaughan's influence is unknown. It is apparent, however, that Wordsworth, Vaughan, and Traherne shared a common reassessment of childhood.

Metaphysical Memory

Following the examples of Plato, St. Augustine, and St. Bonaventure, Vaughan and Traherne reasoned that the Good, or God, is recoverable through memory. In turning the pages of the Book of the Soul backwards, they found the opening chapters the most portentous.

For Vaughan, who grew up in the gentle grandeur of the Welsh valley of the River Usk in the early 1600s, the beginning appeared closest to the source:

Happy those early dayes! when I
Shin'd in my Angell-infancy.
Before I understood this place
Appointed for my second race,
Or taught my soul to fancy ought
But a white, Celestiall thought,
When yet I had not walkt above
A mile, or two, from my first love,
And looking back (at that short space,)
Could see a glimpse of his bright-face;
When on some *gilded Cloud*, or *flowre*
My gazing soul would dwell an houre,

And in those weaker glories spy
Some shadows of eternity.[37]

In a similar spirit, Thomas Traherne read in the Book of the Soul
the lines:

Those Pure and Virgin Apprehensions I had
from the Womb, and that Divine Light
wherewith I was born, are the Best unto
this Day, wherein I can see the Universe.
By the Gift of GOD they attended me into
the World, and by his Special favour I remember
them till now.[38]

Vaughan and Traherne combined personal ecstatic memories
with Platonized Christian beliefs to arrive at a series of equivalences:
the garden of Eden, the golden age of the human race, the inward paradise of a blessed soul, and childhood are comparable conditions.
Where one condition is stated, the others are metaphorically implied. For these two poets, their childhood experience of the world
was the closest analogue that they knew to Eden, the golden age, and
the felicities of a fervent soul. Therefore, like Augustine, they
searched for the Good that is God through autobiographical reminiscence; but unlike Augustine, they found what they sought in
their beginnings.

The Bible presented two images of childhood: choosing either
required selective reading. According to the dominant doctrine of
original sin, children were vessels of error and ignorance that must
be cleansed and filled with knowledge through the authority of parents, preceptors, and priests. The words of Paul epitomized this position: "When I was a child, I spoke like a child, I thought like a child,
I reasoned like a child; when I became a man, I gave up childish
ways" (I Corinthians 13:11). On the subject of childhood, Vaughan
and Traherne read not Paul but the Gospels. In Matthew 18, when
the disciples come to Christ demanding "Who is greatest in the kingdom of heaven?," he sets a child in their midst, replying, "Truly, I
say unto you, unless you turn again and become like children, you
will never enter into the kingdom of heaven." Echoing this passage,
Vaughan exulted that childhood is "an age of mysteries! which he /
Must live twice, that would God's face see."[39]

Convinced of the divine harmony of the cosmos, Vaughan and
Traherne concluded that only human beings, who have the power of

free will, can fall out of grace, but as infants we enter the world as innocent as bird or beast or lily of the field. Therefore children enjoy a special attachment to dumb creation, and remembrance of childhood accord with the world can serve as a guide to mature perfection. In Vaughan's words:

> Some men a forward motion love,
> But I by backward steps would move,
> And when this dust falls to the urn
> In that state I came return.[40]

Vaughan and Traherne inhabited the bright ring of the Neoplatonic circle in which beginning and end meet. For them, Paradise Lost and Paradise Regained were neighboring estates. Christian, both poets accepted that after childhood innocence, people fall into experience and loss. They acknowledged the human race's "blessed sin" that brought Christ to earth as a redemptive savior. Unlike orthodox Christians, however, Vaughan and Traherne emphasized blessedness rather than sin. Although they would not gain full reunion with God until death, they could anticipate it in maturity by reexperiencing their childlike apprehension of the world. In Traherne's terms, the divine light by which he saw the world in infancy was the same light by which he viewed it with his highest reason.

Wordsworth's Task

Receptive as he was to Neoplatonic ideas, Wordsworth could not easily enter the Neoplatonic circle. Vaughan and Traherne worked in an age that still tolerated Neoplatonic belief in an animated world in which all things are joined by a divine "tye of Bodyes." Wordsworth and Coleridge worked in an age increasingly disdainful of these "superstitions."

Wordsworth's writing suggests that he was acutely aware of his dilemma. By his own account in *The Prelude*, he had grown up nurtured by nature's powers: first as a young child, playing along the banks of the Derwent River under his mother's indulgent eye; later as a motherless boy at Hawkshead Grammar School, roaming the borders of Lake Windermere; then as an orphaned young man, visiting his sister Dorothy at Penrith. As it was to Vaughan and Traherne, for him his childhood envelopment in nature was:

> a time when meadow, grove, and stream,
> The earth, and every common sight,

> To me did seem
> Apparelled in celestial light,
> The glory and the freshness of a dream.[41]

Into this concord, the ambivalent note "dream" appears. Wordsworth's memories of nature were at odds with orthodoxy both in and out of church. The age in which he worked showed a new appreciation of individual development as a process by which the adult progressively emerges from the child; and this accentuated sense of individual history both fostered, and benefited from, the burgeoning new genre of autobiography to which Wordsworth contributed. Yet the same growing prestige of science that encouraged autobiographical consciousness challenged the validity of Wordsworth's consciousness. By the time that he matriculated at Cambridge in 1787, the mechanical universe of Locke and other "Mechanic Dogmatists" had been generally accepted to be fact. According to the premise that the universe operates like an inanimate machine, there could be no significant encounter between a living child and dead matter. Therefore Wordsworth's memories of childhood experience must be delusive.

The paradox was deepened by other characteristics of his time. According to the literary historian Josephine Miles, English verse of the eighteenth through the nineteenth century exhibits an increasing reliance upon the physical world's capacity to convey ideas and emotions.[42] In premodern metaphysical and courtly poetry, objects, plants, and animals carried standard heraldic associations: for example, the lamb signaled innocence; the lark, gaiety; the lion, valor; the rose, love. Traherne and Vaughan read the landscape in this way. In their work, as in texts before them, a cock crowing signified the soul's awakening to the resurrection; a fountain, freely flowing grace. Reviewing attributions of emotion to physical things in major works of English poetry since 1700, Miles found that standard symbols gave way to a closer look at the object itself, along with a more variable, individual response.

In this respect, poets kept pace with the new empirical emphasis upon the close observation of facts. Seemingly in flight from science and industry, yet in keeping with secular attention to the things of this world, eighteenth- and nineteenth-century poets, including Wordsworth (with some borrowing from his sister Dorothy), kept notebooks that revealed as close an eye for the details of nature as naturalists' reports. Wordsworth worked in a period that instructed him to observe nature with a new fidelity, and to record the emotions evoked with a new subtlety, at the same time that it denied what he saw and felt sanctity.

According to Raymond Williams's analysis of eighteenth- and nineteenth-century British culture, nature, childhood, and poetry came to appear solaces from the pressures of industrialization and urbanization. Therefore poetry about childhood in nature offered escape and restoration.[43] The irony is that British society idealized nature and childhood even as it let villages be engulfed by manufacturing cities, the rural poor pushed off their land through enclosures, and children sent into factories and mines. Wordsworth worked in an age that encouraged him to recollect and record the very things that it threatened to destroy.

From Wordsworth's perspective, at issue was not only the sanctity of his memories, but the sanctity of his vocation as a poet. The influence of Locke and other empiricists trivialized poetry as well as childhood. Locke's theory that an infant's mind is an empty slate upon which experience inscribes sensations erased the doctrine of original sin, but it introduced the restriction that perception must be passive to be true. It made ideas valid to the degree that they are either empirical—meaning in strict correspondence to sense observations—or logicomathematical. As this chapter's preceding summary of Locke demonstrated, his philosophy relegated poetry to light entertainment, and stripped poetry and childhood of the possibility of religious intuition.

According to Locke, the existence of God and the content of God's laws are as evident as a Euclidean proof. Therefore sober souls schooled in mathematics can deduce the existence of God from a systematic study of the order, harmony, and beauty of the universe. "The illiterate bulk of mankind," Locke advised, must rely upon revelation as it is imparted in the Bible and by ministers of sober faiths.[44] By this logic, religion became not a matter for experience but solely a matter for reasoned demonstration or compliant faith. Mystical intuition was denied poet, peasant, and child.

Romantic Reasons to Remember Childhood

To find defense for poetry, Wordsworth and Coleridge studied German Romantic idealism as well as Neoplatonism. According to Fichte's extreme form of idealism, the mind itself generates the world it knows. According to the moderate idealism of Kant, the mind makes essential contributions to what it perceives. Wordsworth was moderate. "What then does the Poet?" he asked, and answered:

"He considers man and the objects that surround him as acting and re-acting upon each other, so as to produce an infinite complexity of pain and pleasure."[45]

To chronicle the actions and reactions of people and surrounding things, Wordsworth needed to grant the mind and nature mutual dignity. Lockean empiricism conceded the world's reality; but by prescribing that sensations passively register the impressions of a dead, soulless world, it condemned the mind to accumulate impressions with no moral significance. By this same logic, if the mind enlivened the world by projecting its own pleasures, fears, and moral values, it was condemned to live among the ghosts of its own fancies. This second risk was similar to that of Fichtean idealism, which asserted that there is no world outside the mind's conjurations.

Wordsworth avoided the risks of empiricism on the one side and Fichtean idealism on the other by reviving the Neoplatonic function of the imagination. In the *Enneads*, referring to the work of the great sculptor Phidias, Plotinus observed that "the arts do not merely copy the visible world but ascend to the principles on which nature is built up."[46] Wordsworth, Coleridge, and other Romantics across Europe invested the imagination with insight into "the principles on which nature is built up." Because Wordsworth wrote, on the whole, as if he assumed an external material world, for him the imagination had a twofold role: it apprehends the orderly principles of nature, and the coordinated principles of the responsive mind. Graced with insight into the operation of nature and the mind, the artist shapes a medium to reveal their harmony.

Like Locke, Wordsworth was prepared to give importance to sensations. He believed that poetry, in keeping with the operation of the mind itself, must begin with careful observation of the visible world. He also believed, with Locke, that these sensations give rise to complexes of ideas and feelings within memory. Like the associationist psychologist David Hartley, he considered childhood primarily a period of sensation.[47] But he had no use for associations that were passive at best or fanciful at worst. In his words:

> Whose mind is but the mind of his own eyes,
> He is a Slave; the meanest we can meet![48]

Wordsworth believed that images, ideas, and feelings must be ordered by the imagination, because it sees into the essential significance and moral influence of things. It does so because it is "conversant with or turns upon infinity."[49] The imagination best accomplishes its task, Wordsworth believed, in the tranquility of recollection, when it integrates sensations registered by a responsive sensibility.

The great bequest of childhood is that it is a period of fresh, passionate response. Not yet burdened by adult inattention, convention, and worldly worry, a child absorbs sensations that give life to the growing imagination and help sustain it in maturity. Referring to basic objects of nature such as a fine day, flowers, a storm, the sky, and heavenly bodies, Wordsworth observed:

> How dead soever many full-grown men may outwardly seem to these things, all are more or less affected by them; and in childhood, in the first practice and exercise of their senses, they must have been not the nourishers merely, but often the fathers of their passions.[50]

In his preface to the *Lyrical Ballads* of 1800, Wordsworth noted that a poet is distinguished from other people by never losing this passionate response to the visible universe. According to Coleridge, Wordsworth himself exemplified this quality. It was his genius "to carry on the feelings of childhood into the powers of manhood; to combine the child's sense of wonder and novelty with the appearances, which everyday for perhaps forty years had rendered familiar."[51]

Beginning with a childlike sense of wonder, the task that Wordsworth set himself was to observe, respond, and awaken moral sentiments by reflecting upon experience in the serenity of memory: for in the quiet of memory, imagination is responsive to the promptings of the heart—"the one human heart" common to young and old, rich and poor, literate and illiterate. "In a word," he said:

> if I were to write a sermon, and this is something like one, upon the taste in natural beauty . . . all that I had to say would begin and end in the human heart, as under the direction of the divine Nature conferring value on the objects of the senses, and pointing out what is valuable in them.[52]

For Wordsworth, the powers of the heart and the imagination are allied: they confer value on outward things by heeding intrinsic moral values.

In effecting this reconciliation between the human spirit and nature, Wordsworth fell back upon the same premise that fired Vaughan and Traherne. As it was for the Metaphysicals, nature for him was a book that the human spirit may read for its edification,

because a unifying spirit forms and breathes through all things, joining nature to humanity. In "Lines Composed a Few Miles Above Tintern Abbey," he recalled:

> And I have felt
> A presence that disturbs me with the joy
> Of elevated thoughts; a sense sublime
> Of something far more deeply interfused,
> Whose dwelling is the light of setting suns,
> And the round ocean and the living air,
> And the blue sky, and in the mind of man;
> A motion and a spirit, that impels
> All thinking things, all objects of all thought,
> And rolls through all things.[53]

In these "Lines," Wordsworth recorded the process of meditation that he wished to encourage in his readers.[54] In returning to a
once loved place, he found that nature safeguarded his memories
through the permanence of landscape and unfailing seasonal renewal. He himself had changed from what he was as a boy when
"like a roe" he "bounded o'er the mountains, by the sides / Of the
deep rivers, and the lonely streams"; but he did not mourn the loss.
He appealed to readers to remember childhood "spots of time" not
for their own sake but as the source of their highest sympathies in
adulthood. Contemplated in retrospection, the beauty of nature im-
presses serenity and beauty upon the mind. Therefore in later life in
sadder settings, memories of childhood immersion in nature bring
"tranquil restoration." These memories have a moral influence encouraging "little, nameless, unremembered acts / Of kindness and of
love." Because they rekindle communion with the spirit pervading
creation, they have power to lift the spirit to the "serene and blessed
mood" of imaginative insight. Then:

> the breath of this corporeal frame
> And even the motion of our human blood
> Almost suspended, we are laid asleep
> In body, and become a living soul:
> While with an eye made quiet by the power
> Of harmony, and the deep power of joy
> We see into the life of things.[55]

In confronting the paradoxes of autobiography, like the eye and ear in "Tintern Abbey," which half create and half perceive, Wordsworth partly drew upon earlier traditions and partly reworked them. Like Vaughan and Traherne in the face of the mechanistic nature of the New Science, he reaffirmed the Platonic tradition that all things are pervaded by a divine spirit. By this means, his childhood perception of an active universe remained sense, not nonsense. He broke away from this tradition's reading of conventional religious symbols in natural things, however, to directly observe the qualities of things themselves.

According to Coleridge's account of the creation of the *Lyrical Ballads*, Wordsworth's principal intent was "to give the charm of novelty to things of every day, and to excite a feeling analogous to the supernatural by awakening the mind's attention from the lethargy of custom, and directing it to the loveliness and wonders of the world before us."[56] By finding the supernatural within the natural, Wordsworth assimilated the secular spirit of his age, yet spiritualized it, maintaining the sanctity of his experience. He went beyond Vaughan and Traherne by finding the growth of a poet's mind fit subject for attention—to the extent of the fourteen books of the 1850 edition of *The Prelude*, which detailed his personal process of development with a degree of self-consciousness that the Metaphysical poets never dared. By Wordsworth's time, the supernatural was no longer easily discovered in the natural. The simple Metaphysical plot of a pilgrimage had to be replaced by an open-ended exploration in which life's significance is deciphered as it unfolds.

The Romantic Model of Development

The literary critic M. H. Abrams has argued that the meaning that Wordsworth discerned within his life is broadly representative of a new Romantic pattern, which can be described as the opening of the Platonic circle into a spiral.[57] Vaughan and Traherne maintained a sense of memory comparable to Plato's doctrine of anamnesis, in which the soul's learning is a recovery of original perfection. Therefore they sought to repossess their native state of "Angell-infancy" in maturity. For Wordsworth and other Romantic writers, there could be no going back, given the challenges of a more recalcitrantly secular world in which the miseries of industrialization and social upheaval pressed heavily upon them. Direction became determinant, and the end that they aspired to became a higher point than the beginning. This new model of development can be represented by the following figure.

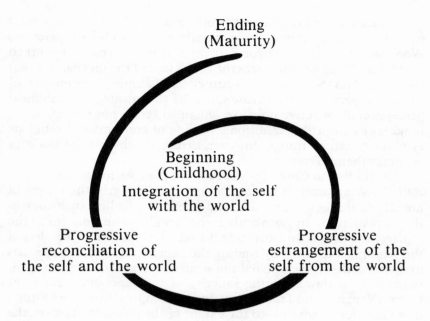

Ending
(Maturity)

Beginning
(Childhood)
Integration of the self
with the world

Progressive   Progressive
reconciliation of   estrangement of the
the self and the world   self from the world

Figure 1. The Romantic Model of Development

Without violating Christian tradition, this spiral imaged the nineteenth-century spirit of progress and history more accurately than a circle. On a universal scale, a spiral mapped the Creation, Fall (as the curve descends), Redemption (as it rises), and Apocalypse. The pattern of an individual life parallels these events through birth, sin, salvation, and final resurrection. Abrams has argued that when Wordsworth and other Romantic writers secularized Christian history by comparing it to individual autobiography, they also secularized the meaning of paradise. The great Romantic transformation of the circle was that the goal came to represent—not a state to be granted by God in moments of grace, after death, or on the millennium—but a present potential to be won through spontaneous intuition or creative labor.

Different Romantic writers emphasized different aspects of this spiral. Some, unlike Wordsworth, considered the curve of social history and individual history inseparable. Blake, for example, considered the world of nature itself fallen, and believed that it would take a more beneficent form, along with human life, after an intervening mental and historical revolution. In Germany, Schelling, Hegel, and Schiller drew comparable connections. Therefore Schiller acknowledged that attraction to nature, childhood, and rural or primitive society is inevitable. But he warned the poet "not to lead us back to our childhood," but to "lead us onward to our coming of age, in order to allow us to feel the higher harmony which rewards the fighter and blesses the conqueror." For, said Schiller, "that nature which you envy in the non-rational is unworthy of your respect or longing. It lies behind you, it must ever lie behind you."[58] (Hear how his admonition echoes in the work of Freud.) Depending upon a poet's emphasis, the Romantic spiral either demonstrated proximity between the spirit of maturity and childhood, or their distance.

New World Variations

From England and Germany, the Romantic synthesis passed to the American Transcendentalists. They read Romantic tributes to the power of the imagination and to the value of the child, the local, and the commonplace as a self-confirmation. Ralph Waldo Emerson called the position that he adopted simply Idealism, but he attributed "Transcendentalism," the name by which he and his followers became known, to Kant's use of "transcendental" to signify the a priori intuitions of the mind by means of which sensory experience is admitted and arranged.[59] Trusting the value of their intuitions and their local material, Emerson and his colleagues proceeded to write a new American literature.

Although the historical conditions under which the Transcendentalists came of age paralleled those of the Romantics, in some respects their relationship to their place was distinctively American. They were the descendants of Puritans and other immigrant groups who had left Europe's social and political disruptions in order to create a New World. Nurtured on the Bible, they were accustomed to the sublime mode of poetry, the poetry of praise.[60] Intensifying their gratitude for this land of refuge, the Puritans arrived with the conviction that the land they encountered was raw material for the New Earth promised in the book of Revelation. According to Revelation, after the second coming of Christ, Satan would be chained and God's chosen flock would enjoy one thousand years of earthly bliss, in preparation for the end of human history and eternal bliss in heaven. New England settlers saw the landscape through the coloring that they had been chosen to prepare for the Apocalypse by transforming the wilderness into a New Earth, and by building cities that would become a New Jerusalem.[61]

Puritan enthusiasm is exemplified by the "Contemplations" recorded by Anne Bradstreet, as she watched the sun set upon an au-

tumn landscape. Her reflections formed a popular theme in sermon
as well as verse:

> I wist not what to wish, yet sure, thought I,
> If so much excellence abide below
> How excellent is He that dwells on high,
> Whose power & beauty by his works we know!
> Sure he is goodness, wisdom, glory, light,
> That hath this under world so richly dight.[62]

Despite these panegyrics, the orthodox maintained the fine line of
theism that, although God created and governed the world, and sustained it by His continuous presence, and wrote upon it so that
everything was a symbol or moral parable of the divine, He was not
in it. How could it follow?

The Transcendentalists followed Puritan premises straight into
heresy. Crossing a New England common on another twilight
evening, through the medium of "the bare ground," "the blithe air,"
and "infinite space," Emerson had an unmediated experience of the
divine. "I become a transparent eyeball. I am nothing. I see all. The
currents of the Universal Being circulate through me; I am part or
particle of God."[63] The human soul perceives the divine in nature,
according to Emerson, because it enjoys a direct relationship with
both God and nature: the individual soul is part of the Oversoul of
the Creator.

Given that innate intuition, not labored logic, is the preemi-
nent means of knowledge, a child may be as wise as a seasoned sa-
vant—or wiser. If nature is a book of wisdom that reduplicates the
form of the spirit, then a child's ingenuous, receptive wonder is the
best instrument for learning. A writer, in turn, needs to preserve a
childlike spirit in order to see into the essential character of things.
Emerson observed:

> The sun illuminates only the eye of the man, but shines into
> the eye and the heart of the child. The lover of nature is he
> whose inward and outward senses are still truly adjusted to
> each other; who has retained the spirit of infancy even into the
> era of manhood.[64]

Through Emerson, this Romantic image of the child's special
perceptiveness passed to succeeding generations of American poets.
As it was conferred, it converged with the trend in modern poetry
that Josephine Miles has identified: an increasingly empirical, varied

use of objects and events as vehicles to carry poets' meanings. The result became "a wider universe of possibilities" in poets' images of the child as well. For example, Walt Whitman's poems, "There Was a Child Went Forth" and "Out of the Cradle Endlessly Rocking," report his childhood assimilation of blows as well as morning-glories, his premonition of death as well as poetic power. Emily Dickinson frequently adopted the persona of a child in her verse and letters, where it sometimes signified the playful freedom necessary for her art, sometimes her fragility and fear in the face of death, but most often, the biblical promise that a childlike nature is required for admission into paradise.[65]

A Contradictory Tradition

Contemporary American poets, and all contemporary literate people in the West, inherit the contradictory legacy of the preceding "science of childhood" and "poetry of childhood." On the subjects of childhood and nature, modern Western society maintains conflicting assumptions. On the one side, nature is a mechanism to be known through passive perception and logical reasoning: powers not yet developed in the child, who is thus primarily defined by deficits. On the other side, childhood is a time of strong sensation and intuition, when spiritual harmony between the self and nature is vividly apprehended, forming a pattern of renewal to be drawn upon in memory.

As members of Western society, we may maintain these two sides of tradition in unresolved contradiction. We read poetry, novels, biography, and autobiography that describe childhood as a time of formative perception. We seek restoration in parks, gardens, and woodland hikes, where we can be "close to nature." We send our children off to camp in the country, because we believe that experience of nature is good for them. Yet we consider ourselves modern rational beings who know that nature is a mechanism that operates by laws that empiricist science has already half-deciphered. As science progresses, we expect to have remaining mysteries resolved. When children show signs of animism or poetic fancy, we smile indulgently. In contrast to sober adult reason, imaginative perception and wonder over nature's simple everyday events make children divertingly appealing.

The preceding assumptions coexist in an uneasy balance. By not thinking about these discrepancies, we can maintain them. According to either Wordsworth or Heidegger, however, one of the distinguishing characteristics of poets is that they ponder first principles.[66] The chapters that follow will present the work and thought of five contemporary poets who confirm this expectation. Well read in their literary heritage, they are familiar with the preceding Romantic and Transcendentalist connections between childhood and nature. At the same time, they live in our modern secular culture in which science defines the value of childhood perceptions. As these poets make their way among these conflicting claims, they illuminate our culture's assumptions with rare clarity. They also illustrate new relations to nature and childhood that contemporary diversity affords. In the pages that follow, these poets define their place within the cultural context that this chapter has reviewed, sometimes echoing positions that have already been reported, sometimes suggesting new possibilities of connection.

The chapters that follow have been broadly conceived. To acquaint readers with who these poets are, each chapter covers basic biographical material, philosophies of nature, and views on language and style. Choices of philosophy, language, and style regulate how these poets admit childhood memory into their writing.

To borrow a hermeneutic metaphor, the purpose of the following chapters is to create a clearing—an open space in which all attention is focused on hearing and understanding—in which each person's work and thought can stand out in its own light.[67] To this end, in the presentations that follow, each poet has been solicited to speak, with minimal interruption by commentary. It is hoped that as each person's words follow in turn, readers will begin to hear these authors concurring or taking exception to each other. By the time their versions of nature and childhood are compared in chapter 6, readers will arrive as informed participants in a dialogue of insight. In this process, the people presented here will assume their rightful role as poets if they come to be heard speaking not just for themselves, but for many. Taken together, they exemplify some of the major understandings and perplexities of our time.

Chapter Three

Confrontations: William Bronk and Henry Weinfield

   This chapter presents the work and thought of the poets William Bronk and Henry Weinfield. They are presented together because they share an essentially common confrontation with nature, with similar consequences for their use of memory. In characterizing what is common between these two poets as a "confrontation" with nature, this chapter seeks to emphasize the word's etymological meaning of standing face to face with something. It may be something resistant that presents an obstacle; and to some degree, this undertone of a threat to the fulfillment of desire runs through both poets' accounts. The word *confront*, however, does not necessarily imply hostility. One also confronts a lover; and the ambivalence of this relationship, which captivates even as it threatens independence, suggests their relationship with nature more accurately than simple opposition.

Given these connotations, this chapter also presents confrontations in the sense that these poets' work and ideas are brought
together for comparison. Beginning with basic points of agreement,
the two men have diverged widely in the forms of poetry that they
have written and in the images of nature that they incorporate.

This chapter opens with William Bronk, because he has articulated the seductiveness yet threat of nature with the most compelling
single-mindedness. People's relationship with the world, which for
him means predominantly the natural world, is his great theme.
Childhood, on the other hand, is perspicuously not. His views on people and place provide clear reasons why it should not be. He rejects
the Platonism of Romanticism and presents a scientific account of
nature, but he has pushed modern scientific assumptions to their ultimate end, beyond popular credence in the stability of the self. His
conclusions, however, are implicit in his premises. Therefore his reasons for avoiding memory compose an important part of this book's
reflections on the contemporary significance of childhood memory.
He has unsparingly presented the modern dilemma with which the
poets Weinfield and Ignatow also contend.

WILLIAM BRONK

Since the 1950s, William Bronk has been publishing poetry and
prose in little magazines and alternative presses. For almost all these
years, his center of work has been his home in Hudson Falls, New
York. From this location, he has not pursued a wider audience, trusting that, "if the poems have any real vitality and stability, as long as
they're around where they can be discovered they'll make their own
way."[1] One sign that time has begun to work in his favor is that *Life
Supports*, his collected poems, won the American Book Award in
1982. In 1983, his prose essays, some written in the 1940s, were reis-
sued under the title *Vectors and Smoothable Curves*. His latest
books of poetry are *Manifest;and Furthermore* (1987), *Death is the
Place* (1989), *Living Instead* (1991), *Some Words* (1992),and *Mild
Day* (1993).

By place as well as preoccupation, Bronk remains in the line of
inheritance of the Transcendentalists. According to an old gazetteer,
at the turn of the century his home town of Hudson Falls was "one
of the principal commercial centers of the country and one of the
most notable places in northern New York. . . . principally noted for

its great industries."[2] The first colonists came to build sawmills and gristmills on the seventy-foot falls at this point where the Hudson River changes course from east to south. In the nineteenth century, paper manufacturing became the dominant industry, using pulpwood floated down the river from the Adirondack Forest. In its building stock, in its industry (and relics of it), and in the proximity of farms, fields, an old feeder canal, and the Old Champlain Canal, the town still evokes the nineteenth century within the twentieth.[3]

The Bronk family, who gave their name to the borough of the Bronx, were established in the Hudson Valley by the 1640s. Bronk takes no special pride in his ancestry, which was not wealthy nor high placed; yet his connections to the nation's past may have created an affinity in him for Thoreau, Melville, and Whitman, the subjects of his first book of prose. A paternal great-uncle lived in the household when Bronk was growing up, and he entertained his great-nephew by recounting his own upbringing in the 1870s and 1880s on an Albany County farm. His stories about slaughtering and smoking meat, growing, spinning, and weaving flax, and husbanding seeds from year to year recalled not only the nineteenth century, but a world more ancient than modern.

Bronk's father improved the family fortunes by going into the lumber, fuel, and building materials business and investing in real estate. One sign of his success was his acquisition of a large Victorian house with surrounding fields and wood lots that were in time partially sold off. The son still lives in this house, which he moved into two years after his birth in 1918.

Whereas many contemporary poets, such as Williams and Ignatow, have confronted urban environments beset by violence, banality, and ugliness, Bronk has escaped this burden. Certainly there are many features of Hudson Falls that might strike outsiders as ugly or banal. The town has been marred by decaying buildings, dumping, haphazard planning, and hard use. These man-made blemishes, however, are encompassed by the region's essential gracefulness. Like Mistress Bradstreet contemplating the autumn sunset, Bronk remains in a locality where he is assailed by landscape and light. His poem "Where It Ends" gives testimony to it.

> The gentleness of the slant October light
> Cancels whatever else we might have thought.
> It is a hard world, empty and cruel;
> but this light, oh Jesus Christ! This light!

> The maple leaves, passive in front of the house,
> are laved in it, abandoned, green gone.
> That nothing else should matter but this light.
> Gentleness, gentleness, the light.[4]

The transformation between Mistress Bradstreet's period and his is that the tone of the contemplations has changed. The poem contains no couplet comparable to hers:

> Sure he is goodness, wisdom, glory, light,
> That hath this under world so richly dight.[5]

For Bronk's work, one could adopt the same subtitle that he applied to his youthful essay on Melville: "The Ambiguities."[6] By Melville's time, Mistress Bradstreet's underworld and other world were already beginning to come unpinned. The faithful theme of Bronk's own writing might be put in the one word *world*; but by his time there are worlds and worlds. Bronk's world is clearly ambiguous.

The underlying world is the "hard world, empty and cruel" of the poem "Where It Ends." This foundation encompasses all human and natural events, as human affairs are subsumed in the universe of nature, which takes away everything it gives. As a defense against this all-inclusive world of nature, people fabricate alternative worlds through stratagems of reason. In this sense, Bronk's writing often equates the words *world* and *reason*; and he has never tired of contemplating how rationality plots the worlds in which we believe. He has examined the alliance of world, reason, and belief so closely that Cid Corman, his friend and first publisher, once wrote objecting that he did not value either belief or reason, and that, therefore, all of Bronk's talk about them seemed irrelevant. Bronk wrote back:

> Belief and reason. Yes, as you say, I am clearly doomed by my very approach. You know, maybe, someone who isn't? But I'm sure you do know the old story of the inveterate gambler who was warned away from a certain game on the grounds that it was crooked and replied that he knew it was crooked but that it was the only game in town. Belief and reason, God help us, are the only game in town. Who knows better than I know, how—so to speak—crooked they are. But this is what it is to be human.[7]

Point by point, Bronk's poems analyze how belief and reason continuously construct worlds, which continuously fall apart.

Fabrications

One method of construction that people attempt is the idea of place. "As others before / and after, or in other worlds, I have loved / my native places as if, without them, / I should be lost," Bronk has confessed. "But our homes are contrivances, coverings / for emptinesses."[8] People impose place identity on what is in fact unbounded terrain. Bronk has suggested that his very rootedness in one locality that is so atypical of the present age—living in the same house since the age of two, in a region with over three hundred years of family connections—has allowed him to be radical in his evaluations. "If you haven't got them," he has said, "you're likely to think that there are roots and they're very meaningful. But, if you have them, you realize their limitations."[9] Everyone, everywhere, inhabits unmeasured space.

Another fundamental strategy of rationality is time. Bronk has rejected the reality of time for the same reason he has rejected the demarcation of space. "You talk about time," a poem observes, "but time requires a line / from one point to another, time requires / direction and distance."[10] In the world itself, there is no point, line, direction, or distance. In Kantian terms, time and space exist only in our minds.

Another great flaw in rationality is that its foundation—names and terms—is weak. "How almost like the beasts, with only barks / and cries we are, so tangent is any speech / to all we know,"[11] another poem exclaims. Language is an insubstantial human invention, incapable of communicating embodied experience in the world.

Behind all these methods of rationality—time, space, place, language—our guiding intention is to give things form, but the forms we give are fabrications. In Bronk's words:

> World, world, I am scared
> and waver in awe before the wilderness
> of raw consciousness, because it is all
> dark and formlessness: and it is real
> this passion that we feel for forms. But the forms
> are never real. Are not really there. Are not.[12]

After place, time, names, and forms have been exposed in this way, there is no basis left for autobiography, another exercise in ra-

tionality. Accordingly, Bronk has never written any. The nearest
that he has come to autobiography is a one-verse poem entitled "The
Antibiograph," in which he gently parodies Freudian free association. In an interview, Bronk has said that he finds the intensity of
feeling and the irrational freedom of dreams a close approximation
to the way we experience the world even in waking hours.[13] The
poem exposes the dreamlike desires that would give life form, in
contrast to the chance waywardness of actual occurrences:

> I look a long time now—years
> longer than my father ever lived—
> where life used me, pushing for purposes
> I never understood and purposes
> it never had, perhaps. I let it do
> and it did, did all it did in spite
> of my not being able ever to set up house
> somewhere with youthful mother for fear
> young father will one day want to take me
> to all the places he always goes himself.[14]

The poem plays with the fact that Bronk's own life history
loosely fits Freud's scheme of dream interpretation. As an only son
with two sisters, Bronk was closely attached to his mother and distant from his father. For one reason, the older Bronk was always busy
with some new business enterprise. For another, there was a strain
between father and son similar to that which Freud attempted to explain. Close resemblance between the two, which Bronk has come
to recognize more and more as he himself grows older, perhaps increased their awkwardness with each other. Whatever the reasons,
his father never, as Bronk recalls it, talked with him. The poem suggests, nevertheless, that Freud's interpretation of dreams is another
inventive effort to give reason to an irrational world.

In addition to rationality, the other great element of ambiguity
from which Bronk finds the world created is desire. The final section of *Life Supports* contains the poem "Questions for Eros," with
the verse:

> Eros, have I ever called your name?
> Always, in all the calling, I had thought
> to call you. Is there a name? Or have
> I always called it wrong? Wrong? Is
> there a right? What name is not diminishment?[15]

In some respects, Bronk's Eros is like the one addressed by Socrates at the banquet in Plato's *Symposium*. This Eros was the squalid child of Poverty and Plenty: homeless, poor, and always in distress like his mother; but enterprising, fertile at intrigue, and terrible as an enchanter and sophist like his father . . . therefore a philosopher at all times. Socrates' Eros, however, stung the soul so that it could never be satisfied by the transitory objects of the natural world, thereby impelling the soul to seek its heavenly identity. Given Bronk's disbelief in anything beyond the impermanence of nature, Eros impels him futilely.

Like the poet who projected him, the Eros in Bronk's poems makes no boasts or self-displays, so he can be easily overlooked. After readers and reviewers repeatedly remarked that Bronk's poems are short of love, he wrote a brief rejoinder, "Yes: I Mean So OK—Love":

> Some people say, "Well good,
> now you write about love."
>
> "Yes," I say, "what else,
> I always have; what else?"[16]

The Real World

Despite Bronk's relentless analysis of the pretences of rationality and the desires that impel them, he is not a skeptic about the world itself. Sometimes, in his writing, *world* means a false fabrication of reason and belief; but at other times, it means nature's reality which reason cannot contain. Behind our fumbling apprehensions, Bronk is certain that there is a real world. It tantalizes him directly through the place where he is.

Bronk finds desire a door in and out of this world. In imagining shapes and possibilities of fulfillment, we leave reality for invented worlds. But when desire remains unsatisfied—as it must be, being desire—our invented worlds fail us and we are left confronting nature's reality again.[17]

In his attempts to speak of this real world, it appears as formidable as the God of medieval theology: uncreated, infinite, eternal, independent, self-existent, indestructible, ineffable. The absurdity of rationality is that it attempts to limit this limitlessness. Buildings, plumb lines, the layout of cities, the naming of places and things—all of our geographic mapping, all of our invention of a concrete spatial world—are efforts to contain ourselves within this world without boundaries. "A kind of cage for the sake / of feeling the bars around us."[18] Calendars, clocks, time schemes, histories, biographies, and autobiographies are efforts to put starts and stops to this beginninglessness and endlessness. "We want the mark of time."[19]

Words, being finite, presuming finitude, can barely approach reality. The poem "The Real World" asserts words' inadequacy before this world that activates the senses, even as it escapes human sense:

> There is a real world which does make sense.
> It is beyond our knowing or speaking but it is there.[20]

Belief in this infinite world makes Bronk reject finite belief or reason. He maintains that any idea of the finite is a contradiction of the infinite. Feeling ourselves finite, we pretend as though the infinite does not exist, but our real experience, our real existence, in a real world, is in an infinite field.[21]

This real world is the only true basis of identity that we have; but the difficulty for us is that—infinite—it is so much beyond us that, in one sense, it has nothing to do with us. "The real surrounding is a medium more than man / can will, despoil, or even reckon with."[22] The difficulty for us is compounded because, in another sense, this medium has everything to do with us. It, on its side, wills, despoils, and reckons with us. One certainty of reality is that it will undo us:

> We are in the real world as nothing in ourselves, as a skin on that world, as a network of nerves, an awareness not of ourselves but of that world, even as though we might be that world's awareness of itself. In this act of union, the self is shed like an exoskeleton and we lie so close against the real world our identity lies there.[23]

Despair in response to this reality runs through Bronk's writing. Against the charge that people call his poems pessimistic or dark, he has invoked the defense of truth. "I deal with despair because I feel despair," he has said. "Most people feel despair but they are not prepared to deal with it except pretend that it's not there. I think it's there metaphysically. . . . It's in the nature of reality and not to be denied."[24]

Sanctifications

Despite Bronk's preceding convictions, his world remains ambiguous. It is not all mocking silence and dark despair. He titled his first published book *Light and Dark*. For a reissue of early pieces, he again chose chiaroscuro, *Light in a Dark Sky*. Against the title *Silence and Metaphor*, he has placed *To Praise the Music*. Music, which expresses ravishment by the world's beauty, is one of Bronk's most constant metaphors. Defying nature's randomness, music imposes order on feeling. So does poetry. Thus many of Bronk's poems have been inspired by the experience of music—the most temporal of all activities, as precisely quantified as mathematics, which must be played against silence.

One of Bronk's most memorable phrasings is that "I am the instrument of the world's passion."[25] Unable to possess any identity of any consequence for himself, he yet lives in the world with feeling, recording poetry filled with response to the real physical world that surrounds him. Love may be a terrible power that sweeps him up one moment and drops him into despair the next, but sometimes love holds him captive in simple adoration. Consider another colloquoy between his reason and the world, entitled "The Lover as Not the Loved." The poem places him among the woods, fields, canals, and towpaths that he has walked since boyhood: a setting that he still haunts, that haunts him. The "T" that it refers to is the junction where a feeder canal runs into the Old Champlain Canal:

> What am I then, because in a sense, I am
> though clearly not? Compared to what there is,
> there could never be comparison because
> I am wholly absorbed in it, am nothing more.
>
> Something other though, something apart.
> A feeling instrument. How else?
> Tonight, in April, I stood on the bridge by the T
> in the late, faint light, worshipping.[26]

Bronk has accepted twentieth-century science's cosmology that the real world of nature is an incalculable field of energy in which humans form transient sentient parts. He has also accepted the Kantian division that the mind imposes space, time, and other categories of reason on a world that is an unknowable and hence unsayable thing-in-itself. He has added the contemporary conclusion that there is ultimately no intact "thing." In the poem "The Annihilation of Matter," Bronk compares naive belief in the substantiality of objects with a physicist's world of dematerialized energy exchanges: in the case of vision, exchanges of light energy. Echoing the poem "Where It Ends," which was ignited by the sight of maple trees in autumn light, he reduces knowledge of the world as a whole to tricks of light. "Examined," the poem says of objects, "they yielded nothing, nothing real":

> They were for seeing the light in various ways.
> They gathered it, released it, held it in.
> In them, the light revealed itself, took shape.
> Objects are nothing. There is only the light, the light![27]

In the mystic traditions of all religions, sincere seekers after God are rewarded by a transcendent vision of light. In Buddhism, this vision effaces the self. In Hinduism, it reveals that the individual self is a mask of the Self of God. In Christianity, selfhood is a miracle of grace: God in his mercy saves the self. Christian mysticism demonstrates three responses to this dependence upon God. Focus on the figure of the self inspires ecstatic gratitude for the miracle of individual consciousness. It is this ecstatic, wonder-struck self in the act of discovering the world that Vaughan, Traherne, and Wordsworth celebrate and identify with childhood memory. When focus is divided between the figure and the field, there is contrition over the self's smallness, as in St. Augustine's *Confessions*. When a full gaze is turned upon the field, consciousness of the self is obliterated by the revelation of God's infinity.

Bronk's poetry highlights the contemporary paradox that as faith in scientific reason has demolished religious faith, blow by blow, it has whittled away an infinite, eternal, uncreated, ineffable divinity by replacing it, discovery by discovery, with an infinite, eternal, uncreated, ineffable real world. This newly discovered field of force may be graceful, but it performs no interventions of grace. The empiricist impulse, which at first seemed to foster a new selfhood with a sharply defined individuality, has proceeded to the conclusion that this selfhood is mere semblance. There is no figure. There is only field. Strictly applied, this logic leaves no basis for autobiography or childhood memory. Our relationship to nature is dubious because there is no self to relate to it: there is only it.

Bronk works on this ledge where the perspectives of modern physics have dropped him. One of his most beautiful poems, "Virgin and Child with Music and Numbers," observes that in this condition of enlightenment "we are held somewhere in the void of whole despair." There, it also observes, we are held "enraptured, and only there does the world endure."[28] When a friend asked Bronk whether he thought of this luminous reality beyond human fictions as sacred, he answered, "Oh, of course, sacramental." When he was asked if he felt its sacredness constantly or momentarily, he replied, "I feel it in varying intensities, the way you feel anything." As he ages, however, he has found his consciousness of immanence intensify:

> In the course of time I am more frequently or more constantly aware of that. And also feel more and more able to speak of it directly, in the kinds of terms which we are likely to shy away from and be embarrassed by, particularly as what becomes for this civilization a more and more secular world becomes less and less so for me.[29]

No Time or Place for Memory

The modern vision of nature that Bronk has assimilated dissolves the stability of memory as well as the self. Although Bronk's poetry contains the characters of Our Lady, the Baby, Joseph the foster father, and the Three Wise Men, his philosophy makes no place for epiphanies, in the sense of the crystalized moments of revelation that Edith Cobb attributed to childhood memory.[30] No more than recurrent images in dreams, his memories can never be firmly apprehended and detained. In the poem "Out of Context," for example, he compares memory to familiar phrases of music that possess us because we cannot recall the name of the piece from which they come. After the poem asks, "what of our days the same way?," it describes ineffectual efforts to place the day's repeating phrases, and it concludes: "The context that the music of our days / seems barely out of is one it was never in."[31] Therefore Bronk avoids the pretence of inventing contexts for his memories.

He also finds no nostalgic attractions in childhood. When children appear in his poems, they are caught in the same condition as adults, and as futilely, they seek the comfort of believing that they are somewhere at sometime. "In the automobile, in the dark," one poem observes, "the children ask, / 'Where are we now?' " Distracted by energy and desire, they cannot comprehend their situation. "Our / young glee drove us, heedless, and we went, / heedless, and dropped down where the force was spent." Bronk would never exchange the watchfulness of his philosophic years for this ignorance. "When I was little," he notes, "the lights in the natural world / were not so beautiful as they are now."[32]

Perhaps he also feels no nostalgia for childhood, because he would allow that his sense of nature as an awesome, incommunicable force dates back to childhood in some form, although he did not consciously articulate it until he was around twenty. In "Home Address," the only poem in which he makes overt use of early memory, he recalls an unspecifiable dread of his family's overlarge, unmanageable Victorian house, which he later identified with his dread of nature's unmanageable force. He and his sisters hesitated to enter the house alone:

> And, in the winter, coming alone from school,
> we waited outside till there was at least a light
> and someone else inside. We hated the night.
> We hated the big, disordered, incongruous house.
> It was beyond our power. But we stayed on there.[33]

The house has become one of Bronk's most enduring metaphors. When it provides comfort, it expresses the positive angles of world making, as in his poem "My House New-Painted."[34] But the house cannot exclude the engulfing horror of nature: it is a product of it. In "The Strong Room of the House," he compares his sense of nature to the secret in Bluebeard's castle, locked away but eerily present:

> Something nourishes
> As a plant might, in the dirt of the floor, grows
> in the light from the window or in the dark at night.
> Horror is what it is called. It is the whole
> strength of the house, will be there when we move out,
> hang deep in the cellar-hole when the house is gone.[35]

Having noted Bronk's reasons for rejecting the pretences of memory, it can be added that he has little practical need for memory, because he lives *in* its context. His dismissal of reminiscence is mitigated by the fact that he remains in the same house that he has inhabited since the age of two. Therefore his surroundings everywhere recall the past and maintain his continuity with it. In this Proustian sense, he would allow that some poems sweep in feelings that go back to childhood, activated through the actual fact of his world through *mémoire involuntaire*.

An Unpremeditated Life

It was never Bronk's deliberate intention to remain in his childhood place.[36] As a young man, he left home for Dartmouth College.

There, under the guidance of an English teacher, Sidney Cox, he conceived the ambition of becoming a writer. He anticipated that through writing he would win fame and fortune in the bright lights of big cities far from Hudson Falls. From Dartmouth, he went on to the graduate program in English at Harvard. In contrast to Cox's humanism, he encountered the heyday of New Criticism. In Bronk's terms, "The graduate work in English was conducted on a kind of semi-scientific basis that way as though you were studying chemistry." Repelled, he dropped out of school and moved to Greenwich Village in New York, with the plan that he would establish himself there as an author.

Regarding his youthful expectation that he would soon secure such success that he would not need any other trade except writing, he now says simply, "But we learn." After service in the Eastern Defense Command during the Second World War, he taught English for one year at Union College in Schenectady. His father had died in 1941, and the family assets were tied up in his father's business. Bronk returned home to take over the business temporarily until he could find a full-time manager. This temporary job lasted some thirty years. He never married or moved away again, caring for his mother until she died in 1982.

Bronk's themes as a poet correspond to his physical centeredness in Hudson Falls, which signifies at once the frustration of his youthful desires and the fulfillment of his attachment to his native place. Merely by reacting to his surroundings, he enjoys continuity with his past even as he details the impermanence of human affairs. His method of composition consists of unpremeditated responses to his place and reflections on his situation, in the course of which poems often take him by surprise and he writes them down as they come, hardly revising at all.

Bronk avoids literary theory of any kind for the same reasons that he avoids autobiographical memory: it is another fiction of rationality, and it creates a self-consciousness that distracts a poet from his true calling of attention to the world. Therefore he never seeks to understand how personal experience, such as childhood experience, contributes to his work. For himself:

> It is this poem and it is that poem. And how it all ties together, I wouldn't know. And I think it is not well for a writer to know things like that. I think we shouldn't be self-conscious about our writing. We shouldn't write about ourselves. We should write about . . . well, you say it's about the world, and a lot of

people wouldn't feel that the world I write about is their world, but it is *my* world I write about.[37]

He is convinced, nevertheless, that it is their world as well as his. "Most people don't know what's going on and I point out to them what the universal is," he has said. "They don't know that's what's happening to them, but I tell them."[38]

Bronk's attitude to writing conforms to his conception of fictional worlds that deny reality and the real world of nature beyond them, and his belief that "any serious statement, artistic or not, is about the world beyond."[39] His approach is also in harmony with his declaration that "I am an instrument of the world's passion." Pressed on this issue, he can be exasperating, although illuminating, as in the following exchange between himself and his friend Henry Weinfield:

Weinfield: The way you're talking, it's as if the poem exists outside of you and you're transcribing it.

Bronk: Of course, where else? Do you think it's something in your goddamned head?

Weinfield: Well, who wrote it then, if it exists outside of you? Where does it come from?

Bronk: It's like the universe: it was not created; it's simply there. . . .

Weinfield: Let me play the devil's advocate for a moment. Maybe you like the fiction that it's out there, outside you, that you're not creating it yourself.

Bronk: Yeah, I may; that might be so. But it doesn't bother me. If I am deceiving myself at that point, it doesn't bother me. But it's like, all right, you walk out the door, and you hadn't been paying too much attention to the weather, and there's a tremendous light. The sun may be going down; it's been a cloudy day, and it's been dark all day, but there's this clear area just above the horizon and you're astonished: here's this light. You didn't invent the light and who the hell did? Nobody; it wasn't planned; it just happened.[40]

Witness the source of poems like "Where It Ends" and "The Lover as Not the Loved." Having no identity apart from the world, Bronk has no agency to calculate a career or to compose theory and verse. He considers himself no more than a particularly watchful aggregation of nerves that registers the world's occurrences.

In the age of Hesiod and the muses, the poet's role as an instrument of composition was attributed to divine possession, in the Middle Ages, to grace. According to this rhapsodic tradition, poetry is an ecstasy—*ek stasis*, a standing out of oneself—in which the poet is lifted out of mundane human limitations and ordinary autobiographical identity. The word *inspiration* assumes a similar belief: to be inspired is to in-spire, to breathe in, the *spiritus* or divine animating power. Whether the poet be shaman, sibyl, prophet, or saint, he or she is a mere medium that the spirit passes through. The poet's personal distinction is to be empty and to invoke the spirit in. In modern terms, Bronk has reclaimed this ancient vocation.

In doing so, he has aligned himself with one aspect of the Romantic and Transcendentalist conception of the imagination; in other respects, he has distanced himself. If we go by a textbook definition of the Romantic imagination as "a feeling, a sensibility, an intuition, immediate and intense, by which the ego apprehends the character of something outside itself," then Bronk is a textbook case.[41] If we note the conviction of Wordsworth, Emerson, Whitman and other Romantic figures that the imagination "ascends to the principles on which nature is built up" and "is conversant with or turns upon infinity," then Bronk remains in their company. He too has said that "I point out . . . what the universal is," and that "any serious statement, artistic or not, is about the world beyond."[42] He also holds with the Romantics that the receptive power of the imagination soars as worldly distractions and preoccupations sleep.

Bronk parts company with the Romantics over their faith that the imagination apprehends a transcendental order that generates "the world beyond." For the Romantics, the imagination mediates corresponding forms in the perceiving self and the external world, because it is inspired by one universal spirit that animates and coordinates the self and nature. For Bronk, for whom the world of nature is all there is, there is nothing for the imagination to mediate: there is only nature; there is no self. Finding neither creative spirit nor creative self in the world, he has no personal future and no past.

As this chapter began by suggesting sexual parallels to human confrontations with nature, it will end this discussion of Bronk's work with his own sexual metaphor. In the brief poem "The World as a Thieving Woman," Bronk wryly confesses his helpless dependence on nature, and the perverse satisfaction that nature gives him:

The things I love you for
are things you stole from me.
You come at every door
and take my surety.
When you have stripped me bare,
then you must take me too,
that I get back a share
by having you.[43]

HENRY WEINFIELD

Like William Bronk, Henry Weinfield finds music, which is autobiographically mute, inspiration and analogue for his work. He allies himself with a different musical vocation, however, which involves a different relationship to nature and childhood. The method of composition that Bronk describes is akin to the ancient role of the rhapsode, the human instrument that a spirit of greater power and duration plays upon. Weinfield associates himself with a second, more artful vocation that has coexisted with rhapsodic possession at least since the time of Homeric minstrels: that the poet is the music-maker himself, a gifted master of meter and verse who spellbinds his audience by transporting them into magical worlds beyond the everyday. Such a poet transcends his individual history by dwelling in poetic myth, imagery, and form itself. Through epic and lyric arts, he creates an alternative world to the natural world of change and loss. Through art's long-lasting forms, he enters the suspended time of cultural memory: enjoying in this way the "forgetting of ills and a rest from sorrow" for which Hesiod gave the Muses credit.

Weinfield's different conception of his role involves a different relationship to Romantic tradition, which this section will explore. Bronk, in youthful prose essays on Transcendentalism entitled *The Brother in Elysium*, submitted Walt Whitman's faith in an external world "in which whatever existed was right and perfect" to subdued scorn.[44] Nevertheless, in his faithful attendance upon the details of his local world, Bronk has remained loyal to the famous counsel of Whitman's mentor, Emerson, that "I become a transparent eyeball. I am nothing. I see all. The currents of the Universal Being circulate through me."[45] Behind this advice to be transparent stands Wordsworth, who directed poets to perceive the divine spirit within the objects of the senses. American Transcendentalism conforms to Wordsworthian Romanticism. Bronk has remained true to

American poetry's roots by seeking to be transparent, if not to the Universal Being, then at least to the universe. In addition to rejecting Whitman's faith in the perfection of the natural world, Weinfield has distanced himself from Wordsworth's and Emerson's emphasis upon present perceptions. He has done so in keeping with an alternative Romantic impulse that sought solace from nature in the world of artistic creation itself.

As Coleridge recalled his and Wordsworth's co-authoring of the *Lyrical Ballads*—the book whose publication in 1798 is widely held to mark the beginning of the Romantic era—they decided to form an amicable alliance of two complementary poetic roles. As Coleridge described the book's plan, he himself was to create characters romantic or supernatural:

> so as to transfer from our inward nature a human interest and a semblance of truth sufficient to procure for these shadows of imagination that willing suspension of disbelief for the moment, which constitutes poetic faith. Mr. Wordsworth, on the other hand, was to propose to himself as his object, to give the charm of novelty to things of every day . . . by awakening the mind's attention from the lethargy of custom, and directing it to the loveliness and the wonders of the world before us.[46]

American poetry has predominantly followed Wordsworth's direction by concentrating upon the world before it. European poetry has more frequently taken liberties like those of Coleridge by investing the shadows of the imagination with poetic faith. It is this course that Weinfield has pursued.

This appeal to poetic faith has its own universe of custom and tradition to contend with: the universe of preexisting literary forms. These two poles of romantic ambition are ambivalently evident in the critic Clarence Thorpe's description of the Romantic imagination:

> Such is the power of the creative imagination, a seeing, reconciling, combining force that seizes the old, penetrates beneath its surface, disengages the truth slumbering there, and, building afresh, bodies forth anew a reconstructed universe in fair forms of artistic power and beauty.[47]

This statement can be applied to Wordsworth to describe his effort to awaken "the mind's attention from the lethargy of custom" and "to give the charm of novelty to things of every day." Thorpe, however, is describing Keats, who belonged to Coleridge's company; and in this case, the old he is referring to is myth, story, and preceding artistic achievement.

Weinfield's alliance with Keats and Coleridge is evident from the titles of his three books of poetry: *The Carnival Cantata* (1971), which alludes to eighteenth-century music; *In the Sweetness of the New Time* (1980), which alludes to the "sweet new style" of Dante and Provence; and *Sonnets Elegiac and Satirical* (1982), which varies old sonnet forms. He has also written a prose study, *The Poet Without a Name: Gray's "Elegy" and the Problem of History* (1991). He is currently translating the complete poetry of Mallarmé for the University of California Press. Mallarmé, of all modern poets, epitomizes the habitation of language itself as a release from material constrictions.

Music and Books

Weinfield's beginnings prepared him for the company he has elected. He was born in Montreal in 1949 to a family with deep Canadian roots on his father's side.[48] His paternal grandmother's ancestors were among the first Russian Jews to emigrate to Canada in the 1800s; and his paternal grandfather came from Austria in the early 1900s. His mother, in contrast, emigrated from Nuremberg, Germany, just before the Second World War. She came from a wealthy Jewish family that had moved within the imperial circle, with a colorful history and a castle hung with originals by the Old Masters. She fled the total destruction of her world by the Nazis. For her, resettlement in Canada represented a tragic uprooting, the annihilation of her past. In a sonnet about the Jewish diaspora, her son has explored the confluence of longing for "home," Jerusalem, the promised land— a paradisal ideal of peace and stability that has been as persistent as it has been elusive. The poem denies its possibility of fulfillment:

> I said that home is just a metaphor
> For everything that we must leave behind.[49]

Through family stories, the mother transmitted to her two sons a sense of connection to their family's German past, and a sense of irrevocable loss for a world left behind.

Home was also problematic because Weinfield's parents never managed a happy marriage. When he was nine, they divorced. From the beginning of his life, the place that came closest to the ideal of home was his paternal grandmother's house. It was the childhood place that he felt to be *his* in a special way; and he has said that if he were ever to write an autobiography, it is the one place above all others that he would have to include to account for himself. As in Bronk's case, it was a large Victorian house, but unlike Bronk's house, it lent itself to comfortable possession. In addition to his grandmother, two great-uncles lived there, and it was the center of gravity for the whole family. The back gate opened onto a hauntingly beautiful path with a semirural feeling, that wound its way to the summit of Mont Royale. As a boy, Weinfield often took walks there with his great-uncles.

Inside, the house was filled with reading and music. Gray's *Elegy*, the subject of one of Weinfield's books, was a favorite of his father and his grandfather, which his grandfather was remembered to recite by heart. In addition to literature, the family's great pleasure was music. Weinfield's father, a lawyer, came home from work to play the piano with serious dedication, and his brother also became a pianist. Every Friday evening, all of the family gathered at the grandmother's house for dinner. After dinner, his father and other relatives gave informal piano recitals. Like Bronk, Weinfield loves music keenly and it is a common figure in his poetry. Unlike Bronk, he also knows it technically; so that it serves as a pattern as well as figure, as he works comfortably with sonnets and other metrical forms whose roots go back to music and dance.

A precocious reader, Weinfield soon began to work his way through his family's library. Imaginary plots and settings in books transported him into magical worlds. By kindergarten or first grade, he had begun his own versifying, mostly in the form of limericks and ditties motivated by the sheer pleasure of playing with language.

Word play and voracious reading did not keep him from play outdoors, where he was allowed free access to the city. With a bicycle, he enjoyed a wide range, and he played outdoor sports through even the severest winters. Every summer, he was sent to camp, so that Canada's woods and lakes were part of his childhood too.

Weinfield still loves Montreal without qualification. He describes it as a city with an expansive sense of freedom; a city of human scale instead of skyscrapers; an amiable, graceful city with beautiful parks everywhere. Despite its greater openness in the sense of freedom, air, and sky, he describes it as more "closed" than New York, in the terms that it is more private, more a mosaic of *vieux faubourgs* and a reticulation of small streets than a grid of vast public avenues. If ties of work and family did not now keep him in the United States, he could gladly resettle in Montreal again.

He moved away from Montreal when he was sixteen. His mother decided to make a total break with her past once again by making a new beginning in New York. Although her son did not come to New York by choice, given an age when he was ready for adventure, neither did he come with reluctance. The small family of mother and sons settled in Rego Park, Queens.

Weinfield was shocked by the contrast between New York public schools and the excellent secondary school that he had left behind; he remedied the situation by often skipping school to explore the city or read on his own. During this period, he came successively under the spell of William Butler Yeats, Ezra Pound, and T.S. Eliot. He went on to major in English and philosophy at the City College of New York, where the teacher who most impressed him was Julias Elias, a philosophy professor who confirmed his idealism. Elias taught that whether or not the ideal world is the real world, as Plato may have believed, we must spend our lives trying to create and inhabit it. Whereas Wordsworth emphasized the Platonic doctrine that the mind is able to apprehend the world's divine character, Weinfield has emphasized the Platonic teaching that fulfillment is found in the beauty of the intellect's own creations.

While working on the college literary magazine, the *Promethean*, Weinfield heard about William Bronk, and wrote to him, initiating a correspondence and friendship that continue. After several years spent editing various literary journals, he returned to school for a doctorate in English at the City University of New York Graduate Center. He now teaches in the Program of Liberal Studies at Notre Dame University.

A Life of Letters

Given Platonism's and Romanticism's contradictory search for immanence in the world of nature and transcendence in the world of ideas, Weinfield's emphasis on transcendence has drawn his attention away from sensory experience, including childhood experience of nature. Words that he has applied to the poet Thomas Gray apply equally well to himself. Weinfield noted that Gray's *Elegy* begins as twilight is obscuring the poet's perception of his country setting:

> In Plotinian or neo-Platonic terms, in order for the mind to take hold of its true object there must be a removal from the narrow experience of the senses. And since the visual and the vision-

ary are inversely related, the fading of the landscape . . . is a prelude to meditative *clarity*.[50]

The distance from poetry about nature or childhood that this position implies is already evident in Weinfield's first book, *The Carnival Cantata*, which consists of mostly undergraduate compositions. With the caveat that it is something of a fiction to impose an abrupt beginning upon a history of steadily developing involvement, Weinfield traces consciousness of becoming a poet to a space of eight lines in the title piece of the collection. The sources of inspiration of his first "real" poem were entirely human creations—film, music, and language itself. Its impulse had nothing to do with a remembered childhood sense of paradise. On the contrary, its catalyst was the film *Les Enfants du Paradis*. He saw the film several times, and concurrently, he listened to a Bach cantata with music suggestive of a carousel. The images of the carousel and the actors and actress in the film fused into a poem in which the decisive eight lines are:

> The little mimist with the hands,
> And the boisterous tragedian
>   are
> vying for position
>   though
> she is dead
>   no
> always dying.[51]

He had no plan to write these lines when he began. It was as if the poem itself took over, playing with the words "though" and "no," and then proceeding to write itself. He suddenly found poetry no longer "out there," a playful diversion, but out there confronting him in the engrossing exchange of the "I" and the "not-I" that German idealism has said constitutes the creative experience, and that the tradition of the muses perpetuates. He accepted the encounter like admission to a *métier*. "I wasn't even trying to express myself. Poetry was something outside me that I could tap into, and I was aware that I had a gift of some kind. It was some kind of work that I understood that I had."[52]

Reflecting on his engagement in the play of words, Weinfield accepts the position of the critic Harold Bloom that a poet develops through other poets. He believes that it is particularly true at the beginning of a career. "I really love poetry, and I love English poetry,

and it's my language. I am very moved by it. And I develop that way."
He has expressed the all-consuming exclusiveness of this identification in the refrain of one of his poems:

> The lives of the poets are my life—
> I am the lives of the poets.[53]

This formative environment of words removes Weinfield from
attention to his personal past and the physical world around him. In
his case it is particularly true to say that his work develops within an
existing community of words because he has an unusually retentive
verbal memory, and effortlessly remembers thousands of lines of favorite poems by heart. He also carries his own work in his head as he
sifts and refines it, not committing a poem to paper until it is complete. Sometimes this process of thinking through a poem, still not
knowing exactly where it will go, still struggling with the language,
extends over a period of years. He is not, therefore, a "writer" in the
physical sense. This cerebral process is probably closer to musical
composition than to a succession of written revisions; and Weinfield
suspects that it is similar to the method followed by early oral poets,
such as Homer. Through the span of time that his poems' creation
may cover, through their musical quality, they have little tie to mundane physical experience of the world.

Rather than the faithful rendering of the world before him,
Weinfield feels impelled to move on to new styles and subjects not addressed before. Branching off into new directions, however, involves
loss as well as gain. He has assessed the exchange in an interview:

> There are certain kinds of poems that I could write, for example,
> that I would never be able to write again. Because that is what
> happens with poetry—when you have completed something, you
> know, you have also lost something. Just like life in general.[54]

Having turned a passing aspect of life into poetry, having created something for someone else to pick up and assimilate, is not a
light loss. Sonnet Ten of *Sonnets Elegiac and Satirical* presents a recurrent theme in his writing:

> For years I sojourned in the Land of Prose;
> With other sojourners I sojourned there.
> It was a land of plenty, I suppose,
> But in the end I was a sojourner.
> I was a person then, a character,

And so I happened to encounter you.
It seemed that I had known you once somewhere,
Though both of us were merely passing through.
How long ago it was I cannot say
That I departed for the Land of Rhyme;
But it was long ago and far away,
And I am finished now with space and time.
When I arrived, I learned that I was dead—
And I am nothing now but what you read.[55]

Because poetry substitutes words for physical existence, it is helpless to contain the people, places, and things of the past or present. In place of material experience, however, it offers something more meaningful, which is spirit. For Weinfield, poetry is the language of the spirit; and the spirit, if there is to be any hope for it, will find itself at odds with the physical reality around it.

Desire and Reality

Tension between reality and desire is the dynamic that drives Weinfield's poetry.[56] It is apparent from the beginning in his undergraduate Platonism and in *The Carnival Cantata.* When he temporarily immersed himself in reading Marx and Hegel, he found a new set of terms to express it.

In Hegel's philosophy of nature and spirit, he found a systematic exposition of many conclusions that he had already arrived at on his own. To express his own sense of the relationship between words and the world, he has referred to the opening chapter of Hegel's *Phenomenology of Spirit*, on "Sense Certainty." Regarding the desire to speak of actual things, Hegel drew the conclusion that: "this is impossible, because the sensuous *This* that is meant *cannot be reached* by language, which belongs to consciousness, i.e., to that which is inherently universal."[57] With this aspect of Hegel's philosophy, Weinfield is in complete agreement. Language appears to point people into the world, but it actually takes them out of it. In some practical ways it can focus attention on objects and orient behavior, but, on the whole, it creates an alternate world that is irrevocably separate.

Language creates a tension between desire and reality because it magnifies desire itself. Beyond contingent, passing desires, which people share with all animals, it elaborates intricate realms of possibility. Thus language makes humans both beneficiaries and victims of a radical separation from the given physical world. For example, language enables people to do what no animal can do: to imagine that someday they will die. It also enables them to imagine that perhaps, by some fate, they will not. Language takes people out of the world by opening doors to an infinite variety of heavens and hells. For Weinfield (as for the Romantics in general, including Wordsworth), language seeks to express this apprehension of infinite possibilities.

Weinfield parts with the philosophy of Hegel because he believes that there is one more inevitable tension between desire and reality. As he has put it, "Hegel confuses harmony with history."[58] Hegel looked backwards to the golden age of classical Greece, and ahead to some future age when the spirit would realize itself in a perfect reconciliation with itself. Weinfield consigns belief in a utopian past or future to our century's dump heap of illusions.

Weinfield's vision is essentially tragic because he finds desire facing two monumental adversaries: nature and history. By the laws of nature, all beauties of person, beast, or plant are condemned to death. By the man-made laws of history, people who dream of social justice and the possibility of paradise on earth are often imprisoned or condemned to death before natural causes can get to them, and they are invariably frustrated. Within these strictures, desire negotiates a temporary truce by weaving its patterns of aspiration on the looms of language and art.

As a result of these convictions, Weinfield finds himself in conflict with the mainstream of American poetics. He rejects William Carlos Williams's famous dictum, "No ideas but in things," as an absurdity: ideas are the product of language, which cannot reach things, "the sensuous *This*." For the same reason, he parts with American poetic convention since Whitman's "Song of Myself," because he finds autobiographical experience inappropriate subject matter. Liberated from the autobiographical and the local, he feels free to take liberties with language that many American poets would deem heretical.

In the enormously influential Preface of 1800 to the *Lyrical Ballads*, Wordsworth announced that his purpose was "to imitate, and, as far as possible, to adopt the very language of men."[59] True to this tradition, Whitman asserted that vivifying words arise out of immersion in the concrete realities of everyday things, and Williams struggled to reproduce American speech patterns.[60] Weinfield belongs to an opposing tradition of word use, which has more adherents in Europe than in the United States. Perhaps his origins in a French city in a British Commonwealth country help to explain his independence from American doctrine.

The model with whom Weinfield agrees is again Coleridge, who, when he read Wordsworth's preface, protested that his friend misjudged himself. In the moments of strong passion that Wordsworth said give rise to poetry, Coleridge countered, men speak in the most unpoetical of languages, in no wise like Wordsworthian ballad or blank verse.[61] Weinfield, like Coleridge, believes that all poets' pronouncements about "writing in the very language of men" are self-delusion. He recommends that theory should focus instead upon poetry's proper sphere, its *musical* resources of sound, rhythm, and sense. For his achievements in this area, he considers Mallarmé, whom he is presently translating, the most advanced modernist. He is of one mind with Mallarmé in his belief that the poet must die as an individual to be reborn as an artist who can transform the accidents of daily life into the universal melodies of verse.[62]

Literary Landscapes

Spirit that leaves the language, events, and things of daily life behind, inhabits its own landscape. Landscape imagery is an important element of *The Carnival Cantata* and *In the Sweetness of the New Time;* but instead of real reference, their images evoke qualities of feeling or allegorical settings. If one were pressed to choose between a dichotomy of nature and city, they conjure up the softer landscape of Weinfield's childhood rather than the hard fact of New York where they were written. In place of either, however, they conjure up a world that is literary from its first moment of creation. More than anything else, this geography, "where mountains barricade the sun," where "trees cleave to the wind," where "the moon casts their shadows on the sand," takes its example from storybooks of the type that enchant both children and adults. They are images of a world created out of words.

As images of a world of words, they represent ephemerality and desolation. The sea figures recurringly, because it suggests the indifferent vastness of nature, which is the limiting margin of a poet's words. Weinfield never plays with the conceit that artistic achievement can secure immortality. Every poet, he believes, is like Keats, who lamented that he wrote on water. All the fire of a person's spirit is no more lasting than a lamp on the sand, all the intricacy of a person's labor no more effective than a net on the sea. The short poem "Slow Steps / The Muddy Shore" is representative of his use of landscape:

> slow steps,
> the muddy shore:
> a silhouette

upon the road.
He left his lamp
upon the sand;
he left his nets
upon the sea.

He left the face
the world had changed:
the world has changed,
has changed,
has changed.[63]

Weinfield's position has already been associated with the division defined by Coleridge in which some poets seek to create "shadows of imagination," in contrast to those who seek "to give the charm of novelty to things of every day." Weinfield himself has characterized the difference between his work and that of most of his contemporaries by reference to more general polarities described by Yeats in his book *A Vision*.[64] Yeats described two types of poets, both potentially great. One category, "primary" (which includes Wordsworth, Whitman, Williams—and the other poets in this study), writes out of objective experience, laying stress upon outward things and events and their interaction with inward thoughts. The other category, "antithetical" (in which Weinfield would put himself, and in which Spenser, Coleridge, Keats, Shelley, and Tennyson fall), writes out of conflict with the world as it is, expressing instead desire and imagination. Poets of this second kind, Weinfield has said, chronicle the history of the soul rather than the history of the body. Therefore for them there is no reason to record factual autobiography.

Antithetical poetry incorporates images from experience that have assumed the force of metaphors of spiritual conditions. In Weinfield's case, for example, the image of the sea is a childhood legacy, seen briefly during vacation trips to Maine. Beyond affording a few images and metaphors, however, his childhood world has never directly formed the subject of a poem.

If antithetical poetry is not to become a dream world of idle desires, it must reflect back upon reality. In rare moments of accord, physical actuality and desire may harmonize. Reality rolls on, however, and these moments of harmony give way to loss. Poetry then becomes elegiac. In moments of discord, desire holds reality accountable for what it is . . . and reality holds desire accountable for its illusions. Poetry is then satirical. *Sonnets Elegiac and Satirical* combines both modes.

The alternate world of desire, which language enlarges, can go by many names. Some common terms are "utopia," "home," and "heaven." In this sense, even a nonbeliever can believe in heaven. In an interview, Weinfield half-facetiously described himself as a "religious atheist" because he rejects dogma that would situate God and heaven in some aerial geography, but he puts a religious faith in poetry itself.[65] He believes that at its best the human spirit reveals an intelligence, purity, innocence, and force of love that gods and angels, if they were to exist, would have to model themselves after. It is poetry's calling to sustain this best side of the spirit.

It might be supposed that Weinfield's emphasis on the power of language puts him in the deconstructionists' camp. Like Derrida, he explores how language constructs mental worlds.[66] The similarity, however, is superficial. In practice Weinfield damns deconstructionism for treating language as a facile and ultimately faithless game. Derrida advocates the deconstruction of ideals; whereas Weinfield locates the origins of poetry in indispensable conflict between the real and the ideal. He argues that not only poets, but anyone who would remake reality to the shape of desire must turn to the "necessary fictions" of literature. Here, in this music, dreams of social justice and earthly harmony are kept alive.

Reappraisal of Wordsworth

When Weinfield was in his mid-thirties and he was first questioned about his relationship to childhood, nature, and memory, he drew a sharp dichotomy between himself and Wordsworth. He saw Wordsworth as a poet who begins with a sense of presence from childhood, as if "the poetry is back here in childhood and he wants to get it out." In contrast, in his writing he felt himself to be reaching for a perfection beyond the present, past, or even any possible future, as if "when I get out the poetry then I restore something that was missing."[67]

In his late thirties, in the book *Poet Without a Name*, he has articulated a more serious quarrel with Wordsworth than this simple conflict between retrospection and aspiration. With regard to both nature and history, he has concluded that Wordsworth sentimentalized his experience in some ways that were duplicitous.[68] When Wordsworth returned to the Grasmere Valley of his boyhood and idealized its impoverished rural figures as pure children of nature *as*

they were in all their misery, he abandoned his own youthful enthusiasm for the egalitarian ideals of the French Revolution and
abetted conservative Tory politics. His politics, with his memory,
became conservative.

Despite this analysis, Weinfield is not insensitive to Wordsworth's
virtues—to which he has found himself increasingly receptive as he
grows older. No one, he believes, compares with Wordsworth in his
ability to show how to use moments of harmony between desire and
reality creatively, how to treasure them and make them "food for future years."[69] For himself, however, this bequest of autobiographical
memory nurtures living, not writing.

Weinfield is no more inert to the enchantments that Wordsworth
found in nature than he is to the resources that he found in memory.
In a long poem on the theme of evolution, he has assigned Western
culture's ambivalent responses to the fugue of nature to two voices.
One voice sings the Christian/Hegelian melody, which Wordsworth
heard, in which humanity and the organic world proceed together toward a transcendent ending. Another voice expresses an alienated
humanity's fears that it is plotting its own holocaust. Like the dialectic
between the real and the ideal that he finds inherent in human existence, Weinfield sets these voices in counterpoint:

> (*First Voice*)
> It is a fugue that hovers in the air—
> all things are ordered in its harmony.
>
> (*Second Voice*)
> I hear that music, but I also hear
> chaos, confusion, and cacophony:
>
> The voices rise and fall, distinct and clear,
> like many rivers running to the sea—
>
> the sounds of desolation and despair
> of those who are afraid that they must die:
>
> where none are lost or languishing, and none
> are swallowed up in its immensity;
>
> that they must die before they have begun
> to realize the myriad destinies

> but all are met in one, and yet each one
> retains its own unique identity.

> that had been promised to them by the sun
> which now glints bleakly from a covered sky.[70]

Weinfield is also not unresponsive to the other great theme of Wordsworth's work: childhood. He has noticed that the innocence that adults must struggle to retain seems native to some children. In his own three children, he has sometimes glimpsed angelic features. He believes that once childhood is over, however, an adult's effort must be directed to new achievements, rather than backwards in retrospection. He has reflected upon general cultural trends that have related poetry to childhood, and presented three reasons why, on the contrary, he has never looked for illumination in childhood memory.[71]

For one reason, there is no going backwards. Cherishing childhood memories is symptomatic of an idealization of the state of innocence that children seem to personify, yet it takes a background of experience to perceive innocence. Innocence, and consciousness of it, are mutually exclusive. This rule applies to cultural history as well as to personal history. One of the central changes in the modern imagination is movement away from the idea of God, so that as a culture we have lost the unquestioning faith required to follow the gospel injunction that "unless you turn and become like children, you will never enter the kingdom of heaven" (Matthew 18:3). Modern intellectuals are too experienced in doubt.

From his Jewish position, Weinfield has added that innocence never was a matter of faith. Judaism never directed him to be a meek child before a heavenly father, but to be a man, which he always understood to be a separate estate. For Jewish men, there never was a retrospective heaven to lose.

He has noted that a second claim for the association of children and poets has been their common use of metaphorical thinking. The observation has often been made that children think like poets, and vice versa, and that they share a common propensity for myth, metaphor, and pathetic fallacy. The argument runs (see chapter 2) that poetry therefore maintains continuity with a childhood sense of the world. The fiction behind this argument, Weinfield argues, is that there is such a thing as a literal language that can be contrasted to metaphorical thinking. Even casual examination, he believes, reveals that all language—including scientific prose—is metaphorical. Thus children and poets lose their special preserve.

His third reason for not seeking inspiration for poetry in childhood memory is that children do not write great poetry.

Weinfield's charge is that modern industrial society has attempted to group poetry with childhood and partition it from adult activities because it perceives both poetry and childhood distortedly. The cause of its distortion is its own rampant childishness. True children try to understand the world, try to piece information together as well as they can. Poetry, used sincerely, struggles for truth and meaning of an adult kind. The society that would collapse these similar commitments to a similar level has exempted itself from the honesty of either effort. It has turned life into a superficial game marketed under a pretense of sophistication, in which people feel free to pursue their own self-indulgence, like spoiled children. When poetry is practiced under these rules, it is turned into an end in itself, a shallow performance, or a flirtation with irrationality. An appreciation of life, including poetry, as a striving to secure an elevated level of beauty or truth has been lost. In this society that is already primitive, irrational, and immature, poets and other artists have felt that they must break out and make something new. But they often mistake their direction and follow in the established path by cultivating greater primitivism, irrationality, and childishness.

In Weinfield's words, there can be heard echoes of the German Romantic poet Schiller, who observed that his contemporaries were tempted by childhood, nature, the rural, the primitive, but who urged resistance. "That nature which you envy in the non-rational is unworthy of your respect or longing," Schiller warned. "It lies behind you, it must ever lie behind you." Therefore the poet is "not to lead us back to our childhood" but to "lead us onward to our coming of age."[72] Weinfield, like Schiller, perceives an antithesis between nature and culture that Wordsworth mutes.

Poetry's Returns

How does a poet speak for a society that is childish, but not innocent, having disregarded the injunction to grow up? In such a society, Weinfield feels no obligation to learn its tongue and speak its parts, in the manner of William Carlos Williams. He takes to heart as intently as Williams that poetry must purify the language, must save it from abuse; but he does not seek saving words in a study of contemporary idiom in response to local things. In his development of open form, or composition by field, Williams felt a mission to forge *the* style for his time and place. In contrast, Weinfield would accept a multiplicity of styles, and he would keep the resources of every period of English poetry accessible for assimilation into the contemporary labor of creation. He believes that every new poet, confronting the challenge of evolving a personal style, should find the field open.

Although Weinfield divides language from the world, it does not follow that he finds poetry empty or unfulfilling. Language may appear meager and bleak compared to the sensory richness of experience, and it is empty to the extent that it cannot contain the times and places of embodied life. Yet ordinary contingent day-to-day reality often yields a sense of emptiness. Poetry then has the power to restore missing meaning. Eternity, which measures our time and place, may not be the eye of a benevolent father. Dead may be dead. But within the space and time we have, life can bear its own weight of fullness—to which poetry is not irrelevant:

> The truth of the matter is that the existence of God was never really a problem to me. I never really cared one way or the other. . . . In a certain way, art is sufficient, music is sufficient to me. I don't experience that kind of emptiness. . . . When you're full . . . I think people do experience fullness, and when they experience fullness the question of God's existence isn't a big issue.
>
> There is some way in which art brings us closer to *home*, whatever that is. And therefore to the world. It brings us closer to Being. That is what I feel about it. It's a question of getting closer and closer to reality. Not that you substitute one world for another world. It's that you're trying to get closer to reality, to the world itself.
>
> Interviewer: Is reality a certain sense of the world, a full sense of the world?
>
> Yes, yes. Assuming that reality is a fullness. If we say that reality equals fullness in some way. And I guess that is my only definition of reality. . . . I define reality in terms of fullness, in terms of meaning, plenitude.[73]

Poetry is part of the world's plenitude. In moments of accord with the world, in childhood or at any other age, we may enjoy fullness, and these memories nourish us. Apart from time, in childhood or at any other age, the Land of Rhyme offers a fullness of its own.

Weinfield has observed that Western culture has usually projected cravings for fulfillment backwards. Western ideals exhale *la nostalgie du paradis*, looking in the past for a vision of the promised land. To pagans, the past meant the golden age or the preexistence of the soul; to Jews and Christians, the time before the Fall; to the Romantics, childhood in nature; to Freud, the infant at the breast. In these ideals, there successively appear as redemptive figures adults companionable with the gods or God . . . the child . . . the newborn: inhabiting different paradises but sharing similar blisses. All exist where there is no death, or it is far postponed, where all desires are sympathetically fulfilled, where nourishment falls from the trees or courses freely from the earth like milk and honey, where it *is* sweet milk. The present age remains susceptible to this retrospective craving; but we suffer the disenchantment that we know that nostalgia requires forgetting as well as remembering, that the past was never entirely paradise. The age of bronze was predestined. The serpent rested waiting in the tree. Infant and child are mortal; and they inherit the fears and frustrations that maturity will magnify.

Weinfield has put this loss and gain of paradise in the elegiac terms of a poem, "Adam and Eve."[74] It begins—as his poems do—with a world of words: words that are all that we have left of Milton, a man of great experience, who said that the finest estate of heaven is found within. The verses meditatively weave around the concluding lines of *Paradise Lost*, at the point when the first children of paradise walk through their primal home for the last time, leaving it behind to go in exile into the world. They have irrevocably lost their perfect place, because when they enjoyed the garden of Eden and all its innocence, they began "to yearn for something / which is only a dim intuition: its location / unknown." Seeking this ideal, they lost what they had, and now must grieve for it, and forever look for it "far beyond the reaches of experience." How can we do less than our first parents, Weinfield has asked, being so closely related to them?

Through these ideas, Weinfield finds himself in essential harmony with Bronk; and it is no coincidence that the two men are personal friends. They share a consciousness that a poet's days are measured against nature's vastness, and that against this scale, every literary measure fails. Both men believe that language creates worlds that exist apart from nature, incapable of communicating physical experience: an inarticulate world of "barks and cries," in Bronk's phrasing; a siren world with its own fulfillments, according to

Weinfield. Therefore neither man considers poetry capable of preserving the past through autobiographical reminiscence; and neither has ever tried to do so.

Beyond these essential agreements, the two men illustrate the very different responses of primary and antithetical poets, to use Yeats's categories. Bronk, a primary poet, writes in direct response to nature, recording what he sees, ephemeral as his feelings and incomplete as his art may be. Weinfield, an antithetical poet, describes worlds remade in shapes of imagination and desire. This chapter has noted that Weinfield presents a position that is rarely heard in contemporary poetry, but that has ancient antecedents. Like Helen on the tower of Troy in Homer's *Iliad*, he finds embodied existence evanescent. From this position of reflective surveillance, autobiographical experience appears as insubstantial as a dream. As Homer has Helen muse to her brother-in-law Hektor, perhaps the gods portion out human passions that they may hear people's stories live on in poets' songs in time to come.[75]

Chapter Four

Reconciliation:
David Ignatow

David Ignatow's perspectives on nature and memory pivot between that of the other men in this study, Bronk and Weinfield, and the women, Lorde and Ponsot. With Weinfield, Ignatow believes that the artist, as a creator of culture, has a responsibility to advance ideals of cultural and political reform, and that no return to unthinking childhood immersion in nature is possible. As a Jewish man, like Weinfield, Ignatow has also related his commitment to forward movement to his understanding that becoming a man means something entirely other than a child. Ignatow also shares with Bronk, Weinfield, and Freud the tragic view that unity with nature, seductive as it may sometimes seem, is ultimately annihilating, so that the fundamental fact of our confrontation with nature is our inability to escape this union.

Despite these similarities, Ignatow has struggled through turmoil and despair to a revised understanding of his relationship with nature that places him, in some respects, in the company of Lorde and Ponsot. His relations with nature in old age may be summarized as a reconciliation, in the double sense of this word. He has achieved renewed harmony and amity with nature after years of estrangement and discord. This hard-won serenity, however, has not been free from reconciliation's painful edge of acquiescence to affliction.

Ignatow's changed relations with nature follow from his understanding of his role as a poet and his commitment to speak for his time and place. He has assimilated the prevailing scientific view of nature, but over his life span, since his birth in 1914, this view has begun to change. Like Bronk and Weinfield, Ignatow began by believing that people's craving for order and permanence alienates them from nature. He internalized a behaviorist view of people as bundles of fictive reactions to meaningless material processes. As he continued to read popular presentations of physics, however, he revised his position in keeping with an emerging new paradigm of a responsive, constructive world in which nature and the imagination cannot be separated. This new view of nature allows no permanence, but it implies order and connection.

An Autobiographical Voice

In struggling from estrangement to reconciliation with nature, Ignatow has followed the Romantic pattern of development that Wordsworth described—with some disenchanted twentieth-century revisions. His life's general conformity to this pattern coincides with his investment in the Romantic tradition, in contrast to Bronk or Weinfield. This alignment with Romanticism explains why his work is overtly autobiographical, unlike his two male contemporaries, and why childhood memory is an important theme in his writing.

Ignatow is as skeptical of Wordsworth's "intimations of immortality" in childhood and nature as Bronk and Weinfield; but he stands apart from these poets and in line with Wordsworth in his commitment to chronicle the social and cultural conditions of his age. Like Wordsworth, he has made autobiographical experience his main material. Wordsworth worked at the beginning of the modern age, when the self was gaining recognition as a creative force in itself, at the same time as it was still presumed to be attuned to powers outside itself. In his preface to *The Recluse*, Wordsworth wrote an apology for the emerging new literature of autobiography:

> if with this
> I mix more lowly matter; with the thing
> Contemplated, describe the Mind and Man
> Contemplating; and who, and what he was—
> The transitory Being that beheld
> This Vision; when and where, and how he lived;—
> Be not this labour useless.[1]

By now, it is customary for poets to describe who and what they are, and when and where and how they lived. The sensitive question is—to what end? To be self-centered incurs the danger that one may be . . . well, self-centered. In the passage quoted, Wordsworth worked to double purpose. He pleaded that it would not be useless to describe the Mind and Man Contemplating, and he gave as grounds for his importance that he had beheld a Vision. The dilemma that Ignatow has grappled with throughout his career is that few modern poets continue to consider themselves a medium for transcendent vision.

Ignatow is one of many poets who have come to the resolution that, as individuals with an individual history, they may epitomize the history of Everyman or Everywoman, or, more restrictedly, Every Man of Letters or Every Woman of Color. Although transcendence may not be this poetry's origin, it may yet be its goal: as the self, in the process of discovering points of commonality with other selves, finds itself speaking for voices greater than the self again. In this tradition to which Ignatow belongs, autobiographical identity is the medium for the message. The result is that, whereas Bronk and Weinfield compare their work to music, Ignatow's work may be described as a reading in which the events of his life form the text.

Ignatow's commitment to chronicling his changing relations to his time and place was intensified by his close ties to William Carlos Williams—the poet with whom Weinfield has contended. As a young poet, Ignatow was inspired by Williams, discovered by him, encouraged and promoted by him, and Williams became a friend for life. Just as Williams committed himself to remaining in the Passaic River Valley of his boyhood and crafting a style appropriate to its obdurate realities, Ignatow has defined himself as a poet of his native city of New York. Like Williams, he has struggled to reconcile childhood and adult experience. His changing styles, as he has refined his role as city poet, may be read as alternatives to Bronk's loss of self in poetry and Weinfield's loss of place.

Ignatow is also distinct from Bronk and Weinfield in that he has taken Whitman, and Whitman's vision of nature, much more seriously than they. For Ignatow, *the* crisis facing contemporary American poetry is that belief in a unifying principle in the universe, such as Whitman celebrated, has been lost, but acquiescence to this loss threatens moral diremption. In the sublime Romantic and Transcendentalist mode, Whitman aspired to sing about a divine unity greater than the self through the medium of the self, but this legacy no longer appears plausible. "But to give him up entirely," Ignatow has observed, "is to let ourselves sink into something which we just don't want to imagine":

> So we are at a point now where we talk to him, argue with him, refute him, and when things become very desperate we have an automatic reflex and fall back upon things that he said. We fall back upon the self once more. But that's still not adequate, which is the main problem. We're in a crisis, an intellectual, philosophical, and emotional crisis right now as poets.[2]

This chapter summarizes Ignatow's changing assessments of Whitman as he has talked to him, argued with him, refuted him, and ultimately come to a truce with him. His changing relations with Whitman, it will be seen, correspond to his changing relations with his own early memories of nature.

A Disenchanted Life

There has been more material available to trace the course of thought and feeling in Ignatow's work than there has been for any other author in this study. In addition to fifteen books of poetry and two interviews on the occasion of this research, there is the record of *The Notebooks*—journal selections that cover the period 1934 to 1971, *Open Between Us*—a 1980 collection of essays and interviews, and *The One in the Many*—a 1988 essay collection. During a career that now spans sixty years, Ignatow has lived to see his work widely distributed and acclaimed. It has been possible, therefore, to observe his reevaluations of his childhood past with a rare degree of insight into his spontaneous self-reflection.

Ignatow was born in 1914 in Brooklyn to first-generation Jewish immigrants—the only son, between two daughters.[3] He traces the roots of his writing to his father. His mother was the daughter of an illiterate Austro-Hungarian woodsman: his father, a Russian who was apprenticed to a Kiev bookbinder at the age of twelve. On completing apprenticeship, the father found work at a Greek Orthodox monastery, where the monks collected great works of Russian literature in addition to religious books (presumably to keep up with the opposition). Besides binding them, the young man read them. When he fled Russia to escape pogroms, he brought his fondness for the stories with him. Later, in the United States, when he would rest in his easy chair after work, his son learned how to prompt him into retelling Tolstoy, Chekhov, and Gorky from memory. They made the most enthralling accounts the child had ever heard, and they had clearly won his father's deepest admiration. The child quietly resolved that he would become a writer too. He felt his resolution confirmed when he asked if he could write his own acceptance speech for his bar mitzvah—the occasion on which a boy assumes adult responsibilities—and his father gave his proud consent.

The eventual inheritance that the father gave the son, however, was mind-numbing labor. As a child, Ignatow knew the vicissitudes in the family fortune from a distance, as tense exchanges overheard between his parents. When the father participated in union activities, he was blacklisted by the city's bookbinding management. The father opened a butcher shop, but when his son was nine, he closed it as a bad business venture. By that time, the father was able to resume his bookbinding trade by opening a bindery of his own. Most of the son's recorded memories of home, school, and play in the street belong to this final peaceful period of childhood after his father had reestablished his trade and bought a two-family house in a new development in the Park West section of Brooklyn.

Then came the Depression. Fighting for his economic life, the father expected his son to work for him in his pamphlet binding sweatshop. When Ignatow dropped out of Brooklyn College in the first semester after an English teacher made an anti-Semitic remark, the only job options open to him were in his father's shop or similar menial slots. He spent the next thirty years of his life alternating between work in the bindery and forays for relief in other jobs: night clerk for the New York sanitation department, apprentice shipyard handyman, hospital admitting clerk, shipping clerk in the wholesale fruit and vegetable market, messenger.[4] One thing he learned was that one such job was as bad as another. The following 1940 entry in *The Notebooks* was written during a stint in his father's bindery:

> I hate the whole fucking shop, its noise, its arguments, its problems, its jealousies and intrigues. I hate the mood of the people, cynical, hard and callous, like the working of a machine. I hate the attitude of the boss, carping and anxious for his money, a

sickness, once a game, now a disease eating away life: emptiness growing like spoor over the body. Soon, soon it will reach
out for the heart and the brain and Pouf! you see transfigured
into stone what once was a breathing man. . . .

My hatred of the shop—because of its disintegrating pres-
sure upon the personality. Stand for one hour at a machine band-
ing folders and you will feel the pounding motors and clack of
the folding machine going through you as if to pull you apart.[5]

With these reversals in his fortune, Ignatow's feelings for his
surroundings underwent parallel fluctuations from buoyancy to fore-
boding or disillusionment. His recorded childhood memories reveal
a mixture of vulnerability and assurance, with a sense of ease and security predominating during his peaceful Park West years. Against
the bleak backdrop of reality as he came to know it as an adult, he
judged some of his early memories foolish, some wise.

In early childhood, the world often appeared mysterious, bewildering, incomprehensible. A formative incident that remains
"just as I remember it," that Ignatow has repeatedly described, occurred in Borough Park, Brooklyn, a quiet residential neighborhood
where his father ran the butcher shop.[6] The son had the daily after-
school routine of delivering meat and chicken and collecting orders
for the next day. The routine mingled the friendliness of customers
when they opened their doors to him, his father's satisfaction, and
fear when he had to walk past a cemetery after dark.

During his errands one winter afternoon, he discovered a still,
small, black bird in the snow. He put the bird in his pocket with the
hope that warmth might revive it. When he returned to the store, and
found the bird still dead, he solemnly dug a grave and buried it. This
event combined a complex cluster of associations: his fear of the
night and the cemetery, which "would lead me to think of intangi-
ble, unknown things . . . the mysterious, the something that was always behind me and yet threatened me"; his pity for the tiny soft
animal, which he associated with himself; self-pity; and a sense of
power to confer meaning on the event through the mock serious act
of burial.

This place and its emotions became associated with his first apprehension of poetry. Almost seventy years later, he observed:

I write of death often, and it may be that I have not been aware
that the revelation has been with me for all this while, ever
since I can remember, as far back as my childhood when I stood

leaning against the gate of a cemetery and looked out into the sky and spoke to it, as if it were listening, as if it were the being to whom I should address myself in wonder. I was answered from within by the emergence of a poem.[7]

From the perspective of adulthood, Ignatow found his childhood intuition of death accurate.

On the whole, however, his childhood world was a positive presence. Overbalancing fears and doubts, a certitude of nature's favor infused his earliest memories. Life might rush along in a headlong bewildering way, but he assumed that it must be fundamentally benign. "This is how I felt as a child: / I was high on self-delight / at the touch of the mild sun and breeze."[8] The world beckoned beguilingly, without restrictions or limitations. "In the beginning we think it belongs to us and we belong to it eternally. As children, we feel an immortality clinging to everything including ourselves."[9]

The most common elements in his reminiscences are the sun, wind, and trees in Brooklyn streets. His most common remembered response was at-oneness with a world that appeared animated and benevolent, as in the prose poem "Growing Up:"

> These were among my first thoughts on earth: I had been placed here as some kind of reward, given the gift of being what I was, and I loved my bike, praising it for moving at the command of my pedaling, and steering in the right direction at my touch. The sidewalk lay flat and still, expecting the bike. It, too, cooperated with the powers that be, and no one stood in the bike's path to topple me over. The wind upon my face was like the hand of approval.[10]

Overarching his childhood feeling for the world was the security embodied by his mother. Later, when he was an adult under pressures extreme enough to drive him to the brink of madness, memory of his mother's influence remained a point of calm that could hold everything together.

> I am trying to find out what memories, what experience in the past hold me to life. Not too much hardship. A memory of ease in my childhood. Going to the library, being able to sit at a window and read, being free to leave and enter the house at will. What made me believe life was worth living? My mother's largeness. She wore a corset that reached from her breasts

to her thighs. My mother's largeness felt protection for me against harm. I never saw it in violent motion and I imagined all was well.[11]

The absolute security that his mother represented overflowed across his surroundings; and the Brooklyn that Ignatow encountered lived up to this maternal ideal. From Park West it spread out free of fear, open for him to go wherever he pleased. Brooklyn in his childhood was a borough of *Gemütlichkeit*, of geniality.[12]

In a junior high school English anthology, Ignatow came upon selections from *Leaves of Grass* by Walt Whitman, another Brooklyn resident. He immediately recognized his world. Here was veracity! Here was his place! Here was his man! He sought out the full book and read it ardently. Whitman has remained the great comrade/protagonist that Ignatow's reflections circle around.[13]

The sun, the wind, the trees, the friendly streets of Brooklyn may have offered enough material for Ignatow to recognize his known world in Whitman. But the expanding world that beckoned him was across the river: Manhattan, *the* City. Brooklyn was fine for a child. As an adolescent, he chafed at it. He had begun to write, secretly, privately, but determinedly. It separated him from his companions. He still enjoyed sports and sitting on stoops chatting with friends about baseball teams and local quarrels and rivalries, but he felt that his real self was elsewhere. At the close of childhood, he found his isolation epitomized by a new image:

> The memory of a dank, shadowy school gym on a hot summer day. I am standing at the entrance looking in, having walked from my house one half mile away in search of friends or of something to do. The smell discouraged me but worse was the fact that no one was present, and I walked back, first beginning to sense being alone and having nothing to do but feel my loneliness. . . . I suddenly saw that empty dank-smelling shadowy gym as a metaphor of my existence, even of me as a person. I became identified in my mind with that image, and I carried it around with me silently and often subconsciously as the kind of person I was.[14]

A parallel conflict was developing between his two worlds of school preachment and family practice. In school, teachers taught that everyone has an inalienable right to the pursuit of happiness, and that it is not to be found in money, clothing, and food alone, but in the freedom of the spirit. Whitman's America. At home in the evening, when the boy was presumed to be occupied with homework, he soaked in his parents' America. Across the kitchen table, his father unburdened to his mother the tense drama of the family business, blow by blow. School ideas set him apart from his parents.[15]

After Ignatow dropped out of Brooklyn College at the age of eighteen, he worked in his father's bindery for two years.[16] In 1933, a short story he had written was placed on the honor list in the annual collection, *The Best American Short Stories*. This award led to his being offered a job with the WPA newspaper project. He quit the bindery and his parents' home and moved away to the East Village, anticipating that he was going to become rich and famous as a writer and find true friends. For five years, WPA work enabled him to concentrate upon writing and editing, and escape grinding labor. During this period, he married the artist Rose Graubert, and switched from short story writing to poetry. But fame did not fall into his lap. When WPA work ended, he had no recourse but to move from one unskilled job to another, only to find each become a burden and a threat to his life as a writer. He began to realize that he was up against a different order of reality than Whitman's transcendent harmony.

When, desperate, Ignatow returned to work in Brooklyn in his father's shop, he observed life there with a new clarity. It was Whitman's world turned upside down. The image of the gym was the correct metaphor not only for *his* life, but for the people around him also. To his exuberant childhood memories, he was ready to add a sequel:

> As children we feel an immortality clinging to everything including ourselves, but we are here on earth at the price of being alive. We pay for being alive by work and sweat and tears and patience and endurance, with never a permanent sense of relaxing into security.[17]

Ignatow's other great revelation was that there was poetry in the subject. His first poems, never published, were written in the style of Keats. Friends told him that Williams was a poet to watch; but when he read him, he found him tasteless. Flat and ordinary like prose, his work did not sound like poetry at all. Ignatow was flabbergasted that this man had won a reputation. After years of disillusionment, when he picked up a book of Williams's poetry again, he understood that it was the necessary style for the necessary subject:

I learned soon enough as I began working in industry and commerce in New York City that this was the contemporary subject. There was no way around it. And if you were going to write about things honestly and what was *there*, you had to write about the city and about the plainness and the ordinariness and the tensions, and you had to develop a style which gave the quality of the city. And I went back to Williams, and I saw he had captured it, he had captured all that, and that was contemporary. So I took my courage in my hands and I wrote straight from the facts.[18]

Ignatow sent Williams a copy of his first published book, *Poems* (1948). Williams wrote Ignatow two ecstatic letters and then gave the book a rave review in the Sunday *New York Times*. Ignatow's ecstasy, of course, was more than equal. His dedication to being a poet had been confirmed. Williams became a close friend, who pushed Ignatow on stage at his own poetry readings, who offered criticism and encouragement.

City Rhythms

The self-identity that Ignatow came into was not just poet, but poet of the city. In crafting a flat line with unsparing images of urban life, he rejected the exalted style of the Romantics and Transcendentalists as obsolete. Conventional forms, he concluded, grew out of now outdated illusions about humanity's oneness with nature. With these illusions gone, old forms must go too:

I have only one note to add to aesthetics—about rhythms and diction in poetry, the more or less regular iambic pentameter, the Alexandrine and all the other conventional poetic techniques are the result of an agricultural society which was able to follow the seasons with an assured regularity of necessity, its life depending upon this conformity, whereas in our modern, urban existence neither the seasons nor agricultural influence is felt. The rhythms, the beat spring directly from the excitement, the unpredictableness, the harsh clangor of city life where man is the measure and not the earth or the sky. Man and his consuming drives within a city. The beat we hear is that of a voice in anguish, in conflict with itself and with others, on which it feeds and which it feeds in return, feverish, cruel, hard and loving in one long torrent. The dignity, the poise is gone

from man's posture vis à vis himself and which he drew from
his respect and awe of nature on which he depended for his life
and from which he drew illusory conclusions about himself as
one with nature, a child of nature to be looked upon favorably
and admired.[19]

In addition to repudiating Romantic forms, given that the city,
not nature, was becoming the predominant fact of life, Ignatow re-
pudiated Romantic union with nature, given the very different kind
of union indicated by twentieth-century science. In the spirit of scientific empiricism, he wrote that "I am wrestling with the idea that
this exaltation that we feel is nothing more than physical":

> It is not an extension or hint of God. It is not an intimation of
> divinity. I am in complete rebellion against the use of man as a
> metaphysical object. He is man, a body with a brain, giving
> him his correct signals for living, after which it counts for
> nothing else. It cannot ever be ascribed to sources outside
> himself, unless we say man is made of the earth. This is the
> only fact of which we are certain and it leaves us where we
> have been all the time, on earth exactly, nowhere else, going
> nowhere but back to earth after we die of the exhaustion of the
> materials of which our bodies are composed. I am fighting for a
> philosophy of oneness of man, of singleness of man, man re-
> lated simply to earth and to the cosmos which we believe is
> made of the same stuff. There is no heaven and no hell. There
> is no future after death. There is no intimation of divinity in
> even the most exalted and mystical moments. There are
> merely physical reactions to certain states of mind while the
> mind is a function of the body so that what happens to the
> mind or the body is an interaction. I am fighting for the scien-
> tific view of man.[20]

Ignatow concluded that he had never been able to grasp the
world of Whitman, the secure world of his childhood, because it
was a mirage. Yet although he rejected Whitman's faith in transcendent harmony, he refused to reject him altogether. Ignatow has observed that some twentieth-century poets, such as Charles Olson
and John Ashbery, have responded to modern dubieties by floating
from perception to perception and thought to thought without any
effort to crystallize individual and social meaning. In contrast, he
believes that poets evade their role unless they attempt to preserve

the sense of commonality that Whitman celebrated, that is vital to American democracy.[21]

The life meanings that Ignatow has proposed are existentialist. Against Whitman, he has set Nietzsche, Schopenhauer, and Kierkegaard. Against the radiance of transcendence, he has pinned the backdrop of death, confident that this blackness does not engulf the illumination of authentic human action and reflection. He has held to Whitman's line by committing himself to discovering meaning that can be passed on—even if the meaning is paradoxical. "I don't want to live without meaning," he has said. "But I am living without meaning, which is the meaning of living without meaning."[22] Caught in this paradox, he has found an answer close to Whitman's. "Life still has to be affirmed and expressed in all its ways."[23]

Reappraisals of Memory

As Ignatow moved through successive understandings of the poet's relationship to the city and society, he moved through corresponding poetic styles. Each style, in turn, involved different orientations to early memory. In the beginning, he expressed his discovery of city exigencies through objectivist writing. His use of the city as a metaphor for modern experience, for the society that built it and suffered it, led him to cluster images. Focused on the pressures of the present, his poems of the 1940s and 1950s notably lack reminiscence. As he expressed the principle of objectivist writing in the 1940s:

> Get the gasworks in a poem
> and you've got the smoke and smokestacks,
> the mottled red and yellow tenements,
> and grimy kids who curse with the pungency
> of the odor of gas. You've got America, boy.[24]

Ignatow gradually grew restless with recording observed reality. "No ideas but in things," he concluded, echoing Williams, but added, "and things die, with their ideas."[25] Outward things came to appear too changeable, too ephemeral, to establish commonality. Ignatow then decided that the poet, not the city, is metaphor for society, and he turned his attention inward to concentrate upon observing himself. There he found the evidence equally changeable and deceptive. After a period of perplexity, he resolved "to merge the internal with the external, that is, to write from within out."[26] He learned to embody shifting moods in shifting events. As he recorded this interplay between inward and outward worlds, he began to write poems of reminiscence. Self-revelatory images and events from memory perfectly served his principle of writing "from within out," as they embodied persisting moods and concerns through persistently remembered people, places, and things.

In addition to vignettes about his parents and his childhood home, his poems in the 1960s began to include extended surrealist metaphors, which remain his hallmark. They have tended to draw him back into the way a young child sees the world, as by his own assessment, surrealist disparities are similar to "the child's beginning apprehension of life."[27]

He also began to make the interplay between the internal and the external explicit through prose poetry. As he has explained it: "I broke away into the prose poem to give more emphasis to the intellect, to the search, to the mind, to thought rather than only feeling, only the image . . . the emphasis now fell on developing the metaphor along with an analysis of the metaphor."[28] This method of statement and review is ideally adapted to recalling and reflecting upon memories. Ignatow has made the analysis of childhood memory the subject of numerous prose poems.

These techniques are illustrated by the following poems that reflect upon childhood "intimations of immortality." In addition to mocking childhood illusions, they form ironic counterstatements to Whitman and Wordsworth.

In the poem "Turnings," Ignatow echoes Whitman's ecstatic childhood awe beside the ocean at night in "Out of the Cradle Endlessly Rocking." But turn by turn, he deflates Whitman's rapture. By Ignatow's time, the ocean of the All that lapped at the child's feet has turned into a stagnant pond:

> It is a silent pond surrounded by silent
> woods and shore no animal or man in sight
> Here as a child I tossed my pebble
> and now my stone
> and the ripples fade
> my glance as vacant as the smoothness of the pond[29]

The vacancy of his gaze reflects his inability even as a child to penetrate beneath the surface of things. Ignatow remembers that as a child he sometimes pondered the mystery of how God, whom he was told was the fountain of joy and pleasure and in Himself perfect, could create such suffering, imperfect children. At that time, he attributed his inability to understand to his own weakness and ignorance, still trusting in the world. As an adult, he learned that dread was in the nature of things.[30]

Ignatow's book *Tread the Dark* (1978) takes its title from his poem "Brightness as a Poignant Light," which submits Wordsworth's Intimations Ode to existentialist dissection. Emerson called the ode "the high water mark which the intellect has reached in this age." But in Ignatow's version, its "clouds of glory" and "celestial light" have become a field of light and dark, of consciousness and oblivion. The joy that Wordsworth found prompted by early "obstinate questionings / Of sense and outward things" no longer gushes from "the immortal sea." For Ignatow, it has given way to the "ghostly joy—wildly / free" of knowing that there is nothing beyond sense and outward things. One with the material world, a man engenders himself by treading the waters of darkness. The opening verse observes:

> I tread the dark and my steps are silent.
> I am alone and feel a ghostly joy—wildly
> free and yet I do not live absolutely
> and forever, but my ghostly joy
> is that I am come to light
> for some reason known only to the dark,
> perhaps to view itself in me.[31]

In the prose poem "Growing Up," whose section about bike riding has already been quoted, Ignatow follows his description of childhood euphoria when he felt that "I had been placed here as some kind of reward, given the gift of being what I was," with his reappraisal of the situation now that he is an adult:

> I never thought the bike betrayed me, nor the sidewalk, nor the wind, but now I see them simply as means, and the betrayer is me. I cannot call the bike an emissary. It is a tool, the sidewalk a path, the wind a current of air. We are no longer communicating that I'm aware of, but what does it matter, I tell myself, so long as I am free to use all these for my delight; but I am alone in my pleasures. I am not the child of anyone, for, as I watch myself growing up, the bike shrinks in size and the sidewalk fills with cracks and bumps; the wind on my face in cold weather chills me, and when I eat I know it is because of appetite.[32]

Although Ignatow has concluded that reality invalidates the Romantic and childhood imagination, his commitment to uncompromisingly observe and record his moods has led him to accept shifting moods as the tissue of his life. Between 1955 and 1965, a series of events occurred that prepared him for a new tolerance of the natural world and, with it, a truce with his childhood memories of happiness.

In 1955, Ignatow's only son showed first signs of schizophrenia, which eventually required his institutionalization.[33] The father's constant tension in attempting to combine writing with support of a family may or may not have been a contributing factor: it was enough for Ignatow that he believed it was. It was the lowest possible point in his life, after which anything further must represent recovery. Almost simultaneously, a second book of poetry, *The Gentle Weight Lifter*, came off the press, reaffirming his role as a poet. In 1956 a daughter, new life, was born. Within four years, Ignatow's mother and father died, and he sold the bindery for the price of his father's medical bills and walked away from it for the last time. He found work as a paper salesman to publishers. For the first time in his life, he had what he needed: a job that paid good money in exchange for few hours, that allowed him to write between sales. He was still alive, and the sun was still shining.

In a notebook entry during this period, Ignatow describes walking from one business account to another, enjoying the skyline, the old brick and doorways, the people:

I love my senses. They give me the complete story. I am partly at play myself, in complete ease, thinking automatically of my next business visit, concerned more with pleasure. I am happy, simply happy to find the sun and I are still together, after all. These years we are not lost to each other after all and a man's childhood can be brought into old age and enjoyed more than ever with a new insight. That adds to the pleasure.[34]

He captured the same mood in the poem "Above Everything." After thirty years of struggle, he could take simple childlike delight in the world again. His irony is so gentle here it is playful: seeing beauty in the world is dreamlike, and *should* he have memory after death, he will praise the world:

I wished for death often
but now that I am at its door

I have changed my mind about the world.
It should go on; it is beautiful,
even as a dream, filled with water and seed,
plants and animals, others like myself,
ships and buildings and messages
filling the air—a beauty,
if ever I have seen one.
In the next world, should I remember
this one, I will praise it
above everything.[35]

Reappraisals of Nature

In 1964 Ignatow published another book, *Figures of the Human*.[36] In 1965 he received a Guggenheim Fellowship. Before it ended, Wendell Berry called to ask if Ignatow would replace him for a year while he was on sabbatical from the University of Kentucky. For the first time in his life, Ignatow moved away from New York. After a year in Kentucky, he spent a year at the University of Kansas and a year at Vassar College. In 1969 he came back to New York to teach poetry at Columbia University and York College of the City University of New York. He bought a home for his wife and daughter in East Hampton on Long Island; and after he was mugged in the lobby of the building where he rented a weekday apartment, he became a commuter from East Hampton himself. With these geographic changes, the theme of nature entered his poetry.

To say that nature entered Ignatow's poetry as a salient subject is not to suggest that it excluded the city. Nature claimed his attention for the same reason that he found that he had to redefine his relations to the city: the city that he returned to in 1969 was not the one he had left behind. Like American politics during the Vietnam War, it had become violent. Ignatow found that he had to stay alert, guarded, until, reluctantly, he moved out. Just as he believes that poets had a moral obligation to protest the war, he believes that they need to analyze the changing urban experience. "The problem I face as a poet is not to lose sight of the city," he has affirmed. "Because the city is a fulcrum, the city is the very fulcrum of civilization, in all societies. To dwell upon the country is really to lose sight of the most vital information, the whole vital labor of the city."[37]

Yet despite himself, nature entered his poetry. Since childhood, he had known the trees and bays of Brooklyn, and he had often used natural images as metaphors for human feelings. The great change that came over his work was that meditations upon nature shifted from metaphors and occasional asides to frequent main address. Teaching in the rural states or at home in East Hampton, "I felt a change coming over me. I was learning to relax, to study the trees, the grass, the sky, and the birds, and to write of them with affection and wonder, asking myself how I could have missed it all."[38]

With nature, childhood memories returned, to be seen from a new point of balance. Adhering to plain practical explanations, Ignatow attributes the serenity and peace that he has attained in old age to his having achieved recognition as a writer, a satisfying job, a fulfilling family life, and a safe home. Through this hard-won security he has reestablished continuity with his first security as a child:

> I enjoy this world in its squirrels and cats and birds, its silence after dark, its darkness outside my window and the peace with which it is happening. In other words, that part of my life which I remember from childhood that I love has been returned to me and through my efforts at getting it back.[39]

This new voice in Ignatow's poetry might be called the voice of wisdom. "What's that?," he has asked himself. "Acceptance of natural processes and events, setting history, the city, culture, work, angers and fears, ambition, love and sex in a natural order that I sense—can that be called transcendence?"[40]

In this new mood, he has come to tolerate the impulse to animism that he once tried to exorcise. Trees, sky, furniture, and walls still appear to beckon to him like speaking spirits—although his reason still knows better. The dynamic tension that results has inspired a major body of his late poetry. Accepting that his kinship with nature is real and inevitable, though mute, he responds with a new gentleness that is evident in the title of his 1981 book, *Whisper to the Earth*. He has also concluded that his communication, with nature epitomizes all communication, because we know ourselves only through relations with others. Addressing another—whether it be person, chair, or tree—enables us to hear ourselves. Ignatow believes that his poems addressed to things heighten the reader's consciousness of this dilemma.[41]

Given the preceding conclusions, Ignatow no longer finds material for mockery in Whitman's assurance at the end of "Song of Myself" that if readers want to find him, look for him under their boot soles.

A Changing Paradigm of Nature

Coincident with his hard-won accommodation of his tranquil childhood memories, Ignatow was reading popular presentations of the changing paradigm of nature in quantum physics. Heisenberg's principle of indeterminacy dissolved the mechanical world view that Ignatow had previously accepted. It implied that scientific perception could no longer be separated from artistic imagination. Quantum physics also revealed a universe composed of one undivided field of energy. In Ignatow's words, it demonstrated that "we are, finally, the same being." And it validated Whitman's opening lines in the 1855 *Song of Myself* that, "I celebrate myself / and what I assume you shall assume / for every atom belonging to me as good belongs to you."[42]

In his latest published excerpts from his notebooks, Ignatow has written a passage that could have been written by Whitman himself. The passage was motivated by Wallace Stevens's separation of imagination and reality (or, one might add, by Bronk's or Weinfield's, or Ignatow's former separation). In opposition, Ignatow has proposed the accommodation that reality and the imagination are united by one common principle of metamorphosis. In arriving at this conclusion, Ignatow has suggested that he and Whitman were never as far apart as it may have sometimes seemed:

> Here I am saying that Stevens misses the essential point . . . when he separates the principle of imagination from the principle of reality. Both are characterized by change and the possibility of seeing one thing in terms of another. . . . Since all is matter, we are all in the same cauldron of change, together with the stars and the grass. We are in reality and never out of it. We are reality. We do not form imaginative wholes or fictions with which to defend ourselves against reality. We are doing precisely the same thing as is the chaotic reality, changing, ever changing its face, simply carrying out the principle of being or reality in its constant movement toward and from itself, the very character and nature of reality as we manifest it in our imaginative existence in poetry and all the human arts and events.[43]

Not only is constant metamorphosis into ever-changing new forms the common principle of nature and the imagination, but this change is organized around a common avoidance of pain and pursuit of pleasure. Ignatow's meditation continues:

Chaos is us, if we must have it that way, according to Stevens, but since we live and breathe and function beyond and with and by and against and towards and away from pain, we cannot honestly declare all this chaos, ourselves chaos who live to know, to see, to change which too is within the principle of being. . . .

The division between ego and reality is a false one because the ego manifests exactly the principle which makes reality reality, and that is change, renewal, reassertion, reaffirmation of itself in constantly emerging new forms.[44]

Romantics and Transcendentalists, if they could have read the future, would have read this passage with assent. They too compared artistic creation to natural processes of creation.

Later in the notebook entry, Ignatow observed that science works in this way as well as art: by metaphor and imaginative associations that take constantly evolving new forms. It could be said that Ignatow is still fighting for the scientific view of humanity. But contemporary physics has changed in pace with Ignatow's changing appraisal of his relationship with nature. Socially, politically, materially, personally, and artistically, Ignatow has concluded, the great modern discovery is that what we have is:

not the imagination as some sort of artifact, but the imagination as a way of relating to the universe. It can't be any other way. You can't relate to the universe in any routine manner and still feel that you are living a significant life. You're living significantly if you recognize that the whole world is in process and you recognize that somehow you're contributing, there is something new that is contributing to this process.[45]

On this note of reconciliation with nature, Ignatow has come to accept his own metamorphoses. His new condition of transcendence does not dissolve the fact of death, and his poetry still shows recurring moments of despair.[46] Within the larger scheme of things, however, he has found freedom for memories of his childhood alliances with nature to return on terms of peace.

Chapter Five

Connections:
Audre Lorde and
Marie Ponsot

Audre Lorde and Marie Ponsot, like David Ignatow, follow the poetic method that Wordsworth pioneered: each speaks autobiographically as an individual identified by a personal history. They may contrast with Wordsworth in where they come from or what they conclude, but all three have committed themselves to a deliberate reading of memory to chronicle who and what they are, and when and where and how they live.

The Romantic pattern of relationship to nature, however, obscures these two women's experience. Where Wordsworth stationed "celestial clouds of glory" at the beginning and ending of his life, Ignatow has cast a cold existentialist light; yet he, like Wordsworth, has moved from childhood affiliation with nature to adult distance, regaining acceptance of his bond with nature with the "philosophic mind" of his late years. This Romantic spiral of immersion in nature, estrangement, and reconciliation does not apply to Lorde and Ponsot. Where the men's experience of nature has been described as a *confrontation*, theirs is better described as *connection*. They begin in agreement with major Romantic premises, but they have applied them to independent conclusions. In the sections that follow, the women describe connections to nature and to childhood memory that may have a long history of practice, but that have been historically muted by literature and omitted from psychology.

AUDRE LORDE

Like Ignatow, Lorde was born to immigrant parents who struggled to make a place for themselves and their children in their adopted city of New York. Like him, she turned her parents' determination to survive and succeed in the city into a commitment to remain and write about inhabitants' dreams and disillusionments, convinced that the city is representative of American society at large. Like Ignatow, she found her own life experience since childhood essential material for this analysis, and like his, her life contained a mixture of sweet and painful memories.

Yet the one side of memory may seem to cancel the other out. How can painful and pleasant memories be equally true? For Ignatow, they could not be. As long as the empty gym epitomized reality for him, his recollections of security and self-delight as a "child of nature" appeared naive folly. Lorde, in contrast, made her childhood images of nature the core of the dream that she adhered to, and her painful experiences a guide to the obstacles and opportunities she faced in seeking to achieve her dreams.

Since 1964, when Langston Hughes selected several of Lorde's poems for a collection that he edited shortly before his death (*New Negro Poets*), she has been one of the most anthologized black woman poets in this country. Before her death of cancer in 1992, she published nine books of poetry. She is the only poet in this study who has written a formal autobiography—or, as she calls it, a biomythography (*Zami: A New Spelling of My Name*). She also published collections of essays, speeches, and interviews (*Sister Outsider*), and journal entries that she made during diagnosis and treatment for breast cancer (*The Cancer Journals*) and cancer of the liver (*A Burst of Light*).

All the major themes that compose Lorde's mature vision as a writer evolved out of one fundamental circumstance: that she was born black, of West Indian descent, in the United States. Out of this circumstance came her need to articulate what it means to be an outsider, to specify her resources for survival, and to negotiate conflicts between dreams and reality. Her vitality as a writer is based upon her ability to explore these terms in so many senses that she made them issues of broad human significance. These themes' significance begins, however, in her particular situation as a child growing up in "a country where other people live." Therefore the subject of childhood memory goes directly to the core of her concerns.

"A Country Where Other People Live"

Lorde's parents came to New York from Grenada in the 1920s, expecting that they would work, save money, and return to their island home.[1] In the beginning, her mother worked as a chambermaid and her father as a laborer. Her father went on to real estate school and secured a steady job managing small Harlem rooming houses. Her mother then assisted him, making her the only woman her children knew who had the stature that she "went to business." Despite the couple's combined efforts, the Depression defeated their plans. They never returned "home." But as long as their three daughters were growing up, they cherished the faith that someday they would.

Audre, the youngest, was born in 1934. Through the years of the Depression, her family was one of few in Harlem that never lacked food or clothes, or simple luxuries such as parochial school tuition and summer visits to a hotel on the Connecticut shore that belonged to a real estate friend of her father's. Despite this physical security, Lorde has characterized the primary lesson of her childhood as survival. Her parents paid for the family's physical survival through relentless toil and the denial of their own dreams and highest abilities. They exacted comparable submission from their children, forcing their youngest daughter to fight to survive as an independent entity. As she has put it, when you are born "Fat Black Female and almost blind" in Harlem in the Depression, "survival is not theoretical; it's a day-to-day decision and it's one you make over and over and over again. You can't be theoretical about survival. You live it too often in too many ways."[2]

When her parents arrived from Grenada and encountered American racism, they bought survival by keeping within the lines drawn and denying the price. The message her mother taught was that survival "meant being White or as close to White as possible." To interiorize this message would have been self-annihilating. Underneath this mixed message, however, was the primary one. By itself, "survival was programmed into me as essential."[3]

As the youngest, and most stubborn, daughter, Audre was the most strictly supervised. One sign of her subordination was that she was denied privacy. Unlike her two older sisters who had the privilege of their own room, she was restricted to the public parts of the apartment under "the eternal parental eye."[4] The only room where she could be momentarily alone was the bathroom, but even there, if she dawdled, her mother was sure to intervene.

Under these pressures, from earliest infancy the child equated survival with self-definition. It required defining herself on her own terms in resistance to her parents. She remembers swimming into punishment in the spirit that, "if this is the only way you're going to deal with me, you're gonna have to deal with me this way."[5] In asserting herself within the small circle of the family, regardless of the cost, she learned lessons that she later transferred to her position in the city at large, and in time, to American society at large.

As a child, she was handicapped because she could barely see or speak until she was four. When she was four, she was diagnosed as nearly blind and fitted with eyeglasses. She remembers the moment when she looked up and discovered that the puffy swirl of green in the playground was an aggregate of single, particular, precisely shaped leaves. Given sight, she began to speak and read at the same time. The local librarian learned to calm this unruly, inarticulate four-year-old by sitting her on her lap and reading her picture books. In a short time, the child was working her own way through the children's room collection, committing favorite poems in anthologies to memory.[6] She began to bring the tools that would be essential to her self-definition—clear seeing, speaking, reading, and poetry—under her control.

Denial was not the only method that her parents used to protect their children from the realities of Harlem. There was another, softer form of protection that they interposed. It was the memory of Grenada. In contrast to everything around them, their place of origin was black and proud; it was a paradise of beauty; and it would never cease to be "home." The children grew up under the expectation that someday they would all pack up and return "home," to the good place. New York and the United States never merited better referral than "this place."[7]

Their mother provided inexhaustible resources for fabricating "home." Most specifically, home was the little island of Carriacou off the shores of Grenada, where their mother grew up on a hilltop overlooking the Caribbean. She described every native tree, fruit, and flower to her daughters in detail and taught their medicinal uses. She recounted every daily custom. She told how she and her sisters drew buckets of water in the evening so that they could sit in the night air, growing cool and beaded with dew in time for morning use. She shared the island's ever-present songs.[8] Her youngest daughter lay in bed at night piecing the details together.

One result of these reminiscences was that the child learned that nature was something magical to seek out. Returning home from school or errands, she picked blades of grass that grew between paving stones and tied them into bouquets to present to her mother—like the pictures of flowers that she saw in books.[9]

The children were never allowed to go out to play in the street; but there were two special places where their mother would take them, where she herself could look out at the water and remember home. When they lived on 142nd Street, she would take them down to the edge of the Harlem River, which had not yet been closed off by Harlem River Drive. When they moved to 152nd Street, she would take them to a nearby park attached to one of the first city projects, which had a little greenery and which banked on the river:

> *That* place, the green, the trees, and the water, formed—all through high school I would write about it—my forest of Arden. I would write about beautiful scenes. It was the only green place I ever saw. . . . I will never forget, after my first book, some students said, "Miss Lorde, would you call yourself a nature poet?" And I thought, "What? Me?" And then I realized how wedded to these images I was. And they come from this pocket park. I would fantasize about sun on a red brick roof. It was the shards of sun against the wall, with this new kind of brick that they build with now, but which was totally unlike most New York architecture in the forties. And that became entrenched in my mind as beauty. The sun on a red brick roof. And a rose trellis. . . . I never found the rose trellis. I don't know where that came from. I think perhaps there may have been a white structure through which you went into this park. And I fantasized a rose trellis, because I had never seen one.[10]

For Lorde, such places of particular beauty or security in childhood are generative. Even if they may appear ordinary, even shabby, to outsiders, they are the pieces out of which people quilt their dreams. "I think it informs everything we do, our dreams, our work,

our hopes," she observed of resonant places like the one above.[11]
She also noted that elements of the natural world usually grace
these places.

In childhood, the dream called home and the imaginative elaboration of every scrap of nature both shielded her from an accurate
perception and naming of her world, and disposed her to it. It left her
with the permanent sense of being an outsider. As she has described
her family position, "We were sojourners in a place that was not our
own." As a line in one of her poems later put it, "This is a country
where other people live." Being an outsider was both a liability and
a strength. In one way, it worked against clear perception of her situation by clouding it with the mirage called home. In another way,
it facilitated perception by giving a standard of comparison, "the
sense that this was not all."[12]

As a result of this background, *dream* remains one of the most
recurrent words in Lorde's vocabulary. The tension between dream
and reality remains the underlying dynamic in her work.

Split Worlds / Split Words

Lorde's reconstruction of her preschool years reveals key pieces
of her life, which later combined to make writing poetry a possibility and a necessity. It shows her need for self-assertion in the face of
denial and deception. It shows her fabrication of a world of the imagination, which she identified with the world of nature, in contrast to
her actual surroundings. It shows her absorption in reading, which
fed the imagination. Behind everything, it shows her bond to her
mother and her mother's special relationship with words.

Lorde was prepared for poetry by her mother's way with words.
Her mother's descriptions of Carriacou were lyrical. When she described West Indian fruit, she savored the words as if she were tasting the fruit itself. When she had something particularly firm to say,
or, on rare occasions, something particularly tender, it was poetry of
another kind. (If you go out "in next kin to nothing"—dressed too
lightly—you risk getting *co-hum co-hum*—catching cold, and then
the world turns *cro-bo-so* —topsy-turvy. The risk is worth it if it
moves your mother to *raise your zandalee*—massage your backbone.
But then again, what you might get is *a smack on the bamsy*.)[13]

On the other side, the child needed poetry, because her mother
and others around her often buried their words' true intent. Her
mother expected that her children knew what they should do without being told. Deciphering the real message beneath unspoken or

masked words was a general rule of conduct. "Don't just listen like a ninny to what people say in their mouth," her mother taught, and she herself gave plenty of practice.[14] Her daughter learned to use poetry as her own self-protective code. Even at the stage of nursery rhymes:

> When someone said to me, "How do you feel?" or "What do you think?" or asked another direct question, I would recite a poem, and somewhere in that poem would be the feeling, somewhere in it would be the piece of information. It might be a line. It might be an image. The poem was my response.[15]

Growing up black in Harlem, she found herself surrounded by unspoken words, and there was no one to help her with them. Her parents never explained what "colored" meant, other than clothes that don't take bleach. It was never explained to her why the white children in school never invited her to their homes. She thought that the world had gone mad when she lost a class election designed to go to the smartest girl in the class, when she obviously should have won hands down. Her childhood came to an end muffled in an awkward innocence.[16]

The final episode of childhood came on a family trip to Washington, D.C. in her thirteenth summer. The family made the trip because an older sister had been excluded from a senior class visit to the capital with the words that "she would not be happy" going. The father swore that he would take her himself. On a hot afternoon, dazed from staring up at too many monuments, the family gratefully sought relief at an ice cream counter. When the waitress refused to serve them, they staggered out again, her parents silently raging *against themselves* because they had not foreseen the confrontation in time to avoid it.[17] Lorde came of age in a world she was forbidden to name.

From the very beginning of her experience, she was introduced to the principle that the world, that language, has two levels. On one level, there was the poetry that was learned "out of my mother's mouth."[18] There was a world of nature and a language of love and spontaneous accommodation. Soft-eyed reminiscences of Carriacou. Protective indulgences. There was another unadmitted world and unspoken language of hurt and rage:

> In the center of a harsh and spectrumed city
> all things natural are strange.
> I grew up in a genuine confusion

between grass and weeds and flowers
and what colored meant
except for clothes you couldn't bleach
and nobody called me nigger
until I was thirteen.
Nobody lynched my momma
but what she'd never been
had bleached her face of everything
but very private furies
and made the other children
call me yellow snot at school.[19]

Before she could write these lines of honest memory, she had to learn to close the rift between language and experience. An overwhelming encounter with the reality of nature became instrumental to her healing.

Independence

Lorde began to write poetry in seventh grade. In high school, she made it a habit. She qualified for Hunter High School—then, and now, one of the best public high schools in the country. White classmates still did not invite her to their homes, but they did elect her literary editor of the school arts magazine.

As a high school student, she found herself free to move through the city at her pleasure for the first time. In her autobiography, all her descriptions of childhood outings convey discomfort. Harlem streets were seen through a wadding of winter clothes or through a haze of summer heat, as she was hurried along by her mother or dragged behind her older sisters. In high school, she learned that the city held other possibilities.

She was led through the city through her friendship with a young black dancer named Genevieve, a Hunter classmate. It was a friendship to which her poetry has repeatedly alluded. Genevieve gave her poetry's two great sources of inspiration: love and death. As for love, they were inseparable, irrepressible. Together they took possession of the city. From the Harlem River to Battery Park, the city was their playground. For the rest of her life, Lorde vividly remembered every edge and angle of downtown Manhattan's streets as a result of their roamings. As for death, Genevieve committed suicide at the age of sixteen.[20]

Lorde's first book, *The First Cities*, contains several high school poems that commemorate Genevieve. Anyone reading them would be tempted to observe that here, indeed, we have a nature poet. To speak of her friend, the young writer turned away from the streets that they had explored together in favor of elegiac images of nature taken from other people's poetry and the green vestiges that she knew. An example is "Memorial I":

> If you come as softly
> as wind within the trees
> you may hear what I hear
> see what sorrow sees.
>
> If you come as lightly
> as the threading dew
> I shall take you gladly
> nor ask more of you.
>
> You may sit beside me
> silent as a breath
> and only those who stay dead
> shall remember death.
>
> If you come I will be silent
> nor speak harsh words to you—
> I will not ask you why, now,
> nor how, nor what you knew.
>
> But we shall sit here softly
> beneath two different years
> and the rich earth between us
> shall drink our tears.[21]

Her sense of her vocation as a poet was deepened by poems such as this one, and by her coming into contact with Langston Hughes and John Henrik Clarke at the Harlem Writers Guild. Their introduction to the tradition of black poetry, and their faith in her, affirmed her growth both as a person and a poet. Lorde's parents, however, were unable to accept her self-reliance. Family relationships had become, as she later put it, "a West Indian version of the Second World War." Two weeks after her high school graduation, as everyone else in the family slept, she ran away to a friend's apartment on the Lower East Side. No one made any effort to find her. In a dream, her parent's home itself turned against her, everything in it resisting her or breaking at her touch. Hurt but unconfined now, she was free to establish a new relationship to her place:

When I moved out of my mother's house, shaky and determined, I began to fashion some different relationship to this
country of our sojourn. I began to seek some more fruitful return
than simple bitterness from this place of my mother's exile,
whose streets I came to learn better than my mother had ever
learned them. But thanks to what she did know and could teach
me, I survived in them better than I could have imagined.[22]

Bringing Worlds and Words Together

Paradoxically, Lorde established a new relationship to her native place by striking out beyond its borders in search of a reality
equal to her ideals. Ever since elementary school, Mexico had captured her imagination. It promised the sun on a red brick roof and the
rose trellises of her daydreams. Until she was nineteen, she worked
at different clerical and factory jobs in New York and Connecticut,
accumulating enough money for a year of study in Mexico City. She
found herself unprepared for her exhilaration upon arrival. By contrast, she suddenly recognized that her existence in New York had
been a limbo of salience, as a black person, and invisibility, as a de-
personalized person. For the first time, she found herself in a paradise
where she was recognized simply as a friendly individual among
other friendly individuals. "Mexico was wonderful for me. Wonderful in so many ways. It was so *beautiful* . . . so beautiful. So open. So
self-affirming. All of these brown people in the majority was very
very wonderful for me."[23]

Mexico was also wonderful for her because she learned to affirm her love for women through a lesbian relationship with a jour-
nalist who was a political expatriate from the United States of the
1950s. The woman had made the history and folkways of her adopted
land her own, and she led her protégée into mountains and ruins in
the heart of the country, pointing out archaeological evidence that
suggested ancient contacts between Mexico and Africa.[24]

Lorde made her home in Cuernavaca, which was an easy com-
mute from the university. One morning on her way to the bus to
Mexico City, she walked over a hill into an epiphany that became a
turning point in her poetry.

In order to get to my early class I would catch a six o'clock *tur-
ismo* in the village plaza. I would come out of my house before
dawn. You know, there are two volcanoes, Popocatepetl and
Ixtacuhuatl. I thought they were clouds, the first time I saw

them through my windows. It would be dark, and I would see the snow on top of the mountains, and the sun coming up. And when the sun crested, at a certain point, the birds would start. But because we were in the valley it would still look like night. But there would be the light of the snow. And then this incredible crescendo of birds. One morning I came over the hill and the green, wet smells came up. And then the birds, the sound of them I'd never really noticed, never *heard* birds before. I was walking down the hill and I was transfixed. It was very beautiful. I hadn't been writing all the time I was in Mexico. And the poetry was the thing I had with words, that was so important. . . . And on that hill, I had the first intimation that I could bring those two together. I could infuse words directly with what I was feeling. I didn't have to create the world I wrote about. I realized that words could tell. . . . I used to fantasize trees and dream forests. Until I got spectacles when I was four I thought trees were green clouds. When I read Shakespeare in high school I would get off on his gardens and Spanish moss and roses and trellises with beautiful women at rest and sun on red brick. When I was in Mexico I found out this could be a reality. And I learned that day on the mountain, that words can match that, *re*-create it.[25]

When she tried to write a poem about the way she felt that morning, she was unsuccessful. The memory remained a conviction that words *could* recreate experience, and a challenge that she had to learn to apply.

When Lorde returned to New York at the end of one year, she was no longer in a world of welcoming beauty. If the principle of her revelation on the hill was that words can re-create feeling, then the memory staked a risk at the same time as it gave earthly boundaries to paradise. To believe in earthly paradise and to believe that words and feelings can cohabit, within a limbo where many words and feelings are forbidden, involved a tension similar to that which Lorde had known since childhood as an outsider: a double vision in which alternate possibilities intensify painful realities.

That simple, apparently ordinary connection between poetry and feeling was *terribly* threatening, and very very dangerous. I am black and I am a woman. I took the next step in poetry with the feeling that automatically I was committing myself to exploring a kind a fury that could be totally destructive. How to keep that alive and not be destroyed by it is a tension that runs through all of my work, and I believe the work of every serious black woman poet, every outsider poet in America. I think that is what lends a kind of power and reality to our work. And I think we have reclaimed poetry as a result.[26]

The hill in Mexico remained a sustaining vision, as Lorde gradually began to learn to bring her writing and feeling together. Twenty-six years later, in an interview with her friend Adrienne Rich, she suggested how she learned to extend her conclusions on the hill to painful as well as blissful experience:

The one thread I feel coming through over and over in my life is the battle to preserve my perceptions, the battle to win through and to keep them—pleasant or unpleasant, painful or whatever . . . and however much they were denied.[27]

The possible fidelity of language to experience, which she discovered on the hill, can be compared to the fidelity of behavior to experience, which she learned as an infant in her parents' home. As an infant, preserving her perceptions required physical defiance. On the hill, she discovered that language, too, can defy and preserve.

The converse of Lorde's appreciation for the power of language is suspicion of silence. *Silence,* in Lorde's usage, is a highly charged negative word, which signifies resignation to distortion and exploitation. Silence results when oppressive families and societies have gotten people "to testify against themselves":

What you do is to build it in, so people learn to distrust everything in themselves that has not been sanctioned, to reject whatever is most creative in themselves—to have *them* reject it to begin with, so you don't even need to stamp it out.[28]

The need to preserve perceptions and to save them from censoring silence, it can be observed, is a need for memory.

City Images

When Lorde returned to New York after her year in Mexico, her life moved forward eventfully. She received a bachelor's degree from Hunter College in 1959 and a master's in library science from Columbia in 1961. In 1961 Langston Hughes selected several of her poems for his anthology *New Negro Poetry*. She married and had a daughter and a son, who have been frequent subjects of her poetry. In 1968 she left a marriage that was falling apart to give a workshop as poet-in-residence at Tougaloo College, Mississippi. It was her first taste of teaching, which convinced her that she wanted to teach as well as write. While she was in Mississippi, her first book, *The First Cities*, came out. There she also met the woman who became her lifelong companion. When she came back to New York, she began a career teaching black studies and English, which took her from the City College of New York and Lehmann College to John Jay College, to Hunter College, where she remained until she retired in 1986. She began to publish books of poetry and prose in steady succession.

As she began to bring words and feelings together, she began to explore what it meant to be born into the circumstances of "this place." Just as her parents used to say "this place" to refer equally to New York or to the nation as a whole, she found that she could use her own experiences growing up and living in the city to represent common dilemmas of people of color everywhere. Her commitment to follow wherever words and feelings might lead brought her back to "the center of a harsh and spectrumed city" where "all things natural are strange."

Beginning with her second book of poems, *Cables to Rage*, Lorde established a reputation for her adroit use of city imagery. Most of her images are deliberately harsh. Like Ignatow, she represents this country's cities as concretizations of its profit madness, exploitiveness, hypocrisy, and racism, and its older industrial cities, such as New York, as such condensed centers of this country's pressures and oppressions that they have become symbolic of them. Correspondingly, for years she struggled against her impulse to abandon New York for someplace reminiscent of her fantasy of Carriacou or her youthful experience of Mexico.

Lorde resolved to remain in the city until her children were grown. She agrees with Ignatow that this nation's viability depends upon whether or not it can rectify the problems of its cities, and that it is not an altogether hopeless ambition. Therefore she determined that her son and daughter must not grow up out of touch with the city's realities. When she was debating whether or not to leave, she wrote the poem "New York City," entrusting her children with the hope that they might conceive a new love and faith in the city, like her own as an adolescent, at a point when her own patience was near breaking:[29]

I submit my children also to its agonies
and they are not the city's past lovers. But I submit them
to the harshness and growing cold to the brutalizations
which if survived
will teach them strength
or an understanding of how strength is gotten
and will not be forgotten: It will be their city then:
I submit them
loving them above all others save myself
to the fire to the rage to the ritual sacrifications
to be tried as new steel is tried;
and in its wasting the city shall try them
as the blood-splash of a royal victim
tries the hand of the destroyer.[30]

Her children's knowledge of the city's risks and opportunities, she concluded, would make the difference between their becoming warriors or sacrifices. After cursing all inhabitants of the city "who refuse to recognize their role in this covenant we live upon," she dedicated herself and her children to become warriors, to bring about the city's "death and renewal by fire." She intended them to become swords, not victims.

Coming Home

Lorde did not rededicate herself to the city easily. As she had had to go to Mexico before she could bring her feelings and words together, she had to travel halfway around the world before she was able to reconcile her residence in the city with her childhood ideal of "home." To close the division, she drew upon the West African philosophy of nature, in which memory plays a vital role.

Impelled by Pan-Africanism and the Black Power movement's affirmation of African roots, she visited West Africa in the mid-seventies. Her goal was Dahomey, now Benin, because she believed that her facial features suggested a Dahomean origin. In addition, she had learned that the persona of an Amazon, which she had adopted to steel herself through trouble as an adolescent, which had continued to strengthen her as a grown woman, was not fantasy but Dahomean fact. Historical Amazons included black women outriders who guarded the frontiers of the kingdom of Dahomey. Since women in Dahomey had the status of creators of life, they were also accorded the power of shedding blood in defensive battle: as she imagined herself doing in the poem "New York City." Lorde traveled about the country, drinking in the pride and beauty that she found there. Everything seemed familiar, not foreign.[31]

There she encountered the great African mother goddess, "the Mother of us all," who signifies nature's creative power. Her forms as Afrekete and Seboulisa moved Lorde profoundly. They merged sacrifice and struggle with bonding and power: the combination which she herself was distilling from life. They became abiding presences to her.

When she returned to New York, she intensively studied the history of what she had seen. She concluded that not only her blood was African: so were her modes of perceiving, thinking, and acting. She recorded her vision of Africa in the poetry collection *The Black Unicorn*, published in 1978.

In 1978 Lorde visited Grenada for the first time. She was struck by how African it was. She suddenly recognized that she had inherited her African modes of perceiving, thinking, and acting with her blood. She also realized that it must be true, to some degree, of all black families. Harlem, therefore, was not only a part of "this place." It was a part of Africa and of the West Indies in this place. This place and home were not as distant as she had once believed.

These insights from her travel made it possible for her to write *Zami* (1982), an autobiography of her childhood and young adulthood. Through the example of her own life, she traces an African way of development, which has run from Africa to the West Indies to black America.[32]

In 1978 her identification with the Amazons and her reverence for the African goddess Seboulisa were involuntarily deepened. The Amazons cut off their right breast so that they could draw a bowstring unimpeded. Seboulisa, as a poem in *The Black Unicorn* describes her, had "one breast eaten away by worms of sorrow and loss."[33] In 1978 Lorde underwent radical mastectomy to arrest cancer in her right breast. For urban black women at this time, the prognosis for survival was thirty percent. She did not consider her recovery an accident. When it came to survival, as she put it, "I had been in training for a long time."[34]

Her recovery from breast cancer proved to be training for battle against cancer of the liver, diagnosed in 1984. Confounding medical prediction again, she remained alive and active for eight more years. Her journals from this period show her determination that "there's nothing I cannot use somehow in my living and my work." As she also observed, "It's not like you get a second chance to die the way you want to die."[35]

A Healing Mythography

Out of this confrontation with death, Lorde salvaged a profoundly integrated sense of what survival requires and what it is for. Consonant with her reconstruction of West African philosophy, she combined her identification with women, children, blackness, and the earth with her faith in poetry and political action. Her memory spun the myths that register their connections.

Women, children, blackness, and the earth are elements of integration because they reduplicate and extend the essentials of each other. Each is a source of poetry. The veins of their connection run as follows.

Women's bodies are paradigms of earth. "My body," Lorde has invoked, finding the nature that she craved as a child present in herself, "a living representation of other life older longer wiser. The mountains and valleys, trees, rocks. Sand and flowers and water and stone. Made in earth."[36] During centuries of disenfranchisement and denial of power, women's spirit has preserved itself underground, in blackness, like dormant seed.[37] Like earth, women's bodies bring new life to light and nourish it. Through their identification with children, women carry the potential of a power that transcends sex, race, or age. In the words of Lorde's poem "Now":

> Woman power
> is
> Black power
> is
> Human power.[38]

Children melt all distinctions down to one principle of universal need. Women together with men bear sons and daughters, and together they are responsible for their present and their future. Yet the history of children has been more closely tied to the history of women. Children live at the edge of blackness, where growing is a task of transforming chaos into articulation. They show an affinity for earth, water, open air, and young growing things like themselves.

Blackness is the chaos that recycles material from dissolution into material for creation. It is the color of possibility. A mine for jewels must dig into blackness. A fetus is conceived and grows in blackness. Blackness can also be the color of terror, of suppression, of everything feared. It is the climate of love and death.[39]

The earth lies at the base. Without it, there would be nothing else. The earth nurtures life because it itself lives. Lorde was presented the statement by Alice Walker that "if there is one thing African-Americans have retained of their African heritage, it is probably animism: a belief that makes it possible to view all creation as living, as being inhabited by spirit." Her response was, "I absolutely agree." As she herself has characterized African tradition, "We see ourselves as part of a life force; we are joined, for instance, to the air, to the earth. We are part of the whole life process. We live in accordance with, in a kind of correspondence with, the rest of the world as a whole."[40] When she visited Africa, she found this belief that everything is alive and everything is connected very strong. "And it resounded. It hit something deep inside of me. The whole book *The Black Unicorn* comes out of that consciousness."[41]

Poetry rises in response to each element. Poems of particular love or rage rise from a convergence of all together. One short simple poem that exemplifies all of these considerations is "Coping":

> It has rained for five days
> running
> the world is
> a round puddle
> of sunless water
> where small islands
> are only beginning
> to cope
> a young boy
> in my garden
> is bailing out water
> from his flower patch
> when I ask him why
> he tells me
> young seeds that have not seen sun
> forget
> and drown easily.[42]

In keeping with the African belief that poetry is a chthonic force, Lorde finds the roots of poetry in the forces of the earth and its generativity. For the following reasons, she has said of the source of poetry that "it is dark, it is ancient, and it is deep."[43]

Poetry is unitive, believes Lorde, like the spirit that inhabits and binds everything on earth. It is a mouthpiece of the life forces of the earth. Song surges out of the rhythms of the blood, swelling like sap in synchrony with the earth that feeds the singer along with all other things.[44]

Poetry is primal, the natural mode of thought we are born into. When children make their own attempts to put the world together, they open their mouths and out comes poetry. When her children were growing up, Lorde often dashed for her notebook to save some striking phrase. These records have seeded several poems—as in the example of "Coping." Through openness to children, or to the child in themselves, poets preserve this freshness of insight and expression.[45]

Poetry is emotional and intuitive, motivated by aspirations for human fulfillment "beyond what is now called possible." These qualities are preeminently maternal. Lorde believes that to cherish feeling and a faith in new generations "is the name for a humanity that men are not without."[46] Nevertheless, culture and history have associated this turn of heart with women more often than men.

As a process, poetry materializes in blackness, because it works at the borders of understanding where experience and feeling first birth concepts, ideas, and knowledge. Working against fear, shame, censorship, and preconceptions, it taps the sources of power from which revolutionary knowledge comes. It reaches into the past, into areas which have been forgotten, in order to reach out to the future, to what we do not yet know.[47]

Women, children, blackness, and the earth—when poetry is integrated, it not only rises out of these elements but comes to their defense. They are not only requirements for survival, but the objects of love that survival is for. Lorde maintained her identity as an Amazon; and they are the territory and the citizens that she worked to arouse and defend. She believed that women, children, minorities, and the natural world are allied by their common victimization by systems of power and profit that have exploited everything vulnerable.

Reclaiming Time and Place

To characterize the renewed world that she sought to secure, Lorde chose the term *erotic* in the broad sense of the Greek spirit of Eros, born of chaos, who personifies all human and natural expressions of creative power and harmony.[48] Applied to places, the term implies sensuous color and human openness, such as the Carriacou that she imagined as a child, or the Mexico and Africa that she later discovered. Memory preserves these places for future use.

For Lorde, poetry forms a bridge between need and action, capable of creating a coalition across time as well as across the continents and people of the present. Although the future must make a fresh beginning, she considered the future a bond, rather than a break, with the past. It will not be based upon new ideas or new needs, because there can be none. The dark, deep sources of creative power are ancient; and they have been held in reserve across a history that transcends any individual or any single generation.

Moving into the future, therefore, requires moving in three simultaneous symbiotic dimensions of time. The poem "Prologue" describes the connections. Memory extends the identity of the individual backwards by honoring and attending to past generations of pain and love:

> and through my lips come the voices
> of the ghosts of our ancestors
> living and moving among us

The necessary prologue to amplifying the past is the courage to affirm one's own present feelings, one's own individual moment of time:

> I speak without concern for the accusations
> that I am too much or too little woman
> that I am too black or too white
> or too much myself

The sequel to this effort is that messages that can nourish the future are preserved:

> Here my heart's voice as it darkens
> pulling old rhythms out of the earth
> that will receive this piece of me
> and a piece of each one of you
> when our part in history quickens again
> and is over[49]

This necessity of faithfulness to the past in order to move fruitfully into the future requires two parallel pursuits of memory. At the level of society, it requires history—a retelling that includes all sides. The experiences of women, children, and oppressed peoples must be rescued from silence, whenever traces remain, and restored to the record. When all traces have been lost, that story too must be entered. At the level of the individual, faithfulness to the past requires reminiscence and autobiography. Through the pursuit of unrepressed personal memory, a person learns to interpret history justly. With this conviction, Lorde termed *Zami*, her autobiography, biomythography. To write a life, Lorde believed, is to write a myth: it is to discern the perennial mythic shapes that move under untold lives.

Through the preceding connections, Lorde developed a self-identity that extended forward and backward beyond the limits of her own individuality. This liquid identity softened the prospect of death. In *The Cancer Journals*, she elaborated a description of fishing on a river at dawn with the evocative but not surprising phrase, "tasting the green silence," . . . and then added the exceptional phrase, "knowing that this beauty too is mine forever."[50] Her enjoyment of the sweetness of life acquired the dimension that "I could take this in, and I could own it and use it wherever else I was for the length of my time that is coming to me, and someone else, my children, my children's children, and someone else's children, could stand on that place and see that sweetness also."[51] As she invested herself in all women and children, she felt that a part of herself would remain present in them.

Lorde did not come to this position lightly. *The Cancer Journals* is a record of battles against successive waves of despair. She did not discount death; but for someone who worked within the context that the severest death is silence in the midst of life, she found that a sense of impending death had the positive effect of paring priorities down to essentials.

In a compromise between her bond with nature and her commitment to raising her children in New York, Lorde bought a house on Staten Island, where she could have trees, a garden, and overlook water, like the Carriacou of her mother's stories, yet still be linked by bridges to the borough of her birth, Manhattan, which she came to recognize to be another island home. When her children were nearly grown, she began to explore places closer to the quality of her mother's memories, which eventually led her to her final refuge on the island of St. Croix in the Virgin Islands.

In the early 1980s, she weighed the prospect of change in a poem, "On the Way Out I Passed Over You and the Verrazano Bridge." It was scribbled down on a plane that was to take her to investigate a new location, when the plane got caught in an air jam and began to circle before lift off, over and over, directly above her Staten Island rooftop. After sweeping in imagination from her own home to continents of the oppressed, the poem closes by reaffirming the past, present, and future:

> History is not kind to us
> we restitch it with living
> past memory   forward
> into desire
> into the panic   articulation
> of want   without having
> or even the promise of getting.
>
> And I dream of our coming together
> encircled   driven
> not only by love
> but by lust for a working tomorrow
> the flights of this journey
> mapless   uncertain
> and necessary as water.[52]

MARIE PONSOT

As contemporaries within New York, Audre Lorde and Marie Ponsot knew and respected each other's work. Coming of age in the 1940s and 1950s when women's roles were defined in the service of men, both poets have found redefining their identities in their own terms a central task, and memory their instrument for this purpose. As a minority woman, however, Lorde worked with the conviction that she spoke for other women in comparable positions. Ponsot, in contrast, describes the pursuit of memory as a unique individual exercise. Whereas Lorde became a public poet, Ponsot has maintained a private, domestic identity.

After a first book, *True Minds* (1956), Ponsot wrote poetry in private for twenty-five years without any attempt to distribute her work. In the last decade, her publications reflect some measure of her productivity: the poetry collections *Admit Impediment* (1981) and *The Green Dark* (1988); two co-authored books on the art of teaching writing, *Beat Not the Poor Desk* (1983) and *The Common Sense* (1985); and numerous pieces in literary magazines.

Along with concern for memory and self-identity, the women share worlds of faith. Foreign to each other as the Catholicism of Ponsot and the African philosophy of Lorde may appear, they conform in that they set language and the world in orderly correspondence, as the very nature of things. "God *said*, 'Let there be light'; and there was light" (Genesis 1:3). "In the beginning was the Word" (John 1:1). Medieval and Renaissance metaphysics took these pronouncements literally: God called each being's name, and it came into being. In West African philosophy, *nommo*, the name, directs the life force that activates each thing.[53] In each tradition, language and the world form corresponding orders created by a unitive spirit, so that matching language to the world means matching order to order. Both Lorde and Ponsot have worked with the faith that if they find honest words to recover memory, they will discover a true order inherent in the world.

Their common faith in memory and language is part of their larger faith in the "nature of nature." Their points of agreement regarding their relationship to nature, and their resulting evaluation of childhood memory, will be explored in detail in chapter 6. It is enough to observe here that when each poet was a child, her mother introduced nature to her as an essentially generative force with which she could work in alliance. It follows that the city images that both poets have treasured from childhood and young adulthood are porous to nature; and in maturity, both women have gravitated to places where the city and natural world converge.

A Wordsworthian World

Granting these similarities, Ponsot grew up under circumstances that appear, on the surface of things, a different universe than Lorde's Harlem. She was born in the early 1920s into a white, middle-class, Wordsworthian family in Jamaica Estates, Queens.[54] At that time, the neighborhood was predominantly Catholic. It boasted shops for discriminating customers, a nice park, a large monastery and convent school, and fine public schools, which she attended.

Ponsot's father imported wines and liqueurs for the wealthy. In the 1920s and 1930s, a number of political émigrés from Europe worked in this business. Some French, Belgian, and Spanish associates of her father became intimate family friends. With them, their languages entered the home. French was often the household language of exchange.

Language, in general, was a rich family endowment. Her father
and mother were accomplished storytellers. Poetry, both oral and
written, was a family tradition. As Ponsot recalls it, her mother
found occasion to recite Wordsworth's "Ode to the Daffodils"
"about ten thousand times." Her grandmother's favorite was Tennyson's "Crossing the Bar." Both her mother and her grandmother
wrote verses when they had something especially affectionate to say,
or something especially poignant, and her father contributed birth-
day rhymes for homemade cards. Poetry was a taken-for-granted
strand in the warm weave of everyday life.

Another strand of everyday life was the contemplation of nature. Her mother loved both to walk and to find a beautiful place and
sit still in it. Whereas Lorde's mother sought green spaces to remember home, Ponsot's mother was home in still green Queens. Before the birth of a brother when Marie was six, mother and daughter
often went off exploring together. A public school teacher, her
mother knew how to combine instruction with adventure, and she
taught that part of the pleasure of noticing details of plants, animals,
birds, and rocks is naming them. She enlarged the sense of the area
by sharing geologic history, as well as stories about small changes in
the span of her own lifetime. She described the trillium and dogtooth
violets, for example, that once bloomed in wild corners. To reinforce
the lessons, Marie received a set of Burgess nature books in which
birds and animals described their lives as if they stood ever-ready to
explain themselves to any child sharp-eared enough to listen.

One reminiscence from childhood shows how a sense of the sacred in nature was shared by the whole family:

> I do remember it would be clearly exhibited by just stopping
> and looking at things. I can remember a field of daisies on Long
> Island somewhere. We had driven out to The Hamptons, and on
> the way back my mother said, "We don't really have time to
> stop." But then we came to a field of flowers and we stopped. It
> was a total field of daisies—I can still see it. Everyone got out
> of the car and just stood there, looking at the daisies in the late
> light of a summer's day. Not to pick a lot of them, but just to
> look at them.[55]

Late light also illuminated the sacredness of the world every
evening when the children accompanied their mother when she
drove over the Queensboro bridge into Manhattan to pick up their
father at the office. They rode into the sunset, when the city was

transformed by radiance and the air and river had a softer, floating quality. "And that was a holy city, no question about it." It embodied a sense that grew with her as she grew, that the aggregation of human beings that the city sheltered was somehow inherently holy. If one feels, as Ponsot does, "that if anything is holy it is the human face," then the city is holy at any time of day. But sunset confirmed it, baptizing the city in the sacredness of cosmic order.

Like Lorde, Ponsot retains a strong sense of New York as water-garlanded. She has described it as "my many-voiced harbor city."[56] Not only the daily drives across the East River revealed it. Before her father went into the wine business, he worked in the old Customs House at the tip of Manhattan, which commanded a view of the harbor, and he often took his son and daughter with him to visit friends there. A paternal aunt who worked on John Street took the children on other excursions around this oldest part of Manhattan where city, sky, and water meet. To this day, whenever Ponsot thinks of Manhattan, she thinks of this point where the elements converge.

Before Christmas when Ponsot was eight, her mother allowed her to go into Manhattan by herself to shop for presents. It was an intoxicating adventure. From that time on, she had free access to any part of the city. Its libraries, museums, stores, streets, and parks were open to her to sample as she pleased.

When Ponsot was nine or ten, mother and children began to spend summers as paying guests on a farm outside Newburgh, New York. It was a 220-acre working dairy farm, where the first order of the day was a fortifying farm breakfast. There was no other order of the day. The days stretched ahead with absolutely no claim or responsibility. As it stands out in her memory, she spent most of her time wandering alone on self-appointed searches. She never found the Indian burial ground that was rumored to be on the property, but it drew her through the woods. There was a "fossil field" with fossil-marked boulders, paths and stone fences to follow, an apple orchard, pastures, corn fields. In August the thistles along the fences attracted flocks of goldfinches.

In all, it was an idyllic childhood. At home, there were fond family and friends. Outside, there was Queens in the 1920s, a peaceful borough. Across the river, there was the excitement of Manhattan. In the summer, there were the allurements of the farm. Shining behind it all like a late afternoon radiance was her mother, her namesake: gentle and intelligent, bound to her daughter by such deep bonds that they would bring inevitable deep pain.

Today Ponsot lives a few blocks from the site of her parents' and grandparents' homes. She has also bought a cabin near New Paltz, not far from the Newburgh farm, where she can spend whole summers again. Thus she has remained grounded in her two childhood centers. Devoted to her country retreat, she can say, "I am not a city person." Yet at the same time, she is so much a city person that she must also say, "I am not a country person."[57] As a result, like the river at sunset reflecting both skyline and sky, her poetry mingles both city and nature. Yet if the balance of her poems' images must be admitted, like the river itself, it falls on the side of nature.

Poetry of Praise

When Ponsot was eight, she sent a poem about sunrise to *The Brooklyn Eagle*'s children's column edited by "Aunt Jean" ("that patient lady"). Until the end of childhood, she remained a regular contributor. The *Eagle* was Whitman's old house organ; but the children's column had not maintained the same pitch of revolutionary fervor. In retrospect, Ponsot believes that the advantage of her writing assiduously as a child was that it gave her the opportunity to write every possible cliché out of her system before she knew that the word *cliché* existed. Her parents thought that her writing and publishing were "nice," but nothing special to fuss over.[58]

Given a mother who recited Wordsworth at night as she tucked her daughter into bed, the child deduced that the connection between nature and poetry must be tight. It followed that nature was her most popular theme. She still remembers the beginning and ending of her first offering to the *Eagle*. Her usual technique at the time was rhymed quatrains. ("Hit them over the head with it.") So it opened:

> The dark clouds of night
> Have taken affright.
> The bright clouds of day
> Have flushed them away.

After more of the same, it arrived at a concluding couplet that took her by surprise, which included more subtle slant rhyme:

> Dawn's tapestry
> Defies imagery.

She astounded herself by such finesse. She can remember reciting the lines to herself over and over.[59]

As she grew, she learned to practice a more agile metrical repertoire. Free verse was already the dominant convention, and she accepted it as one possibility, but she has never allowed it to exclude older conventions. As a young woman, she read somewhere that every aspiring poet should write a sonnet a day, so she wrote a sonnet a day until it became second nature, followed by villanelles and each of the other "mean" forms. As this chapter will later show, she is convinced that access to different metrical forms enlarges her freedom as a person, as well as a poet, because it enlarges her access to memory.

Ponsot did her undergraduate studies at St. Joseph's College for Women in Brooklyn, and then went on to a master's degree in English at Columbia University, where she wrote her thesis on the Metaphysical poet George Herbert. Upon completing graduate school, she found work in a publishing company. When she took stock within a few years and realized that the job that she had taken offhandedly as a job threatened to turn into a career, she resigned and left for France, which had just reopened after the Second World War. On the boat crossing the Atlantic, she became friends with a fellow passenger, Lawrence Ferlinghetti. They continued to see each other in Paris, and later continued to correspond and to exchange work.

During the three years that she lived in France, Paris became the second city to take possession of her. She was young and in love in Paris. Many years later, when she put some of her feeling for Paris into a poem, she embodied its beauty in the tiny park at the tip of the Ile de la Cité, the Vert-Galant. As she was describing this place in an interview, she realized that its multiple refraction of Seine, island, and sky is the Parisian equivalent of lower Manhattan that represented New York to her as a child. Where earth, water, and sky meet, she has slipped into her closest skin. In the poem "A Third Thank-You Letter: for the Gift of the Vert-Galant," she acknowledges her identification:

> All islands are
> always being born; each needs
> a like inhabitant, interacting, riverborne:
> here I am.[60]

She married a French painter, Claude Ponsot. Just before the birth of their second child, she and her husband returned to settle in

New York. Because her husband learned English only grudgingly and gradually, French remained the language of their home for many years.

Meanwhile Ferlinghetti moved to San Francisco and started the City Lights press, and he asked his friend to contribute a book. *True Minds*, published in 1957, was fifth in the Pocket Poets Series, appearing between Allen Ginsberg's *Howl* and Denise Levertov's *Here and Now*. The back cover of the book announced: "Marie Ponsot will certainly become known, in the years to come, as one of the most important young Catholic poets of the post–World War II period."

The denomination of a Catholic poet is everywhere evident. The poems' titles and main body of imagery and allusion come from the great fused tradition of Platonism and Catholicism. The subjects are present circumstances and surroundings, but everything is irradiated through the prism of two thousand years of philosophy and faith. For example, the first few pages contain the phrases "intemperate told truth," "passion, miracle, incautious faith," "forever perfected," "forever alive," "the golden diametric," "the danced dimension of the good true beautiful."

Signifier of Platonic *eros*, signifier of Christian *agapé*, signifier of her own new marriage, the word *love* leaps from the book's pages. When words are counted, it appears three times as often as the next most frequent abstract nouns, which are *truth* and *freedom*. A simple counting of these three words is misleading, however, because even when they are not directly named, they are addressed in every poem in some form. The shifting exchanges among love, truth, and freedom, defined against the shadows of their opposites, create the tensions that save the book from a docile faith. Other recurring words are *pain* and *peace*.

An example of the book's simultaneous reference to darkness, radiance, and love is the poem "Downtown." It was inspired by sunset (sunset again) in downtown Manhattan (place of convergence again):

> Surprised, the pursey woman sees, pauses to sham
> Disdain for my folly who am laughing still
> Because the sun's fierce glory roared, to damn
> All murk forever, an instant before it fell.
>
> The street is a passageway dedicated to the alive,
> The being beauty of man and child; I take
> Toll of their lived-in walking; I thrive
> On the grace and gaucherie they, moving, make.

Always among them there is one whose glancing face, unasked,
Fantastic, says, here is a friend of angels; masked,
Yet unmistakable the bright middle creatures move ablaze
About us; and make the intelligence leap with praise,
Rush to claim a breaking joy from joy's created trace.

O good world, God's work, turn, turn, turn in place
Wide in the wild eternal air of His embrace.[61]

Poetry of Riddles

By the time Ponsot assembled *True Minds*, she had given birth
to five children in less than five years. In time, she gave birth to two
more: in all, one daughter and six sons. Her writing had to subsist in
the margin left after mothering. As her marriage began to dissolve,
responsibility for supporting the family also fell to her. She took in
translating, which could be done at home, eventually translating
thirty-two books. They bound her more closely to children's interests, for they included many collections of fairy tales.

It was a valuable apprenticeship. From the *Fables* of La Fon-
taine, especially, she learned how art can have the effect that "its
limits are the limits of a small world, but that world is full."[62] Art
might contain itself within the borders of a small frame—like the
domestic realm itself—but within these borders life might still be
ample (even heroic).

As she has described conditions for personal writing during
those years, "The routine would be to get the babies into bed, do
twenty pages of the work—that of doing translations, and then whatever energy I had left was mine."[63] Somehow, after only a brief interruption, she found the energy for poetry again.

She did not, however, find energy for publishing. Between
True Minds and *Admit Impediment*, her next book, twenty-
five years intervened. It was time enough for gradual changes to
accrue into a metamorphosis. At first glance, it is easy to mistake *True Minds* and *Admit Impediment* for the work of two unre-
lated authors.

An illustration of the difference between the two books is "Unabashed." It is akin to "Downtown" in some of its ideas, but even
they have undergone some removes and reversals. Water, land, and
sky still meet; and the world is still invested with angels, who still
interbreed with human lives: but the mode of their mingling has become more tentative, more patient . . . more like the poem's own
halting yet deliberate new mode of construction:

Unabashed
as some landscapes are
(a lakeshape, say,
lying and lifting
under a cupping sky)
    so angels are,
entire with each other,
their wonderful bodies
obedient, their strengths
interchanging—
    or so
we imagine them
hoping
by saying these things of them
to invent human love.[64]

The watershed in the development of Ponsot's poetry was her divorce. She wrote all but two of the forty-nine poems in *Admit Impediment* after divorce. She selected these poems and rejected earlier ones after reassessing the proper relations of words, things, and memory. She has described her changed criteria by reference to an essay by Northrop Frye in which he discusses two basic modes of word use: charms and riddles.[65] Parallel antinomies are rhyme and reason, sound and sense.

Charms are part of the art of magic. The word's root is *carmen*, meaning *song*. As Frye describes the rhetoric of charm, it is "dissociative and incantatory." Its devices are rhyme, refrain, alliteration, pun, assonance, antithesis. "Such repetitive devices break down and confuse the conscious will, hypnotize and compel it to certain courses of action," notes Frye. "Or they may simply put to sleep." The language of invocation, which seeks to remove the speaker's resistance to the influx of a greater power, follows the same mode. *True Minds* is charm poetry.

The word *riddle* comes from the same root as *read*. Riddles invite the reader to break the spell of charms. They demand intellectual detachment, as they turn concentration from sound to sight, to attention to the given world. *Admit Impediment* is riddle poetry.

Charms originate in the faith that world and word are connected. Therefore words can bend people and things to the speaker's will. Ponsot does not repudiate the tradition that in the beginning was the Word, but she does repudiate the exercise of persuasion or the enthrallment of possession. The poetry of *True Minds* illuminates flashes of emotion, as in "Downtown," but it evades autobiography as much as the poetry of Weinfield, who describes himself as an artisan of song, or the poetry of Bronk, who describes himself as an instrument of the world's passion. In rejecting charm in favor of the self-possessed mind of a reader of riddles, Ponsot has elected the company of this study's other poets who have scrutinized their pasts, Ignatow and Lorde.

Memory the Riddle Reader

In an interview, Ponsot compared the reading of riddles to the intelligence of active memory. She noted that memory is the medium all poetry must travel through: it is impossible to write of anything that has not first been committed to memory. But memory conceals as well as preserves. Therefore Ponsot has learned to rely upon two techniques to reimagine—to re-image—past places and events. Sometimes she begins with a phrase that evokes a fragment of memory, and builds up the poem by association around it. At other times, she begins with a metric form, which she believes taps levels of memory that cannot be reached in any other way:

> The information you get when you are obeying one of these forms, either the sonnet or a sonnet-like form with rhyme, or the sestina where the turn is of a different weaving kind . . . it pulls material out of your head that you can't get out in any other way. You don't "think." It does not "occur to you." You draw on a different matrix of language. You do. And it is a way of discovery.[66]

She believes that free verse, which leaves the choice and placement of each word to the conscious decision of the author, is psychologically less free.

Regardless of whether a poem begins with a phrase or a form, in its first draft it has what she calls a "hum," or dominant incantatory rhythm. "It goes Mmmm, Mmmm, like one of those things of Swinburne's when you can't even remember what he's talking about. There's a big hum. It's great! But what was he talking about?"[67] To discover what an emerging poem is about, she shifts from obedience to song to the discriminative alertness required to solve riddles, which initiates a reconstruction of memory.

In terms of a poem's structure, this process requires that "when I rewrite I try to cut across the hum, both with the idea and with the cadence of ordinary talk."[68] In terms of Ponsot's use of memory, it requires the following course of investigation.

Of course memory has a tendency to both review and revise. Memory edits before you even get to it. So that if you are writing there is a danger in writing too quickly. The thing is to try to get down to wherever that sort of shaped memory is edited and changed. I think then you have to meditate on it a little bit, think about it, puzzle over it, until you get back to the fresher memory. To the less edited version of what really happened. Because somehow . . . clichés must be useful to us. And they will sneak in and blanket things. I'm not sure if any of the Freudian reasons are any good, but they're probably part of the picture. And there are probably just reasons of efficiency, the way a computer can only deal with two poles.

Interviewer: Are you talking in terms of proceeding from one draft of a poem to another?

Yes. And I think that is why, unlike some people who are able to write final versions very quickly, when I write I like to write something and then leave it alone for awhile. . . . I go back through it and can then do that kind of thing I was talking about. See where it doesn't quite ring true somehow.

Interviewer: That is like taking memory as a guide ultimately to what is true if you go into it deeply enough.

Yes, and that means taking experience as a guide, because it is experience that produces memory. . . . Whatever the role of the imagination is in that kind of shaping and reperceiving of memory, I'm not sure; but I know it's an important one, because that is the faculty that is working on memory. To try to push it back toward what you really remember you have to reimagine the first level of memory, and then see the holes in it, and press through the hole and see if it gets somewhere.

The informed imagination gets to know the tricks of the mind, gets to know the bank of your own thought. For example, I am in some very deep way optimistic. Every bottle is half full. And when I am remembering something I have to remember it the way I remember it, and then go back and look at the empty half of the bottle. It's funny the way significance emerges when I do that. I begin to see why I remember what I remembered, and I begin to see something more, or something else, something that completes it all or informed it in some different way.[69]

The tension between first memory and faithful memory that Ponsot articulates here recalls the statement of Adrienne Rich that journeys into the past can be life preserving, but that "every journey into the past is complicated by delusions, false memories, false naming of real events."[70] It also recalls Lorde's insistence on accurate self-definition. Overwhelming emotion may cut through the necessity of patient revisions and go straight to the truth; but for daily writing, this probe for truth remains the guiding rule.

Poems Memories Control

The poem "For a Divorce," which opens *Admit Impediment*, marked the transition when Ponsot made precise memory a conscious instrument under her conscious control. In abandoning the role of self-sacrificing wife, which her church ordained, she gained the role of a critical reader of her own life. In many poems, this reading has examined how childhood people, places, and things haunt or vivify her present experience.

Most of the poems that illustrate her plumbing of memories are long. Her autobiographical poems take many pages to accrue insight around a phrase, or to pursue a musical descent into the past through a metric form. The poem "Late" exemplifies the metrical method of riddle-reading, "Field of Vision," free verse construction, and "Take Time, Take Place," both methods in succession.

"Late," a series of seven sonnets dedicated to her mother, is one of several pieces that Ponsot wrote to exorcise her grief over her mother's decline into senility and death. It revives and relates images of her childhood, her mother, and the nature that her mother introduced her to. Long after writing it, in the middle of a public reading, she suddenly realized that these sonnets had carried her back into early childhood before her brother's birth, when she and her mother shared an idyl of undivided love.[71] What she had taken to be a cross section of her childhood turned out to be only its commencement, when her mother first bound her to nature and to words through the medium of herself.

The poem opens with Ponsot bird-watching—a practice her mother taught her. Grieving, "dark on a bright day," she forces her attention outward, to be rewarded by the sight of a myrtle warbler, "coin-gold." Beginning with this prompt, the sonnets carry her into "the dark poems memories control":

> Once we birdwatched, eyeing shrub & tree
> For the luck beyond words that was our quest;
> Your rings flashing, you showed me day-holed
> Owls, marsh blackbirds on red wings, the crest
> Kingfishers bear. Mother, dreams are too cold
> To eye the dark woodland of your bequest.

Rather than dreams, she elects alertness. Her mother, who led her into woodlands, has returned to them: "Now among boxed bones, pine roots, and Queens sand." Through memory, her daughter searches for her:

> I enter the dark poems memories control,
> Their dark love efficient under day love.
> Down I go down through the oldest unscanned
> Scapes of mind to skim the dim parade
> Of images long neglected lost or banned,
> To root for the you I have not betrayed.

A repeating dark image that she unroots is that of another bird, the elusive ovenbird that she and her mother pursued, who hid under leaves and whistled "Tea / cher!"—her mother's vocation and avocation:

> The call came plain enough to recognize
> And we went out following the sound.
> It went before us in the dusk; its cries
> Go before me now, swerve & dip in shade
> Woman daughter bird teacher teach me. Skies
> Boughs brush tufts; blind I have lost where we played
> All trust in love, to the dark of your disguise.

The final sonnet in the series brings her out of dusk and dark into the bright image of herself and her mother in the family garden. As the series began with a myrtle warbler, coin-gold, which rewarded her faithful practice of attentiveness to the natural world that her mother taught her, it ends with her mother's engagement diamond, set in gold, associated with her mother's other great bequest: attentiveness to words. The ring that flashed upon her mother's hand as she pointed to birds or turned the pages of books rests on Ponsot's hand now, signifying the conjunction of trust in nature, love, and words with which her mother endowed her. The light of her mother's gifts, in her own hands now as she writes, multiplies:

Reading, sunned, outside,
I see your lit hand on the page, spirea
Shaking light on us; from your ring I see slide
A sun, showering its planets across skies
Of words making, as you read or I or we,
A cosmos, ours. Its permanence still defies
The dark, in sparkles on this page; fiery,
It makes its statement clear: light multiplies.[72]

The persistence of this pattern of childhood legacies is illustrated by the long poem "Take Time, Take Place," which concludes
The Green Dark. As "Late" opens with bird-watching, "Take Time,
Take Place" closes with it. It sets her on a New York beach with
cityscape and water before her, like the views of Manhattan at sunset that awed her as a child. Before reaching the orderly sonnets that
close the poem, she struggles through disorderly free verse memories
of lovemaking in early marriage—the deceptively full side of the
half-full glass; and she fantasizes a paradisal reunion with friends and
kin now lost to her or dead. Her challenge is to "haul this place now
up through that place then." She succeeds in being where she is
through attention to a tern's flight. Not willing to sacrifice present
joy for fantasized joy, she accepts that joy "brightens not as I please /
but any instant." As she watches for it, it happens:

On the instant, its innocence accrues
across the cityscape, real and immense.
Here bird and I are each other's news
alighting centered in the present tense.
Inside out I identify bird clues
framed in sun by my binocular guess;
here its lift of head & tail are evidence
its flash of song confirms; here is steadfastness
in single names for thick experience.
"Wren," I say. "Hawk." "Tern." "Luck." "Love." Wingless
and winged we startle then settle, each a view,
alert & modest in our different dress.
I hear unearned joy pay my human dues
and take this passage for my new address.[73]

This triumph of the present reconciles her to the past. The poem's
conclusion affirms that remembered love and desire for love may be
dissolute and drugging—yes—but they are part of nature's redeeming

press of life. She is prepared to receive present joy by her initiation into joy in the past.

A poem that illustrates free verse construction around an initial phrase or image is "Field of Vision: A Map for a Middle-Aged Woman." Given a divorce and grown children, Ponsot assesses her prospects in mid-life. As in "Late" and "Take Time, Take Place," she secures her freedom by establishing new terms with memory. As "Late" and "Take Time, Take Place" find her bird-watching as her mother taught her to do, "Field of Vision" finds her in an old farm orchard much like the Newburgh orchard that she explored as a child. She wakes from sleep in it as if newborn: as she must wake from the past into the present. To meet the world on its own new terms, a world in which "nothing real happens twice," she must shed the casing of rigid memories. The poem's resolution is that she does not thereby shed memory. She gains the agility that:

> Memory's to think with, not daydream absently—
> It should be like light on leaping, rain on water,
> To make the mind run richer, a brilliance
> Merging emerging in the shimmering interchange.[74]

The common theme in these and other poems is that Ponsot secures present joy, or at least present solace, by inhabiting present forms of beloved childhood places and practices. Warbler, tern, orchard, cityscape that she delights in now are resurrected versions of the owl, ovenbird, orchard, and cityscape that delighted her as a child.

Fluid Memory

Ponsot finds the issue of freedom in the use of memory pivotal. After *True Minds* came out, she looked at Allen Ginsberg's *Howl* that preceded it and the other books in the City Lights series around it. She listened to Ferlinghetti read poetry to jazz. She observed that many American poets were competing for the position of public bard that Walt Whitman had left vacant; and she knew that "I couldn't possibly do any of that. I couldn't assert myself, publicly, as 'I am the poet.' I didn't feel like a prophet. I didn't have a definite message that I felt had to be spread."[75] In contrast to poets like Whitman or Ginsburg who seemed driven to proselytize for their beliefs, she found herself moved by questions, by riddles; and she found her material in country retreats and domestic dramas rather than the public stage. Therefore, although she had known since early childhood that she would always write poetry, as she continued writing, she put her work to bed in drawer after drawer.

Just as the publication of *True Minds* was due to her friendship with Ferlinghetti, the publication of *Admit Impediment* was the result of her friendship with Marilyn Hacker, one of this country's most widely recognized woman poets. After years of exchanging work, Hacker finally added to the refrain that "You've got to get those poems out," the conclusion that "I'll be there next Sunday to pick up a manuscript—you'd better have it ready."

Understandably, women's silence has become a major theme in Ponsot's work, as it is in Lorde's. Both poets often use the word in the sense of being frightened into silence or being shamed into silence. Ponsot, however, speaks of silence with the ambivalence that Lorde reserves for blackness. Sinisterly, silence is the reverse of finding one's voice, of sharing memory. In keeping with Catholic contemplative tradition, however, Ponsot recognizes that silence can also be used dexterously as the background against which sound— and memory—resonate: the dark ground, the green dark, out of which deep-rooted memories and necessary words arise. Under the issue of silence, then, the terms that dominated *True Minds*—freedom and truth—have reappeared in Ponsot's work. To be forced into silence is undeniably a negation of liberty. Yet as long as publication requires conformity to a prevailing style, silence testifies to the virtue of truth that she cherishes.

For Ponsot, truth and freedom in writing are essential to truth and freedom in memory. She has phrased her reflections on this subject in terms of Wordsworth's concept of "spots of time." As she interprets Wordsworth, time is preserved through localization in space. Through the permanence of the landscape itself, or through vivid remembered settings, places give associated feelings and events immunity against time. Places and things preserve memory; and memory, in turn, makes places and things sacred. Ponsot would add to Wordsworth's philosophy, however, that these spots in time, being in time, are also in motion. Through the offices of memory, the past may be resurrected in the present; but for the past to win new life, it must keep pace with the motion of the present ("like light on leaping, rain on water, / To make the mind run richer, a brilliance / Merging emerging in the shimmering interchange").

Spots of time, once crystallized, are never lost to an individual, but they must stand a test. The challenge is which form of memory will preserve them.

The easiest answer is memory the ever-ready editor, the cliché dealer, the stereotype seller. Ponsot believes that the great risk incurred in taking the position of the poet as public figure is that the pose may freeze. Public postures make perfect copy for memory the editor.

The more strenuous answer—insofar as questions can be an answer—is memory that seeks truth. This memory may function like either method of her writing: bringing old and new associations to evocative images and phrases, or following old forms into new figures. Then memory becomes not a flight from the present but a flight forward. Every new experience (of love, of pain, of a favorite place) rearranges perception of the present and the past. "Very intensely, something in the moment changes the way you remember the past, and then the way you remember the past informs the way you're seeing the present. None of it stays the same. It jumps around."[76] Her many poems that seek to "haul this place now up through that place then" illustrate this process.

Fluid Identity

Around these two possibilities of memory, the sensitive terms in Ponsot's work—truth, freedom, silence—coalesce. Memory is integral to identity, because whether our identity is free or conscripted depends upon its use. If the truth is kept silent because memory declines to probe for it, either through fear or through the acceptance of clichés, freedom is forfeited. To achieve freedom of identity, according to Ponsot, we must keep faith with memory, with the roots of our identity, by keeping in time with its changes.

When Ponsot committed herself to this open inquiry, exchanging the charm poetry of *True Minds* for the riddle poetry of *Admit Impediment* and *The Green Dark*, she altered the role of images of places and things. Settings and things in *True Minds* are transfigured by the force of words, as if they have to be artificially illuminated through poetic virtuosity. The actual world is sacrificed on the altar of the ideal. Things remain consecrated in her later work, but now it is understood that they are so simply by being themselves. No longer symbols of something more significant, they are named for their own sakes.

When this difference was remarked upon, Ponsot was pleased that this deliberate reversal was evident. Between the first book and the second, she said, she exchanged "the truly vain idea that I could create something" for a desire to make "the importance of things and our connectedness, and the use they are to us, the incredible use that things are to us . . . to stand for itself by itself."[77]

Unlocking the meaning of things, she has noted, is like unlocking memory. Just as memory can edit, censor, and conceal, or disclose for rediscovery, there is a similar distinction among images. When a writer selects established symbols and metaphors, as she did in *True Minds*, she keeps within the confines of edited memory. She produces what she intends to find. Ponsot distinguishes this practice from the discovery of metaphors that unexpectedly reveal a new understanding, which emerge when memory is trusted to disclose the meaning of experience through patient surveillance. Then, in the revelation of immanence, the transcendent incarnates itself.

As material for metaphor, Ponsot assigns natural things a privileged status. They have an essential aspect of surprise which defies prediction and control, not having been brought into existence by human hands. Therefore, although a city street may embody her sense "that if anything is holy it is the human face," to try to express something as mysterious as holiness she finds herself cast upon natural things.

"Riverborne," by her own choice of words, Ponsot uses water as her primary image for the fluid continuity that she seeks in her life, her memory, her art. Christian symbol of grace, water receives her close attention in its incarnations in rivers, creeks, fountains, thirst-quenching drinks. Like Lorde, she associates water with the cycle of the generations and the act of receiving something precious to pass on. A long poem to her children, for example, describes her bequest to them as the water of life. The poem begins:

> The water:
>   I pour it
>   with care
> into these seven jars for
> you seven,
>   sacred voyagers
> soon to be launched.
>
>   One of you will
> one day need it;
> I have seen signs
>   in your faces; one
>   will need it.
> Each of you is
> I judge able to need it.

It ends:

> What we know for certain
> is that this is water
> —mine to give you
> what I may of it—
> that nothing
> can spoil.[78]

The titles of Ponsot's books imply how to find direction within life's liquid course. The phrases "true minds" and "admit impediment" are taken from the opening lines of Shakespeare's Sonnet 116: "Let me not to the marriage of true minds / Admit impediments." "Love is Not Love," the title of a section of *The Green Dark*, alludes to the sonnet's claim that "Love is not love / Which alters when it alteration finds." Ponsot's juxtaposition of these phrases may seem to mock Shakespeare's exaltation of love: "the star to every wandering bark / Whose worth's unknown, although his height be taken"— as the sonnet proceeds to say. Ponsot maintains, however, that she intends no irony.[79] A marriage of true minds is possible only if impediment be admitted and attended to; and pain over life's inevitable alterations is proof that love has not altered. Only if we accept that we are adrift on a sea of change can we follow the course of honest admission necessary to navigate by the sonnet's mark.

In her own memory, Ponsot has attempted to follow this course. Steadfast love has been her guide through her childhood world, as her childhood world has been her guide to the newfound places and things that she loves. Mother, child, grandmother—each passage of her life has held its form by flowing freely into the other.

Chapter Six

Childhood and Nature Reconsidered

In childhood, the universe is active. In early childhood, every part of the world appears alive, purposeful, willed. Clouds and rivers make their way as deliberately as dogs and people. Trees feel winter cold. A stone trips an intruder. The moon and stars commune. Young children may know fear, but they avoid meaninglessness and chaos by creating intentional worlds. This characteristic of childhood, which was documented by Piaget in the 1920s, continues to be reported by contemporary developmental research.[1]

Fundamental to how we evaluate our childhood memories is how we evaluate the world itself. As children, did we see the world in a way that was somehow essentially true or essentially false? Was childhood a period of insight or ignorance? According to this book's evidence, our answers to this question define our use of early memory.

One certainty at this point is that this book's opening question can now be answered: whether Wordsworth can be cited as a timeless authority regarding the creative significance of childhood memories of nature? The answer is *no*. The preceding five poets' accounts show that the autobiographical paradox that Wordsworth labored to heal has intensified. As it has fallen upon our selves to give life form and meaning in an increasingly secular world, we have gained a new appreciation for the creative power of the self, and we therefore study its circuits inexhaustibly. The last two centuries have seen the development of autobiography, psychoanalysis, and academic and clinical psychology. We now assume that childhood experiences influence us to a degree previously unimagined. Yet the same modern turn of mind that has magnified the importance of childhood and autobiographical memory, that Wordsworth encouraged, collides with the childhood world that we remember. A child's sense of an animated, dynamically interactive universe conforms to adult worlds of the Romantic, Renaissance, or Medieval eras, but dominant contemporary attitudes deny this world reality. The same trend of thought that teaches continuity with memory teaches discontinuity with memory's beginning. Faced with this paradox, the five poets described here present a variety of responses.

Their examples suggest that how we relate to childhood corresponds to how we relate to nature—to this vast field of matter and energy that transcends human intervention and control . . . "the world beyond our world that holds our world" in William Bronk's phrasing[2] . . . "Mother Nature" in familiar terms. According to dominant scientific conceptions of nature, childhood perceptions are imaginative impositions. It follows that to affirm connections with childhood, one must elaborate an alternate conception of nature.

This dilemma is compounded because natural objects receive disproportionate attention in early memories. Even in the memories of the four city poets studied here, nature figures prominently. Stone and concrete also composed their worlds; but in response to general questions about place memories, the elements that these poets singled out in talk, which also form persistent images in their writing, are sun, wind, water, and trees. This focus has proved as tenacious as the blades of grass pushing up from sidewalk cracks, which Audre Lorde garnered. This emphasis is consistent with other collections of childhood reminiscence.[3] Skyscrapers and city streets may narrow down attunement to nature, but they do not screen it out.

The Idea of Nature

How we relate to nature is one of the most critical intellectual and existential stories in Western history. Texts of intellectual his-

tory converge in recounting a gradual decline of a religious world
view that set the self and nature upon a common foundation, as
Descartes and succeeding empiricist philosophers worked out the
epistemological premises that allowed the world to be conceived as
a soulless, and, in time, godless mechanism to be manipulated for
technological ends. In protest against this mechanization of the
world, the Romantics sought to accommodate scientific theories to
a revised spiritual vision.[4]

According to M. H. Abrams, in attempting to effect "Reconciliation from this Enmity with Nature," the Romantics fell into the
same two-term scheme that they protested. As Abrams has characterized the tendency of Romantic thought in general, it was "to di-
minish (sometimes to the point of eliminating) God, and leave as
prime agencies man and the world, mind and nature, spirit and
other, or subject and object."[5] Stated in these generalities, Romanticism sounds little different from the mechanistic dualism that it
opposed. The great distinction is that, where Cartesian dualism established a division between the mind and a mechanized nature,
the Romantics established a "vital and productive" dialectic with a
spiritualized nature.

This dualistic tendency can be traced in the work of Bronk, Ignatow, and Weinfield. They too have analyzed the world according
to a two-term scheme of mind and nature. Caught, however, in the
currents of the twentieth century, they have found neither faith in
the efficacy of Cartesian dualism nor Romantic faiths credible. A
tragic strain in their poetry is that they find themselves caught in a
confrontation between mind and nature, when they are conscious
that, in the final analysis, neither any human mind, nor any human
ends, can survive nature's engulfment.

This sense of futility is epitomized by the men's experience of
silence. For them, it is not a social and political term, as it is for Lorde
and Ponsot. It is environmental, signifying nature's indifference to
human exertions and ambitions. Attentiveness to silence so much
dominates Bronk's writing that all human efforts stand exposed as
vain echoes against it. Ignatow has never tired of recording the silence of trees and walls in response to his persistent communing. In
Weinfield's poetry, this sense of silence is concentrated in the image
of the sea. Projected against it, the shadows of passing figures waver
and dissolve.

The significance that these poets have given to autobiographical memory conforms to their philosophies of nature. Ignatow, who
believed until late in life that no meaning can be found in nature's

swirling forces, determined, in opposition, to give life a purely human meaning: "Life has to be lived, no matter how meaningless it is
. . . Life still has to be affirmed and expressed in all its ways."[6] Whatever meaning his life has, then, depends upon autobiographical
analysis. According to this analysis, his childhood presumption that
it is a sympathetic universe became material for irony.

Given a similar sense of nature, Bronk concluded that any attempt to ascribe meaning to memory can never succeed. Therefore
he has never tried it. Weinfield, in contrast, defines nature as a fullness, not a chaos. This fullness, however, exists within the world of
time, which is ephemeral and inevitably a world of loss. Therefore
he seeks meaning by transcending loss through art's enduring forms.
Because language, or any other artistic medium, cannot reproduce
the world of time, he achieves transcendence through the creation of
an alternate world apart from nature, where he himself as a historical individual is "dead." His childhood self has never entered into
this Land of Rhyme.

Women's Place in Nature

Where are the women poets in this quandary? They are not in
it. The scheme of intellectual history that illuminates the three
men's poetry fails to fit the women's work. This conventional
scheme neither accounts for the women's presuppositions nor their
conclusions. Their sensibility controverts it, as they never introduce
a conflict between the self and nature. From the beginning, they define themselves as existing and working in alliance with nature,
which exempts them from the men's tragic opposition.

There are two possible explanations for the women's deviance.
Either women have dodged the last four centuries of intellectual
progress, or intellectual history as it has been written never effec-
tively applied to women.

By the time that Lorde and Ponsot were interviewed, it had become apparent that they expressed a different orientation to nature
than did the men. Therefore it was possible to bring up this observation at the end of their interviews and to ask them to reflect upon
it. This chapter will present their reactions, and propose several explanations for differences that, in this small sample of five, have
turned out to be gender differences.

Marie Ponsot noted that men, in their poetry, usually express
"a way of identifying nature as something outside oneself," as an object over against the self.[7] Men may conclude that there is no self that

can survive in the face of nature, but they begin by introducing the aspiration that there might be one.

"How can you separate from nature, from the rest of nature?," Ponsot continued. "I am not very good at holding distinctions, at making distinctions that would hold. I don't think I have a mind and a body, for instance."

"As two separate things?"

"Not really."

In finding nature something integral to herself, that she cannot separate from, she is at odds not only with the dominant temper of Western poetry and philosophy, but also with the dominant temper of Christian theology, which teaches the separation of body and soul. As a result, she recalls feeling heretical when she studied Thomas Aquinas in college. Intellectually, as an abstract exercise, she could follow his theological dualism well enough; but she could never really understand it. The more collaborative side of his argument, that the ideal expresses itself, moves, and acts through incarnation in the real, she readily absorbed.

Not finding her sense of divinity adequately embodied by "our Father who art in heaven," she has turned to other religious models. She has proposed her own version of nature and transcendence in a poem entitled "Skambha, Guess-Worker, Both Within and Beyond," which borrows from Hinduism the archetype that divine energy embodies itself as a Great Mother. Her interpretation of this figure is her own, based upon her experience of connection, as a child, to her mother and, as a mother, to her children. These connections create a vivifying sequence. "If you're going to make up matriarchy," she explained, "let's just make it up—out of what we know, and that is that mothers have daughters, and daughters have daughters, and daughters have daughters; and that is really a mind-boggling experience." To express this natural miracle, the poem has played with the myth that at the fall of every great cycle of time, the goddess who is Worldtree and Lifemaker is reborn as herself, as her daughter:

> Nothing perishes forever:
> in her fall the mother frees the daughter
> who is herself again when the dream is over.
> After her disaster the Sibyl speaks to us:
>
> See, these are the Same and the Different.
>
> Same and Different meet to keep
> light streaming through the mothercord,

its unrelenting energy
comes here.[8]

This identity between mother and daughter incorporates two
dimensions of Ponsot's own experience. Out of herself, a mother
gives a child life: body out of body, and a convergence of interests and
sympathies out of love. Reciprocally, as she gives nurturance, the
mother's own childhood is reborn within herself. The sum is a sense
of life focused upon birth and rebirth.

Audre Lorde characterized the difference between men's and
women's sense of nature—which she too believed exists as a general
rule—precisely in these revitalizing terms:

> It has to do with renewal, with a belief in renewal . . . The earth
> renews itself over and over again. None of us lives three hundred
> years is another way of saying it. You can't have one without the
> other. A renewal requires a going into dust, to rise again.[9]

The loss that goes with this reality wounds everyone, but, through
children, women find themselves linked to renewal more than loss:

> I often want to move it beyond the question of maleness to
> speak of that principle which is in all of us, that is on the line
> more for men than it is for women. I think women are capable
> of alienation too. Although I think the thing we have built in
> that guards against it has very essentially to do with the giving
> of birth, the giving of life.

Lorde believes that this rule holds regardless of whether or not
women actually give birth. That their bodies are adapted to child-
birth predisposes them to an anticipation of fruitfulness and a sympathy with children, born of woman, and with nature and the earth,
which also bear. The word *nature* suggests this identification, deriv-
ing as it does from the Latin *nasci*, to be born.

As a result, like Ponsot, Lorde finds despair something essentially out of tune with nature, rather than a logical consequence of
it. The identification of mind, body, and nature, which Ignatow and
Bronk have found occasion for despair, both women find occasion for
resilience.

In the course of my interview with Lorde, I repeated a line from
one of Bronk's poems: "Sometimes, I could go in anywhere, not / to
see the stars."[10] Lorde's response was, "When you said that line, my

spine shook. But I suspect that we came to that line from different places. I thought, yes, sometimes we do give in to despair. We do retreat from power. That line represented to me a retreat from power." Power, to her, signifies an affirmation of connection, an acknowledgment of relationship to nature, to other people, and to different parts of ourselves, including maturity to childhood, and the utilization of these connections for the advantage of the whole.

In place of futility, she derives from nature a lesson of indispensable continuity:

> I am myself, and I must define myself; but I am connected, I am part of . . . and I get this sense more and more and more the older I get . . . I am part of a chain, I am part of a continuum. It did not start with me and it will not end with me. But my piece is vital. I feel this so strongly now.

Finding nature an essentially meaningful sum of parts, defined by a common denominator that is renewal, Lorde and Ponsot both find meaning "natural" to their memory. Defining their connection to nature through their connection to children, they maintain continuity with their own childhood. Through the attention that they give to children, they repeatedly reexperience what they themselves once felt; and they accept the sense of relationship to a responsive world that they reexperience as an essentially valid intuition.

Romantic Resonances

In some respects, the position that Lorde and Ponsot express parallels the Romantic position. Like Wordsworth, they have stressed connection with nature. Like him, they have also stressed connection with childhood, which they respect as a period of special sympathy with nature. In *The Prelude*, Wordsworth, like Lorde and Ponsot, has attributed his bonding with nature to the mediation of his mother:

> Blest the infant Babe
> (For with my best conjecture I would trace
> Our Being's earthly progress,) blest the Babe
> Nursed in his Mother's arms, who sinks to sleep
> Rocked on his Mother's breast; who with his soul
> Drinks in the feelings of his Mother's eye!
> For him, in one dear Presence, there exists
> A virtue which irradiates and exalts

> Objects through widest intercourse of sense.
> No outcast he, bewildered and depressed:
> Along his infant veins are interfused
> The gravitation and the filial bond
> Of nature that connect him with the world.[11]

Wordsworth found his infant self an intermediary between the love given to him and the love that he gave to the world. As he learned to notice nature, to reach for it, and in time to name it, he transferred to it the powers of identification and sympathy that his mother taught him:

> Is there a flower, to which he points with hand
> Too weak to gather it, already love
> Drawn from love's purest earthly fount for him
> Hath beautified that flower; already shades
> Of pity cast from inward tenderness
> Do fall around him upon aught that bears
> Unsightly marks of violence or harm.[12]

Wordsworth observed that as he was loved, he learned to love the world. In the arms of his first caregiver, he absorbed the principles and practice of love, which he generalized to all of nature. In terms compatible with Lorde and Ponsot, his passage avoids a duality of mind and nature by unifying perception, action, and emotion on the grounds that all are expressions of nature's creative and sustaining processes as they are passed on through the relationship between mother and child.

Like Wordsworth, Lorde and Ponsot have sought to maintain some aspects of premodern faiths in modern form. Although African philosophy and religion and Christianity have their differences, they have the similarities that they see one spirit infusing all things in the world, including world and word, and that they allow death no final stopping place. According to Wordsworth, these faiths are the necessary precondition for sympathy with his sense of memory. In an 1814 letter to a friend regarding the Intimations Ode, he noted that "this poem rests entirely upon two recollections of childhood." One was "splendour in the objects of sense," and the other "an indisposition to bend to the law of death, as applying to our own particular case." "A reader who has not a vivid recollection of these feelings having existed in his mind in childhood," he cautioned, "can not understand that poem."[13]

Ponsot's poetry leaves open the possibility of "outlands," territories essential to Christian faith. In "The Great Dead, Why Not, May Know," she speculates:

> Some suppose that this post-natal life
> where all we have is time, is fetal life,
> is where as we bounce and flex in time
> our years of moons change us
> into beings viable not here
> but somewhere attentive.[14]

As Ponsot describes these outlands, they are the boundless spaces of a general love in "a universe where love's not crazy," inhabited by the "great dead" who have endowed the earth with legacies of care and creativity during their presence on it.

The African philosophy and religion that Lorde said resounded, that hit something deep inside her, make room for attentive outlands with a different topography than Christian territories, yet these lands too sustain life. In keeping with an emphasis upon ancestry and tribal connection, West African tradition holds that as long as the dead are remembered and spoken of by the living, they form a class of "living dead" who watch over and guide their descendants. When all traces of the dead are lost to living memory, they pass into the elements of the earth itself. Since all things on earth are spiritually animated, the dead remain assimilated into life.[15]

Romantic Divergence

This comparison of Wordsworth with Lorde and Ponsot has stressed their similarities. In the case of all three poets, their adult beliefs have perpetuated their childhood assumptions because they have continued to believe in a spirit that sets alight the "splendour in the objects of sense" and in an unmeasured futurity. It is possible, however, to emphasize other passages of Wordsworth that differ, in which he follows the basic Romantic dialectic of the mind's struggle against nature, ultimately prevailing over it. At the close of *The Prelude*, he concludes that:

> what we have loved,
> Others will love, and we will teach them how;
> Instruct them how the mind of man becomes
> A thousand times more beautiful than the earth
> On which he dwells.[16]

We can imagine Lorde and Ponsot reciting in chorus with him up to the semicolon, but not after it. The Romantic dialectic reflects ambivalence regarding relations between mind and nature. Although Lorde and Ponsot would also like to see enmity between the self and nature assuaged, both women have begun by presuming an essential unity that obviates such a system of alienation and reconciliation. Correspondingly, when they have expressed the basis of their connection to nature, they have not used the agonistic terms of this mental system, but terms of generativity taken directly from nature itself as process.

After these reflections, the words of Edith Cobb quoted in this book's preface, which instigated this study, acquire a new meaning. If they are reread now, two heritages can be heard. Creative thinkers return to childhood in memory, she claimed:

> to renew the power and impulse to create at its very source, a source which they describe as the experience of emerging not only into the light of consciousness but into a living sense of a dynamic relationship with the outer world. In these memories the child appears to experience both a sense of discontinuity, an awareness of his own unique separateness and identity, and also a continuity, a renewal of relationship with nature as process.[17]

Liberal quotations from Wordsworth in Cobb's writing show that she accepted his Romantic conception of the benefits of early memory, and with it the modern stress upon "unique separateness and identity." In her equal stress upon the terms "continuity" and "renewal of relationship with nature as process," she can now be heard adding her own words, as a woman.

In justifying their sense of memory and nature as they have, Lorde and Ponsot have reached back to a body of connections that antedate the history of philosophy that standard texts converge in telling. The women's experience conforms to mythologies that this history appears to have superseded. The mother who gives birth to herself again as her daughter, who is simultaneously material nature and divinity, is a recurring figure in ancient myth, some forms being Afrekete and Seboulisa whom Lorde excavated, or Skambha whom Ponsot reclaimed. The celebration of these connections is believed to have been a core part of the Eleusinian mysteries, which went underground in the West just as Platonic philosophy gained ascendance.

Carl Jung's analysis of the mother-daughter relationship that the Eleusinian mysteries commemorated closely accords with the experience that Lorde and Ponsot have articulated:

Demeter and Kore, mother and daughter, extend the feminine consciousness both upwards and downwards. They add an "older and younger," "stronger and weaker" dimension to it and widen out the narrowly limited conscious mind bound in space and time, giving it intimations of a greater and more comprehensive personality which has a share in the eternal course of things . . . We could therefore say that every mother contains her daughter in herself and every daughter her mother, and that every woman extends backwards into her mother and forwards into her daughter. This participation and intermingling give rise to that peculiar uncertainty as regards *time*: a woman lives earlier as a mother, later as a daughter. The conscious experience of these ties produces the feeling that her life is spread out over generations—the first step towards the immediate experience and conviction of being outside time, which brings with it a feeling of *immortality*. The individual's life is elevated into a type, indeed it becomes the archetype of woman's fate in general. This leads to a restoration or *apocatastasis* of the lives of her ancestors, who now, through the bridge of the momentary individual, pass down into the generations of the future. An experience of this kind gives the individual a place and a meaning in the life of the generations, so that all unnecessary obstacles are cleared out of the way of the life-stream that is to flow through her. At the same time the individual is rescued from her isolation and restored to wholeness.[18]

Jung regretted that the "rejuvenating effects" that "must flow from the Demeter cult into the feminine psyche" have been lost from our culture, "which no longer knows the kind of wholesome experience afforded by Eleusinian emotions."[19] The experience of Lorde and Ponsot suggests that these effects may never have been as lost as Jung believed—only lost from the dominant written culture. Lorde and Ponsot also diverge from Jung by arguing these connections on the basis of their own autobiographical experience as daughter, mother, and earth dweller, without appealing to a collective unconscious as he did.

Reconnected Selves

The connections that Lorde and Ponsot express may explain a long-standing puzzle of memory research: in study after study, women have reported more childhood memories than men. In a study by Douglas Hermann and Ulric Neisser, they also rated the quality of their childhood memories significantly higher than men.

Noting this discrepancy, Neisser lamented that he wished it were understood.[20] At least part of the explanation may be the sense of connection presented here.

This pattern of experience also conforms with results of longitudinal research on memory and personality development. A study conducted by the Institute of Human Development at the University of California uncovered similar gender differences in orientations to childhood memory.[21] Retracing the records of a group of men and women from adolescence into their fifties, Harvey Peskin and Norman Livson found that, on the whole, men distanced themselves from their childhood memories in their twenties and thirties, but began to recall childhood again in their forties. Women participants, however, never showed this pattern of disengagement.

To explain the differences they found, Peskin and Livson proposed explanations compatible with those of Lorde and Ponsot. Drawing upon the work of Erik Erikson, the researchers suggested that the women's involvement with children made their early sense of self relevant through mid-life. In contrast, the men's initial ambition to succeed in a man's world made their childhood self irrelevant and nonadaptive. The men were not disposed to reminisce until their mid-forties, after they had already achieved the security of success, or after they had given up hope of greater achievement. By this time, both men and women faced the challenge of approaching old age, which is to understand and accept all parts of one's life, including beginnings. Peskin and Livson have called for a phenomenological verification of this proposed explanation. The present study constitutes one such confirmation.

This longitudinal research, in turn, may help to account for the different responses to childhood shown by Henry Weinfield, who was thirty-four at the time of the first interview for this book, and David Ignatow, who was sixty-nine. That Weinfield showed little interest in his childhood, but Ignatow, at twice his age, showed integration of his present and past, is in keeping with these suggestions. Certainly if these interviews had caught Ignatow in his mid-thirties, he would have shown a much stronger rejection of early memory than Weinfield's general dissociation of childhood and poetry. Weinfield, in his early forties now, finds his appreciation for Wordsworth growing. For every pattern, however, there are anomalies. Bronk, in his seventies, has never permitted himself autobiographical return.

Of these five poets, Ignatow best illustrates the Romantic shift from estrangement to reconciliation, and comes closest among the men to the women's sense of extension through generations. In his last phase of writing, he has come to an acceptance of nature as metamorphosis and renewal, after battling against its changes throughout most of his career. In his last published notebook entry he has written:

> The division between ego and reality is a false one because the ego manifests exactly the principle which makes reality, and that is change, renewal, reassertion, reaffirmation of itself in constantly emerging new forms.[22]

Rather than annihilating the ego, Ignatow's altered sense of nature provides for individual creativity:

> You're living significantly if you recognize that the whole world is in process and you recognize that somehow you're contributing, there is something new that is contributing to this process.[23]

As this study has shown, as Ignatow came to accept natural cycles, he became more tolerant of his early memories. Nevertheless, as the Romantic spiral suggests, this laboriously achieved position differs from its point of beginning. Ignatow's moments of accord with nature have been momentary, and his underlying ambivalence has prompted him to write a dark parody of Wordsworth's Intimations Ode.

Remembering Death

One of the most telling evidences of the men's and women's different attitudes to nature is their different attitude to death. Despite his moments of affirmation, death has become Ignatow's primary theme. That trees and birds never answer his attention and addresses, that earth and grass always lie silent but accommodative, that the identity that he must feel his way into is what it must be like to be stones and dirt—these perspectives on nature dominate his work. Consciousness of death unifies Bronk's sense of nature also. Death is the subject of many of his poems, in which he has also moved from defiance to imaginative participation. Death itself is not a subject in Weinfield's poetry, but a recurrent image in his work is the waiting void.

Death is a salient subject in the writing of Lorde and Ponsot as well. Yet neither poet has published a single poem on the subject of her own death. Ponsot has written about death in terms of the pain of losing family and friends, or as the dynamic that drives poets to use their talent urgently and faithfully. Lorde's entries in *Cancer Journals* and *A Burst of Light* record fear in the face of surgery, the difficulty of coping with physical pain, rage against the duplicity of a society that tolerates carcinogens and expects women to conceal their scars, and gratitude for other women's healing support. Nowhere does she stop to consider her own death as such—except, like Ponsot, to observe that it illuminates priorities. Although both women acknowledge that nature incorporates death and decay, they present it as an essentially life-giving force.

Like the women, Ignatow has concluded that "it is enough for me to leave behind a child, some books, memories of myself with some friends."[24] He has accepted that through children, books, and memories, the dead can remain a present force: a "great dead," a "living dead." In his poems that draw upon a modern consciousness of ecological cycles, such as "Invocation," he has also addressed dirt and stones with something close to a primitive sense of union: "I walk upon and study you as my next brothers and sisters."[25]

The difference between Ignatow's world and that of either woman appears in succeeding lines from the same address:

> I am resigned, if I must say it that way.
> Try as I might, I cannot think myself exactly that.
> I see us each in separate worlds.

From a modern perspective, dirt and stones are only that. From older perspectives—and young children's perspectives—dirt, stones, people, and everything else are animated by life. The first perspective puts nature and human consciousness in separate worlds. The second confuses, or fuses, them.

Feminine Connections

For readers accustomed to conventional accounts of history that chart inexorable movement away from belief in a spiritual universe toward a secular world of individuated selves who seek meaning despite nature's meaninglessness, the preceding analysis may suggest the following questions. To remain in sympathy with a childhood sense of the world, is it necessary to hold a religious world view, as Lorde, Ponsot, Vaughan, Traherne, and Wordsworth have done? Can it be said of Lorde and Ponsot that their vision of the world fails to fit standard interpretations of history because they have, in effect, escaped the conflicts of modernity by holding to older beliefs? Is it now the case that to feel disposed to hold older beliefs, it is necessary to be a woman?

A simple affirmative answer to any of these questions begs more questions than it answers. The positions of Lorde, Ponsot, and their Metaphysical and Romantic precursors cannot be explained away as religious anachronisms; because at issue is not a religious world view, but a special complex of views. In emphasizing alliance with nature and sympathy with childhood, in finding in childhood and the world signs of original innocence rather than original sin, all of these poets have, in fact, held minority—even dissident—positions within religious orthodoxy. That Traherne and Vaughan were unconventional in this respect has been noted. Wordsworth, when he became older and more conservatively Christian, attempted to delete the deep strain of Platonism from his 1805 version of *The Prelude*. Ponsot's interpretation of Catholicism, as she herself confesses, is unorthodox. Lorde's rendering of African philosophy and religion is similarly her own.

What appears to be at issue is not conformity to an older tradition, but a certain turn of thought and feeling that has adapted different philosophies and religions to its own expressive ends at different moments in time. Even when these poets have drawn upon established beliefs, they have personalized their borrowings. Rather than holding to religious orthodoxy, these poets have contributed to the progressive modern effort to express thought and feeling in secular terms.

The explanations that Lorde and Ponsot have given for their connections to childhood are largely secular. In part, they confirm the proposals of Jung, Peskin, and Livson: that women feel a sense of extension through time through their ties to their children, and that raising children encourages them to remember what it is like to be a child. In addition, Lorde and Ponsot have advanced an explanation that these male psychologists have ignored: that women's sense of connection to past and present generations and to their own childhood is fostered by their sense of connection to the earth. It was of the essence of the Eleusinian mysteries that the reunion of Demeter and Kore signified the earth's fruitfulness, yet Jung has omitted this dimension in his analysis. Peskin and Livson have also left it out, in keeping with its absence in Erikson's thought. Yet this bond with nature has been pivotal to the women's self-understanding.

Both Lorde and Ponsot have linked their sense of nature to their memory of their early relationship with their mothers. Both of them have described being taken by their mother's hand to be introduced to nature as something essentially constructive and benign. As they learned speech from their mothers, they learned to name nature gratefully. When Lorde's mother catalogued Carriacou plants, she instructed her daughters in their healing uses. When Ponsot's mother led her daughter in search of birds, rocks, and wildflowers, she taught her to observe and name all the fine details of this world that embraced them both. The daughters remember these excursions into nature as moments of peace and accord. In these moments they intuited what, years later, they made explicit: that their mothers introduced them to nature as something akin to their own way of being. Their mothers, themselves, nature—alike agents of renewal. In these memories, in the details of nature that their mothers singled out—details of grace, durability, fertility, healing—the daughters understood that they were being taught the essentials of their own role. In these moments, their childhood self, their mothers, and the natural world met to form one unity of nurturer and nurtured. And how, in such moments of peace, are nurturer and nurtured to be separated: any more than infant, mother, and their common feeling for the world, when the infant is at the breast?

Through the manner in which their mothers introduced them to nature, Lorde and Ponsot learned the two forms of identification that Wordsworth believed to be the great endowments of early childhood: naming and sympathetic knowing. At the same time, these poets learned two other forms of identification: identification with their mothers, through the bonds of love and teaching, and gender identification. In their childhood memories of nature, the women united these four forms of identification in one persuasive combination. As they learned to name nature and to project themselves imaginatively into the life of its plants, animals, and elements, they learned to name and know the character of both their mothers and themselves. How natural, therefore, that they should continue to identify with nature, and that they should continue to find their childhood sense of the world valid. Their mothers taught them that it was.

As they grew, their culture reinforced these first lessons. From prehistoric fertility figurines through millennia of myths, paintings, sculptures, and figures of speech, nature has been symbolized as a woman. Children's stories and the tradition of poetry itself perpetuate this feminine personification. Complicating this ancient inheritance, however, is the Cartesian model of the world that nature is an indifferent, amoral mechanism. Caught between these conflicting paradigms, it is not surprising that both women have rejected an impersonal scientific world view in favor of older beliefs.

Masculine Ambivalence

None of the men in this study report memories comparable to those of the women. Perhaps, being sons and not daughters, their mothers did not introduce them to the world in this way. Had their mothers attempted to do so, in a culture in which men must not be defined as motherly—that is, like their mothers—for fear that then they will not be manly, alliances between mother, child, and nature could not fluidly proceed.

The identity of these poets' first literary role models must have intensified these differences. As all five poets have traced the origins of their vocation, they attribute critical importance to another person's teaching and encouragement; and the men's mentors were their fathers or a father figure, the women's mentors their mothers. Ignatow and Weinfield had fathers who set the example that storytelling or poetry was something to be cherished and imitated. Bronk remains so much indebted to his teacher, Sydney Cox, that he cannot imagine how he would ever have written without him. Lorde and Ponsot have said that they learned poetry out of their mother's mouths. This convergence of literary and gender role models probably accentuated alternate reluctance or readiness to identify with the feminine worlds of early childhood and nature.

If the different parts of the men's stories are compared, it is apparent that they add up to dissonance. If their sense of their mother imbued their childhood world, as Ignatow remembered it did and as psychologists have said it will; if society at large personifies nature as a woman, as it does; if the ideal of manhood is to become something radically distinct from a child, as both Ignatow and Weinfield have said it is—then it follows that identification with childhood experience or with nature must be resisted. Either identification involves maternal influence and feminine imagery, which can imperil male identity. Under these terms of tension, it is to be expected that, in the case of the men, childhood memory will face either of two fates. It can be detached from adult concerns, as Bronk and Weinfield have done; or, if early memory is conserved, it can be kept at a distance and diminished by the power of reason, as Ignatow has done. It also follows that the discovery of ultimate inescapable identification with nature will be occasion for despair.

These observations fit the psychoanalytic theory of Dorothy Dinnerstein, Nancy Chodorow, and Jane Flax.[26] According to their argument, the standard course of gender development encourages women to learn connection to people and the surrounding world, whereas men learn individuation and separation. Everyone begins with the common ground that they first come to know and name the world, and to know themselves, in a woman's arms. As a daughter grows, she learns that she is indeed like this person with whom she first identified, and thus self-definition through connection is fostered. A son, however, learns that he is unlike this person who first nurtured him into consciousness of the world and of himself. Even worse, he may learn that this person with whom he first confused himself has inferior social status and is dominated by men who control power and prestige. He grows to play his part in a society that enforces this potent, but precarious, separation.

Within the philosophy of religion, *From a Broken Web* by Catherine Keller supports the correspondence that this section suggests: that mother-child relations influence views about nature, which influence the way in which we relate to our childhood past.[27] Writing in a language akin to that of Lorde (whom she repeatedly quotes), Keller challenges the entire tradition of heroic separate selves that Hellenic mythology, Jewish and Christian theology, Cartesian philosophy, and Freudian psychoanalysis have reiterated. She advocates a new sense of self that defines itself through active memory in response to fluid relationships with the changing world of immanence. To explain why a heroic self has historically sought transcendence at the expense of connections to the body, the earth, women, children, and childhood memory, she relies upon the preceding feminist analysis. She also notes what Lorde and Ponsot neglect: that an emerging new philosophy of science (which Ignatow's late work reflects) and process theology validate this revised self-understanding.

"That Principle That Is in All of Us"

The preceding analysis of gender illuminates the alternate orientations to nature shown by the contemporary men and women poets in this book. It also illuminates the *apocatastasis*, or "flowing of the soul"—the sense of extending backwards and forwards through the generations—that the women show. It conflicts, however, with the observation that remembered childhood bonds with nature were originally expressed and defended by three male poets: Wordsworth,

Traherne, and Vaughan. This discrepancy underscores what feminist psychoanalytic theorists have stressed: that engendering is social learning that cannot be reduced to sex.

To maintain connections with childhood and nature, it is not adequate to be a woman. As Lorde has noted, women too are capable of alienation. Therefore Lorde, as the mother of a son and a daughter, and Ponsot, as the mother of six sons and one daughter, have pondered what determines connection for either sex. They have both hoped to see discussion move beyond the question of maleness or femaleness to "that principle that is in all of us," in Lorde's words. Between them they have proposed two general explanations, and the example of their lives suggests a third.

The explanation that they share refers to an activity that has been almost exclusively consigned to women in the past, although it does not preclude men's participation. It is the phenomenon of *child watching.*[28] Both poets have noted that women's investment in children attunes them to early memory, as their attending upon children repeatedly prompts them to resee the world through children's eyes. To the degree that they respect children (a disposition that the bond of love fosters but not compels), they respect childhood intuitions. An overlay of experience is set in motion—the reshuffling of past and present, "the shimmering interchange," that Ponsot has characterized as memory to think with. In the act of sympathetic child care, caretakers' memories are evoked and reasons to retain them are established.

Ponsot has suggested another condition for maintaining childhood bonds with nature, which is implicated in child watching. It may be described as *redoing time,*[29] and it comes with the disposition, in Ponsot's words, to "expect nothing for work well done." In the poem "Sois Sage O Ma Douleur" written for a self-effacing friend, she describes it as a condition that:

> many women know
> (and some men
> who live like younger
> sons or girls or saints—but most who expect nothing
> for work well done
> are women).[30]

Ponsot has put saints in this taxonomy because they have renounced all claims to worldly success, and younger sons because they were traditionally barred from inheritance by laws of primogeniture, and therefore labored on land they did not own or joined the clergy, who preached, even if they did not always practice, the virtues of saints. Into these categories fall Traherne, a member of the clergy; Vaughan, a younger son; and Wordsworth, a younger son who elevated poetry to a new saintly vocation, who publicly acknowledged his close bonds to his mother and his sister.

Ponsot has noted that, through the millennia, women have been most consistently denied worldly position, power, status, and property, despite their hard labor. All in this condition, who have been prevented from "being something," in worldly terms, have been left free to identify with other things that exist outside the spheres of ambition: with children and elements of the natural world. Ponsot is acutely conscious, nevertheless, of the vulnerability of this position of "unspeakable sanctity." A major motive of her poetry has been to explore the dilemma that, too often, the burden of this blessedness has been self-denial and martyrdom.

Those who are excluded from worldly achievement "redo time" in the sense that they are relegated to the cyclical world of physical necessity: a world of daily and seasonal tasks that are never completed, for which no name, fame, or great wealth accrue. Expressive of both men's and women's bondage to this world, the reunion of Demeter and Kore in the Eleusinian mysteries signified both human and agricultural fertility, and both men and women were initiated into its mysteries. The cyclical world of birth and child rearing has been predominantly women's work—thus these feminine goddesses. Men as well as women, however, labor at agricultural cycles.

Ponsot's category of those who live without worldly expectation is Eleusinian: women, girls, younger sons, laborers, priests, and religious aspirants. The common experience that this diverse group shares is a rhythm of returning certainties without finality. According to research in child development, young children are so busy working out the general scripts of daily existence that they have little mind or memory for out-of-the-ordinary events. As they are learning this quotidian background of sense certainties, the repetitive, not the solitary, absorbs them.[31] Women and laborers are absorbed in the all-too-well-known world of sense certainties that exact unending toil. Priests and acolytes perform daily rounds of spiritual offices.

This rule is not all-inclusive. Ponsot's category shows poetic license in the sense that it is a loose generalization. Certainly it does not include all members of each set without exception, nor conflate these sets. As women poets, Lorde and Ponsot are distinct from these other groups in fundamental ways. They are maternal, unlike children or priests, and literate, unlike young children and most laborers. Each distinction implies differences in self-understanding and in memory's content and use.

What Lorde and Ponsot share with each other and with members of these other groups is an attitude to time: attention to natural daily cycles in which time is repeatedly redone, where they are bound within the here and now, which is like yesterday and tomorrow. This attention to objects and events that pass out of experience, only to return, practices the pattern of memory. Their world invites the image of the Neoplatonic circle, to which Vaughan and Traherne found that their own lives conformed. In this world of recurring time, like points on a circle, the Same and Different are One.

Another common element apparent in Lorde's and Ponsot's lives suggests a third condition for maintaining connections to nature and childhood: an *adult role model* who teaches appreciation for the natural world. Both women have described how their mothers explicitly and implicitly instructed them in their ties to nature. There is no reason, however, why only women can fill this role. As the philosopher Sara Ruddick argues, "maternal" describes a practice, not a sex, and the essence of this practice is protective care, which can be given by men as well as women, and devoted to many things as well as children. She also observes that those who model care, whether they be male or female, tend to perceive nature as an ordered, resourceful ally.[32]

According to the three preceding lines of connection—child watching, redoing time, and models of care—standard texts of intellectual and literary history are obscuring parts of men's experience as well as women's. The dualities that these texts have featured exclude Ponsot's male as well as female cast of exceptions, and Ruddick's male as well as female "mothers."

My own research and experience confirm these observations. I have heard different combinations of these three forms of connection echoed by both men and women among conservationists who work to preserve places that they love, and by farmers with deep affection for their land.[33] These people almost invariably tell about an adult who bound them to nature as a child: typically, when they are men, a father, grandfather, or male teacher. These respondents also often express a sense of connection to past and future generations—sometimes, in the men's cases, illustrated by their own accounts of child watching. Those who are farmers talk about the satisfactions of seasonal tasks. Informally, among men and women friends who practice a craft, I have heard the same connections when they discuss their commitment to reviving old techniques of work with natural materials. The relations with nature that have qualified for intellectual histories fail to express the actual range of men's and women's relations.

Common Ground

This book has charted the history of the modern dichotomy between mind and matter that makes the self salient in a universe of impermanence. The Romantics attempted to secure the self through an idealism that gave the mind ultimate dominion over nature. Romantics like Wordsworth and Emerson emphasized that nature corresponds to divine ideas, whereas Romantics like Schiller stressed that art creates a world of ideas that triumphs over nature. As science and popular notions of scientism won allegiance in the nineteenth century, modern materialism gave nature ultimate dominion over the mind. Under this condition, the relationship between mind and nature became more difficult to reconcile, and lonely existentialist figures who confront nature's void became modern heroes.

Lorde and Ponsot articulate a new position, which strikes a balance between these modern extremes of self-gain and self-loss. They emphasize the natural basis of their connection to the world through their bond with their mothers. They make this bond the model for their link to their parents, grandparents, the generations of the great dead who have brought them into being, and the earth itself, going back into the past. They have projected this pattern of connection ahead into the future through their children, grandchildren, generations to come, and the enduring earth. Through these means, the women have proposed an alternate course that balances the pain of loss with an investment in renewal.

It is true that both women have left open the possibility of older philosophies—that there is something called spirit that does not die—but they have chosen not to phrase their sense of nature, death, or memory in these terms. In the certain present world, these poets have found enough certain present reasons for the sense of connection by which they have defined themselves. Compared to either the tradition of Romantic self-knowledge or the tradition of scientific self-knowledge, Lorde and Ponsot present a new alternative. According to either woman, they have applied new words to well used ways by which people have maintained connections and survived for a long time.

In reviewing the relationships to nature and childhood that these five poets have presented, this chapter has stressed forms of connection, because they have been historically obscured. This emphasis, however, is not meant to imply that other perspectives are groundless. Each poet presented here has assessed childhood in the light of an incontrovertible realization of maturity. Each has expressed a different facet of the human condition: that nature is infinitely greater in time and extension than we are (Bronk); that our bodies will return to the dust from which they came (Ignatow); that living entails loss (Weinfield); that our lives are a link between past and future generations (Lorde); that to exist is to be connected to all things (Ponsot). No one perspective can be pronounced more "correct" than another; but given these coexisting truths, people gravitate to different existential emphases of feeling.

At a time when gender differences make popular reading, there is a danger that this book may be read as a reification of differences: that it may appear to dictate a new set of natal fates. Like Lorde and Ponsot, I would like to move beyond the question of maleness or femaleness "to speak of that principle which is in all of us." This chapter has suggested that different existential emphases reflect different processes of socialization and enculturation. Therefore they reflect developmental possibilities that are open to change, rather than inborn sexual dichotomies that are not. What these differences recount are stories of a first sense of the world, which continues to conform, or which works at cross purposes, to the social and cultural roles that a child grows into.

The different positions presented here are visible because they exist against a background of essential similarities. It is what unites us that makes differences meaningful. The very words that distinguish us join us, as "man" and "woman" name, not separate species, but variants of one. Both words derive from the same root: the Sanskrit *man*, which means "to think."

There is a stereotype that men think, whereas women feel. Not only the words *man* and *woman* but all the words that compose this book belie it. No reader can have reached this page without having noticed that when the five poets presented here—male and female—have written about thinking, it has been saturated with feeling, and when they have written about feeling, it has been saturated with thinking. This book was begun with confidence that it would be so, because beneath our identity as men and women lies our fundamental human identity; and the origin of our common stock as *humans* is the foundation that we cannot fail to think and feel about:

the Latin *humus*, the earth. How the earth permeates memory and poetic creativity has been this book's theme. Regardless of whether we are man or woman, regardless of any other distinguishing characteristics, we are united by our derivation from this common ground. The pain occasioned by this bondage is known to all of us. Each poet, in his or her own way, has expressed it. Yet it is the precondition of all accomplishments. Whatever thinking and feeling this book has reviewed, without exception, has been made possible by the grace of this bond.

The logic of hermeneutics, which has dictated this book's method, affirms similarities more than differences. If any reader has followed the presentation of all five poets or the preceding discussion with any degree of understanding, it is a sign of the hermeneutic principle of re-cognition: a sign that we have understood the different sides of the arguments because, on an essential human level, we already know each side.

Chapter Seven

A Recollective
Psychology

What we want to know . . . is how people use their own past experiences in meeting the present and the future. We would like to understand how this happens under natural conditions: the circumstances in which it occurs, the forms it takes, the variables on which it depends, the differences between individuals in their uses of the past.[1]

The opening chapter of this book presented this proposal of Ulric Neisser along with his criticism that memory research has generally skirted these fundamental questions. The basis of his complaint, the chapter noted, is psychology's adherence to the British empiricist model of science. This book has taken up Neisser's questions, with an emphasis upon past experiences of the natural world.

Empiricist psychology, however, must avoid this topic in particular. If what we want to know is how people use their childhood experiences of nature in meeting the present and the future—and nature is believed to be a mechanism external to us, or engulfing us—then the answer is predetermined. To the degree that people remember a vital, responsive world, they should not use these memories. Between human consciousness and a mindless nature, there can be no true relationship.

Empiricism allows two lasting effects of childhood experiences of nature. According to the stimulus-response theory of behaviorism, responses established in childhood may condition lifelong patterns of preference and avoidance. B. F. Skinner, for example, partially attributed his career as a research psychologist to the reinforcements he received in the Pennsylvania woods of his childhood, where every leaf and stone that he turned over in play rewarded his actions, so that he acquired a habit of curiosity.[2] By this standard, memories have value insofar as they reinforce present desirable behaviors. Another possibility that an empiricist model of the world allows has been worked out within the relational theory of psychoanalysis, which says that lasting feelings for nature derive from associations of fear or trust first learned in primary caregivers' hands.[3] In this case, these associations give memories value. In either case, nature has no value in itself.

There is another, third way in which childhood experiences of nature may have value, which empiricism cannot accommodate. Wordsworth, musing upon the same question this book has taken up, proposed it. After acknowledging that feelings for nature may reflect habit (as behaviorism has since elaborated), or that they may be extensions of social responses absorbed in our mother's arms (as psychoanalytic theory has since argued), he suggested the third possibility that thought and feeling may directly respond to the remembered qualities of things themselves. He expressed this third alternative in *The Prelude*:

> the power of truth
> Coming in revelation, did converse
> With things that really are[4]

Knowing that this explanation would be scoffed at, even in his time, he continued:

> If this be error, and another faith
> Find easier access to the pious mind,
> Yet were I grossly destitute of all
> Those human sentiments that make this earth

So dear, if I should fail with grateful voice
To speak of you, ye mountains, and ye lakes
And sounding cataracts, ye mists and winds
That dwell among the hills where I was born.[5]

That this possibility is rarely considered conforms to the general shift in world paradigms that this book has traced. In a mechanistic world devoid of any values of its own, it is natural to ignore our connections to the physical world altogether, or to concentrate exclusively upon mechanical associations, as in stimulus-response theory, or social associations, as in psychoanalytic theory. So psychology has done.

Potentials of Thought

This book has shown that the philosophy of nature that empiricist psychology assumes, and the uses of memory that it implies, have only a partial hold upon people's actual beliefs and practices. Certainly, people sometimes evaluate their memory in conformity with a despairing monism or a dualism that sets mind and nature at odds—as David Ignatow's, William Bronk's, and Henry Weinfield's struggles with the consequences of these beliefs testify. The examples of Audre Lorde and Marie Ponsot, however, suggest other possibilities.

Together, these five poets demonstrate that a variety of philosophies of nature coexist today, with correspondingly diverse implications for uses of memory. Biblical and classical beliefs in an animated nature remain preserved in customs, institutions, art, and books, at the same time as three hundred years of empiricist science have altered old conceptions. In addition, non-Western cultures have entered the West. When people speak of memory, childhood, and nature now, there are more possible beginnings; and somehow—and this somehow must involve personal history—we choose among them. One of this book's purposes has been to suggest considerations that enter into this choice.

In the sense that they speak for different perspectives in this twentieth-century polyglot of possibilities, these five poets are not remarkable. This book was undertaken on the premise that they express diverse natural attitudes of our age—meaning, in the phenomenology of Husserl, that they give voice to lifeworlds of pregiven assumptions that people rarely take time to articulate and examine.[6] They *are* remarkable, however, in that they are artists committed to this search for expressive form. They are people of thought, of books, of words. They are distinctive in the degree to which they have given thought and form to often unspoken facets of human experience.

According to the philosopher Hannah Arendt, the very practice of profound thinking restrains people from destructive actions. It is fulfilling in itself—an actualization of Aristotle's description of human beings as animals capable of thought. Therefore the satisfactions of thought and its articulation protect people from frustrations. Involving, as thought does, attention to consequences, it also cautions people against inflicting harm.[7] Consistent with Arendt's argument, all five poets—regardless of their philosophies—show personal histories of care for their places and for children.

If the fulfillments and cautions of thinking are removed, however, the implications of these natural attitudes require consideration. Aristotle chose his terms carefully, describing human beings as animals *capable* of thought, not thoughtful animals. This chapter moves beyond the select circle of these five intellectuals to consider the consequences of different attitudes to nature and childhood when they are carried into the often thoughtless rush of daily life. In particular, it suggests how attitudes of connection may be assimilated into psychology, in its two culturally pervasive forms.

One form in which psychology pervades contemporary Western culture is as an academic discipline, a body of theory and practice institutionalized in laboratories and universities, and disseminated through the training of teachers, counselors, therapists, and other members of the helping professions. Even more pervasively—ubiquitously—psychology takes the form of popular processes of human understanding: frames of interpretation that people apply in evaluating and explaining their own lives and the lives of others. To some degree, the two forms overlap, as academic psychology incorporates widely shared natural attitudes, and as popular psychologies incorporate interpretations of nature and childhood, and other subjects, that academic psychology promotes. As this book has shown, however, to some degree these two psychologies operate apart, as academic psychology has failed to reflect the diversity of society at large.

This concluding chapter suggests how both psychology as a discipline and psychology as a practice of self-understanding can acknowledge and promote natural attitudes of connection to nature and to childhood. The Romantics initiated the charge that the mechanistic philosophy of empiricist psychology, as it is assimilated into people's thoughtless search for satisfactions, encourages the exploitation of other people and the earth by turning the body of nature and the human body into material for sensory consumption. The literary historian Jonathan Bate has argued that because Wordsworth advanced this criticism and described conserving alternatives, he can be taken as the enduring unofficial poet laureate of the environmental movement.[8] In the twentieth century, a chorus of environmental authors have reiterated this Romantic charge.[9]

This chapter begins by accepting the criticism that an empiricist psychology that separates the self from a mechanistic world allows environmental abuse. At the least, modern psychology as a discipline and dominant forms of self-understanding have passively witnessed the destruction of ecosystems and communities. Beginning with this premise, this chapter proceeds to suggest how psychology—both academic and popular—can acknowledge diversity, but affirm connection with childhood and the earth.

Hermeneutic Diversity

As the Romantics prepared a foundation for contemporary environmentalism, they also prepared a foundation for a psychology that accepts diversity. In keeping with the Romantic interest in exotic and historical settings, in processes of development, in the creative powers of the individual, and in dialectic, the early nineteenth-century theologian Schleiermacher extended hermeneutics from its traditional function of specialized text interpretation to a general art of human understanding.[10] He required the dedicated study of the history and context within which people as well as texts speak, and an openness to what they say (confident that each person's perspective is a unique window on the infinite truth of God). Members of the twentieth century may be apprehensive to follow the method of a Romantic theologian; but Schleiermacher required only tolerance, not doctrinal correctness (assured that all human efforts tend to evolve into higher forms because they move within the all-inclusive circle of God).

Schleiermacher's search for multifaceted truths within a shared universe offers an alternative to the search for a single point of truth. Some historians have argued that the mechanistic philosophy of the seventeenth century provided a new point of certainty in reaction to the chaos and violence of the Reformation.[11] The authority of science replaced the fractured authority of the church. The postmodern world of the late twentieth century—characterized by indeterminacy in physics, feminism and multiculturalism in politics, and global communication and migration—no longer gives credence to universal laws independent of observers' perspective and historical context. The postmodern reality is dialogue as an alternative to chaos and violence. Through Schleiermacher, the Romantic legacy provides a foundation for this understanding of differences as well as a foundation for environmentalism.

It is critical that Romanticism provides a simultaneous base for a hermeneutics of diversity *and* environmentalism. The Romantic dialectic of exchange between the mind and nature, which allows Wordsworth's third possibility that we may "converse / With things that really are," presents an alternative to the often arbitrary relativism of postmodernism. By granting that we half-create and half-perceive in response to a surrounding reality that we must accommodate, the Romantic dialectic escapes the infinite regress of deconstructive relativism on the one side, and a need for timeless universal laws on the other.

As for this book, its motive has been to practice the Romantic spiral of development by practicing hermeneutic phenomenology, circling around the subject of memories of nature until its beginning comes back into view with a new depth not seen before. As this study began by exploring the significance of childhood memories of nature in psychologies of human development, this concluding chapter returns to this theme. It will suggest a revised conception of development that can accommodate the full range of these five poets' life histories, and affirm processes of connection to nature that their lives illustrate.

This chapter presents its conclusions in the spirit that, if this hermeneutic spiral has been elevating, it will leave its area open. In conducting this research, a helpful guide has been Gadamer, who has noted that when the hermeneutic spiral is translated into human terms, the most productive model is conversation.[12] Like good conversation, this study will serve its purpose if it comes to an end with many questions opened, none closed. In suggesting several meanings that childhood experiences of nature may carry under different conditions, this book invites others to introduce new voices and interpretations. In this contemporary world of rapidly changing places, populations, and ideas, this book's goal is to move the evaluation of relationships with nature forward, not to stop with the stories presented here.

To this end, the following sections review the developmental phenomenology of the Swiss philosopher Jean Gebser, who provided a framework for the evaluation of diversity. The final sections suggest processes for integrating childhood identification with nature into adult identity: processes applicable to individual uses of the past, and to academic psychology's efforts to understand.

A Foundation for Connection

The following sections focus on the developmental theory of Jean Gebser for several reasons. Born in Prussia in 1905, Gebser grew up during one World War and narrowly survived another. During these years, he witnessed the implosion of Enlightenment and Comtean faith in unfaltering progress through the accumulation of scientific and technological knowledge. Therefore he challenged Comtean hierarchies by elaborating a productive alternative that is responsive to this book's issues.

Detailed in the two volumes of his work *The Ever-Present Origin*, published in German in 1949 and 1953, Gebser's thought antedates the contemporary environmental movement. Therefore he does not address contemporary issues in familiar terms. Nevertheless, his developmental theory is radically ecological—in the sense that it is so at its root, its origin. It provides a deliberate framework for describing more benevolent human relations with the earth. Correspondingly, it provides a framework for relating adult wisdom to childhood experience.

Gebser formulated his ideas as he participated in the ferment of early twentieth-century science and art that challenged the fundamental assumptions of mechanistic world views and empiricist psychology. In his early years, he immersed himself in the arts and literature—initially inspired by his profound reaction to the poetry of Rilke.[13] As Fascism spread in the 1930s and 1940s, he fled progressively from Germany to Italy and France (where he changed his given name of Hans to Jean), to Spain (where he befriended Lorca), to Paris (where he was welcomed into the circle of Eluard, Aragon, Malraux, and Picasso), to final refuge in Switzerland. From Switzerland as his base, he spent his later years working with many of Europe's leading physicists, biologists, psychotherapists, sociologists, planners, and architects, becoming familiar with efforts in diverse disciplines to reconstitute the guiding ideas of contemporary civilization. In recognition of his work, the University of Salzburg created a chair in comparative civilizations for him. Gebser died in 1973.

Active in the arts as he was, Gebser inherited the critique of science initiated by the Romantics. Attentive to the phenomenology of Husserl and the hermeneutics of Heidegger, he knew how their philosophies extended this critique. As a friend of physicists like Heisenberg and von Weizsäcker, he was also aware that the practice of science itself was changing, making it receptive to different qualities of consciousness and of the world. Therefore Gebser's theory reflects the latest developments in science, which reverse mechanistic assumptions.

The philosopher J. Baird Callicott has noted that the revolution in quantum physics in the 1920s (whose implications Gebser helped to define) created a metaphysical foundation for a new ethics of connection and care for the environment.[14] By replacing the subject-object dichotomy of classical physics with an open field of interactive matter and consciousness, it justified finding inherent values in nature, which are actualized in interactions with human consciousness. (Thus it provided reason to admit Wordsworth's third possibility: that the physical world has intrinsic qualities that may leave lasting impressions in memory.)

Summarizing this change, the physical chemists Ilya Prigogine and Isabelle Stengers describe the new view of reality as a reciprocal dialogue in which experimenter and nature adjust themselves to each other, so that the classical vision of a timeless universe following immutable laws must be dropped in light of evidence that unpredictable reorganizations are constituted in time at all levels, from atom up.[15] As a consequence, human creations of order, history, and identity, far from being illusory impositions on random atoms, become model as well as method for comprehending nature. The stance of a detached observer—not subjective engagement with nature—appears the new illusion. Events can only be understood as unfoldings in historical time. In biology, Gregory Bateson and Rupert Sheldrake have made similar arguments.[16]

In keeping with these changes, the physicist Alfred North Whitehead replaced the mechanistic language of classical physics with a new language of organicism. Using life processes as his primary metaphor, in *Process and Reality* and *Science and the Modern World*, Whitehead defined all events, from atom to mind, as mutual adaptations of organism and environment.[17] Because all events occur within nested levels of increasingly comprehensive wholes, he defined order in terms of dominant relations between parts and wholes. Because these relationships change over time, laws must be stated in terms of dominant conditions of time and place. Whitehead's language of reciprocally defined parts and wholes within historical contexts, it may be noted, is also the language of hermeneutics.

This book has noted the failure of stage models of development to reflect this paradigm change, and consequences for the study of memory. A few authors have noted consequences of this failure for the actual quality of childhood and for adult relations with children. The geographer Kenneth Olwig, for example, has traced how the premodern engagement of people with their land gave way to the distanced view of the landscape surveyor, as Western culture assimilated the universal mathematized space of classical physics. As this view of space continues to be imposed in community planning and design, subsuming everything within rigid grids and predetermined designs, it limits children's creative physical engagement with the natural world.[18]

The philosopher Gareth Matthews has described how dominant hierarchical models of development, which make the abstract universal logic of classical physics the acme of cognitive achievement, tend to denigrate children's experience. Under these conditions, children's often serious questions about life, consciousness, and relations with the natural world—much debated issues in postmodern science—can be dismissed as childish prelogic.[19] Together, Olwig's and Matthews's analyses observe that as the premises of classical physics remain assimilated within the natural attitudes of psychology, geography, planning, and education, children's access to the natural world is limited, and childhood forms of experiencing nature are judged trivial.

Gebser's theory provides a structure to affirm constructive uses of childhood memory, and to revise attitudes to children and the natural world. Up to this point, this book's purpose has been comparative and hermeneutic, as it has explored meanings of memories of nature under diverse conditions. These differences exist, however, within a larger implied phenomenology of common human experience. If this book's concerns are translated into general phenomenological terms, its guiding question becomes: "What would a developmental theory look like that acknowledges all the different dimensions of significance that childhood memories of nature may hold?" Gebser's work presents an effective answer to this question.

The Developmental Phenomenology of Jean Gebser

In the 1940s, more than twenty years before the beginning of the environmental movement, Gebser saw that the crisis facing civilization was ecological as well as political and intellectual. In his preface to *The Ever-Present Origin*, he wrote:

The crisis we are experiencing today is not just a European crisis, nor a crisis of morals, economics, ideologies, politics, or
religion. It is not only prevalent in Europe and America but in
Russia and the Far East as well. It is a crisis of the world and
mankind such as has occurred previously only during pivotal
junctures—junctures of decisive finality for life on earth and
for the humanity subjected to them. The crisis of our times
and our world is in a process—at the moment autonomously—
of complete transformation, and appears headed toward an
event which, in our view, can only be described as a "global
catastrophe." This event, understood in any but anthropocentric terms, will necessarily come about as a new constellation
of planetary extent.[20]

Understanding a catastrophe to mean a turning point whose outcome is unclear, and having a sense of life that was not anthropocentric, Gebser's ideas have central relevance to the intensifying
global crisis today.

At the foundation of leading developmental theories, this book
has shown, is a distrust of nature, evident in a dualist emphasis upon
the achievement of a separate individuated self, and logicomathematical control at the expense of perceived relationship. In the case
of the psychoanalytic theory of Freud, there is despair that separation cannot be maintained. Gebser's phenomenology directs development to "a renewal of relationship with nature as process," in
addition to an awareness of "unique separateness and identity"—the
two bequests of childhood memories of nature that Edith Cobb identified in autobiographies.[21]

It has been this book's contention that people interpret childhood memory in the context of more or less articulated philosophies
of nature, and the base of these philosophies is either trust or dread.
Gebser considered trust and anxiety primordial reactions to the reality of our embeddedness in nature, comparable to the interdependent poles of order and chaos in nature itself. "Life is forever
menaced by chaos, and must restore balance and order with every in-
take of breath," he wrote.[22] Like the psychologist Erik Erikson, he understood the acquisition of basic trust versus basic mistrust, or as he
termed it, primeval confidence versus primeval anxiety, to be a recurring life crisis that begins in childhood, and the conscious affirmation of confidence the challenge of adulthood.[23]

Gebser founded his own system of ideas on trust; and in the
case of his own life, he related it in part to his boyhood experience of

swimming and diving when he repeatedly entrusted himself to the air, the water, the leap. "It was then," he wrote:

> that I lost my fear in the face of uncertainty. A sense of confidence began to mature within me which later determined my entire bearing and attitude toward life, a confidence in the sources of our strength of being, a confidence in their immediate accessibility.[24]

Gebser applied this "confidence in the sources of our strength of being" to his concept of "origin": a concept akin to the classical Greek sense of nature as *phusis,* an ever-changing, ever-renewing field of energy from which all things arise. As he traveled extensively in India and the Orient, Gebser also acknowledged similarities between his sense of "origin" and Hindu and Buddhist concepts of the inexpressible All of which everything is a part. As a participant in debates over the implications of quantum physics, he was well aware of affinities between this fluid All of interchangeable matter and energy, and twentieth-century discoveries of natural science.

At the basis of Gebser's developmental theory, then, is trust in origin. The origin of our existence and consciousness is the field of energy and matter of which we are a part, which people apprehend with different forms of spiritual feeling. It follows that however we try to define this source, we leave out more than we say. Gebser rejected the concept of the unconscious, believing instead that human experience is multifold and inexhaustible like its origin, operating on different levels of consciousness, some of which are inarticulate. The consequence of this rule is the humility that no one perspective can express all experience. Through words or numbers, we can never know all that the world is, or all that we are; but we approach this knowledge more fully when our language and perspectives are pluralistic.

Structures of Consciousness

As he worked out the implications of this principle, Gebser turned leading modern models of social evolution and human development on their heads. According to Gebser, we experience and shape this ever-present origin through five basic *Gestalten*—a German term with no exact English equivalent, which may be loosely translated in this context as "structures of consciousness." A scholar of world civilizations, Gebser argued that different structures of consciousness have predominated at different periods of history; but although some forms may be dormant as others dominate, all remain ever-present possibilities that constitute our human nature. By this shift—that different forms of consciousness coexist as the ever-present potentials of our human nature—Gebser avoided stage hierarchies that suggest that one structure of consciousness is inherently better or worse than another. He focused instead upon analyzing effective and defective manifestations of each, judged by the standard of "the good of the whole": our whole as human beings, as societies, and as members of the built and natural world.

Gebser required that we remember our connection to the natural world through his analysis of the *archaic* structure of consciousness. At one point, he referred to this foundation as "identity with origin," at another as the "wisdom of origin." It is the origin of existence by which we are conscious, but it precedes articulated consciousness. Prelinguistic, and dominant in early infancy, deep sleep, and unthinking absorption in things, it involves autonomic functioning, sensation, and presentiment akin to the world of animals. It is evidenced in health and illness, as the body monitors itself and reacts to the larger body of the world.

With the beginning of a sense of separate existence, consciousness assumes *magical* form, silently intuiting the forces of the world and personal powers of action. Charged with instinct and emotion, magical consciousness makes possible sympathy and awareness of associations and analogies. As a world traveler, well read in anthropology, Gebser believed that magic consciousness also contains real potentials of heightened sensory perception, telepathy, and clairvoyance that can be used for harm or healing. As magic involves a realization of the unity of the world and the unity of the individual with the world, it is a powerful experience in itself. At its best, it is ecstatic (as many of the memories of nature that Edith Cobb collected attest).

This first consciousness of the self and the world's power, however, also exposes us to fear. Gebser found magic's defective form prevalent in the modern world's destructive mass psychologies and obsession with machines and technology, which externalize the fear "that man is compelled to rule the outside world—so as not to be ruled by it."[25]

Mythic consciousness finds expression through the mouth, the spoken word, music, drama, and dreamlike images. ("Come thou, let us begin with the Muses who gladden the great spirit of their father Zeus in Olympus with their songs."[26]) Through these means, mythic

consciousness communicates psychic polarities that are complementary: light and dark, silence and sound, life and death, child and
parent, male and female. It perceives a world of ritual, symbol, deep
religious feeling, sacred time, sacred place, social sentiment, agricultural fertility. In this world, woman serves as symbol for nature.
In the modern world, myth often takes the defective forms of propa-
ganda and empty logocentric rituals.

Mental consciousness makes possible paradox, perspective, abstraction, rational reflection, and self-assertion: all of which may
take effective or defective forms. Its ruling term is "ego," "I." In defective forms, we feel our self concentrated in our mind, behind our
eyes, in isolation from the rest of the body and the world. Duality replaces mythical complementarities, magical union, and archaic identity. The ruling sense becomes sight, the ruling metaphor one-point
perspective, the ruling language quantification, and the world is
atomized and purged of its qualities. ("Memory refers to storing information and to accessing or retrieving information."[27]) In mental-
rational thought, abstract three-dimensional space replaces sacred
place; and time's arrow, an irreversible quantified line of causality,
replaces sacred time. ("The past . . . never really existed: it has always been an illusion created by the symbolizing activity of the
mind."[28]) Man becomes the model of what a person should be, woman
the embodiment of what is to be suppressed. The demands of the
mental world, Gebser noted, fall most heavily on first-born sons.

These successive "mutations of consciousness," as Gebser
called them, involve an increase in the range of consciousness at the
price of a diminishing sense of the qualitative character of things and
a lessening of relationship to the whole. They may be compared to
successive stages in the concept that ontogeny recapitulates phylogeny. As Gebser's friend, Georg Feuerstein, has noted, archaic,
magic, mythic, and mental states appear similar to the prevailing
modes of being of infant, toddler, child, and youth or adult on one
level, or pre–*Homo sapiens*, paleolithic, neolithic, and literate society on another.[29] Gebser avoided evaluating these states as "higher"
or "lower" forms of consciousness, however, by the two simple but
radical moves of focusing on the potentials for good or ill in each, and
by emphasizing a fifth form of consciousness, the *integral*.

An integral consciousness finds the other four conditions ever-
present possibilities that remain open for use "for the good of the
whole": and this alertness to the whole reconnects consciousness to
origin, the natural world, and the foundation of existence. Whereas
archaic consciousness assumes identity with origin, and thus forms

a medium of access to the wisdom of origin, integral consciousness makes this identity the basis of articulated wisdom. Rather than assigning any one form of consciousness supremacy, integral wisdom assesses how the expressions of each are effective or defective by this larger standard of the whole.

It has been this book's argument that a new paradigm is due in developmental psychology—one that will replace the Comtean hierarchy and Cartesian duality that remain embedded in theory and practice with a more integral model that will acknowledge the reality that we live in physical bodies in a physical world, with feeling as well as reason, and that the quality of this world affects quality of life. The axis upon which Gebser's developmental theory turns is the acknowledgment and evaluation of different qualities of connection among potentials of ourselves, among people, and between people and the earth.

Qualities of Time

The way to approach integral goals, Gebser believed, is to shift from a mental-rational obsession with quantification to a new concern for the quality of time. To magic consciousness, the world is present in every part, at every point. To mythic consciousness, it is a two-dimensional world of complementarities. To mental consciousness, it is a world of three-dimensional, mathematicized space. To integral consciousness, the world is alive with the fourth dimension of time. If this integrating shift is made, then qualities of memory, such as this book has explored, become an essential aspect of attention to qualities of time.

Gebser described integral consciousness as a supersession of recollection, in the sense that it does not involve the empty recall of experience—not naming, or counting, without sympathetic identification. Instead, it involves the reclamation of ever-present possibilities. ("Whatever we encounter that is great, beautiful, significant, need not be remembered from outside. . . . Rather, from the beginning, it must be woven into the fabric of our inmost self, must thus live and become a productive force in ourselves."[30]) Gebser believed that one of the major tasks of our age is "to extricate time from its rational distortion," which involves the notion of a "psychologized past," which can be atomized and metaphorically placed in storage. Preoccupation with the mechanics of memory needs to be replaced by attention to its physics, its *phusis*, as it emerges into the embodied present, into life. The goal of development then becomes "not a freedom *from* previous time forms, since they are co-constituents of every one of us; it is to begin with a freedom *for* all time forms."[31]

This freedom remains open to archaic pretemporality, magic timelessness, the cyclical time of myth, and mental measured time, seeking through each an understanding of how to act for the good of the whole. In this condition, what Gebser called "the so-called past" becomes recognized as a present potential. ("The descent beckons / as the ascent beckoned / Memory is a kind / of accomplishment / a sort of renewal / even / an initiation."[32]) The figure that best represents integrality, Gebser proposed, is the sphere.

Whereas dominant stage models of development assume that maturity requires a movement away from childhood forms of experience, Gebser's model prescribes a continuous process of evaluation, which encourages all abilities to perceive connections and wholes, whether an ability be intuitive, emotional, or rational, and at whatever age it appears. Rather than privileging an independent self, Gebser directs development toward a recognition of interdependence. Rather than neglecting places and things except for measuring how they can be maneuvered or manipulated, he observes that interdependence extends beyond social relationships to surroundings, and beyond surroundings to systems of nature. He provides a structure to discuss how the well-being of individuals and the world depends upon abilities to integrate rational, imaginative, intuitive, physical, and spiritual bonds with particular people, animals, places, and things, in the context of the planet's larger wholes that must also be rationally, imaginatively, intuitively, physically, and spiritually apprehended. Like the Romantic spiral of development, Gebser's goal is a wisdom that integrates childhood and adult experience. This integration, however, need not be postponed until old age, or achieved at the cost of intervening alienation.

Models of Understanding

This book has noted the role of concepts of nature in general models of development and in individual efforts to find meaning in life. This section briefly returns to the five poets on whom this work has focused: first comparing their conclusions to the Romantic model of development, and then to the emerging organicist paradigm evident in the new physics and in Gebser's work. Using the examples of these poets' lives and the principles of this paradigm, concluding sections observe how identification with nature may be affirmed in the patterns of individual lives and in the practice of psychology.

William Bronk has imaginatively lived the Kantian concept that time is a human imposition upon nature's immeasurable expanse. Therefore he can find no memories to serve as anchors for his life. In the middle of the Romantic spiral of development, he has observed a hole; and he has excused himself from attempts to net the infinite. Comparing mental models of time to an infinitely recurring point, or to an infinitely extending vector, he has found no way to circle back to childhood. In his world in which nature encompasses everything, there is no self to remember anyway.

Weinfield has lived the Hegelian dialectic that consciousness develops through a struggle against nature. Whether one relates this dialectic to the monism that there is only matter, or to the Hegelian idealism that there is only spirit, the consequence is dualist. Consciousness struggles to create an alternative world apart from nature. Through art, it weaves the most enduring forms of fulfillment that people can know. As he himself has grown older, Weinfield has found his respect for Wordsworth grow, along with his appreciation for how memories may nourish emotional life, but he has emphasized that in this spiral of recollection, the ending fails to touch the beginning by a wide margin of gain and loss.

Only Ignatow's account of memory coincides with Wordsworth's version of the Romantic spiral, and it does so darkly. In keeping with this model, he recalls some memories of childhood security and delight in nature, followed by years of turmoil and disassociation, recovering early peaceful memories in old age. The irony is that, although Ignatow identifies these happy memories with personal ease and peace, his materialist conception of the unity of the self and world has a somber cast totally at odds with Wordsworth's transcendence. Throughout most of his life, his early childhood memory of the eerie cemetery, or his adolescent memory of the empty gym, appeared to him the appropriate images of his place in nature.

What model of development would fit Ponsot's and Lorde's experience? The Romantic spiral partially applies. They do assume an ordered world, so that a circle fits. They also assume maturity and change, so that childhood and adulthood never precisely overlap. In contrast, however, they do not speak in terms of estrangement and reconciliation. The relationship between childhood and maturity that they describe may be better represented by intersecting planes. Their present self and their remembered self—from childhood or any other period—may be thought of as circles in different planes that intersect along a common diameter. Therefore their present can reflect their past at any point in time. This figure also begins to suggest the three-dimensional sphere of the earth with which they identify. Both women have made these connections by essentially ignoring modern scientific images of nature, drawing instead upon African philosophy in Lorde's case, or Christian traditions of the sanctity of nature in the case of Ponsot.

For similar reasons, Gebser represents an integral consciousness through the figure of the sphere, joining its planes through the fourth dimension of time. Like Lorde and Ponsot, he builds upon a fundamentally spiritual faith in the vitality of nature. He does so, however, not by ignoring contemporary science, but by following it closely. Thus he accepts that meaning is collaboratively constituted through the interdependent activity and value of the world, and human activity and values. When Ignatow revised his ideas about the relationship between the imagination and nature, he did so in response to this changing vision of nature in which Gebser participated.

A New Science of Connection

When the Romantics conceived of development as a spiral in which childhood memories of harmony with nature are regained after intervening years of conflict, their internal conflicts mirrored the larger differences between Romanticism and the dominant mechanistic image of the world. According to the scientific world view with which they contended, there were two possibilities: a Cartesian dualism, which put consciousness and nature in two separate worlds; or a monism, which made consciousness an epiphenomenon of an essentially meaningless natural world. Given this prevailing science and scientism, the Romantics' internal struggles to regain a spiritual vision of nature represented not just individual circumstances, but a reaction to the conditions of their age.

Gebser's belief that an integral consciousness—represented by the figure of a sphere—may gradually prevail over the current emphasis upon quantification and abstraction reflects his observations of an emerging new constellation of ideas in all fields, including science. If the organicist, process philosophy of Whitehead prevails and pervades the natural attitudes of psychology and everyday understanding, then ideas like those of Lorde and Ponsot will no longer appear divergent. Childhood memories of a responsive nature will no longer appear mere fancy, but a foundation to refine in adult terms.

Although an organicist paradigm encourages connection between childhood and adulthood, and a sense of generativity in a world of interdependencies, it does not obviate death and loss, nor promise personal immortality. Therefore the polyvocity illustrated by this book can be expected to persist, characterizing as it does a world of multivalence. Correspondingly, Gebser, despite his conviction that the world's civilizations stand at a crossing point, was in no way a New Age philosopher who anticipated utopia. Observing that effective and defective forms of consciousness are ever-present potentials, he believed that risk is ever-present. For this reason, the integral wisdom that he proposed as a new *telos* for development is not predetermined, but a creative accomplishment gained by learning to apply healing combinations of archaic identity, magic intuition, mythic significance, and mental understanding in order to understand the good of the whole and appropriate action.

Like the future, Gebser noted, both trust and anxiety are risks. Either feeling is a primordial leap of faith in a universe of mystery. Yet despite the risk inherent in either faith or fear, for world cultures at the close of the twentieth century, as the planetary crisis that Gebser identified has taken increasingly pressing ecological forms, the dangers of practices that oppose human consciousness to nature present the greater risk. Too much harm has been done in practice by the mentality that nature is something external to the ego, an antagonist to be conquered, to which we tragically succumb. For the interdependent societies of the twentieth century, there is a clear cultural need now to trust the emerging new paradigm that mind and nature work collaboratively, and that creative contributions of individuals are essential parts of a history that people and nature share. In this spirit, the following sections suggest how identification with nature may be fostered through three means: language, empathy, and models of care.

Identification through Language

Three forms of connection or identification with nature have claimed attention in this book. One is identification through language that observes—that identifies—similarities and interdependence between human experience and the natural world. Given this book's scrutiny of poetry, how language distances people from nature or draws connections has been one of its themes. Other forms of identification that have appeared in the poets' accounts are identification in the sense of empathy with nature, and identification with childhood role models who introduce nature. Depending upon how these poets have named nature, known it, and followed role models, their relations with nature in the present and the past have taken form.

These same forms of identification operate in the practice of psychology. If psychology is to assimilate a collaborative, qualitative model of human relations with nature, it will need to become self-aware of its own uses of language, ways of knowing, and role models. This book has shown that psychology has historically stressed certain forms of relationship with nature to the neglect or exclusion of others. Therefore one change required is open-minded attention to all forms of relationship and their consequences.

The language of psychology can encourage this change. Preceding sections have recommended Gebser's integrative scheme of human development as a structure for this descriptive, evaluative study, given his scheme's embeddedness in nature as its origin and healing relations as its goal. As Gebser notes, some dimensions of consciousness are ineffable. Archaic and magic relations can only be suggested by indirect measures of observation and physiological responses (already accepted psychological measures), as well as by language at its most allusive. Mythic relations involve the emotional, metaphoric language that poetry has preserved and that psychoanalysis has admitted. Without predetermined commitments to doctrinal categories, a phenomenological psychology can examine this emotional language, as well as the abstract language of mental analysis, in terms of the relationships with the natural world which they involve. An integral psychology would evaluate these relationships against the standard of human well-being within nature's supporting wholes.

As the poet Marie Ponsot explores in her work, language mediates people's physical engagement with the world. In Wordsworth's terms in "Tintern Abbey," language expresses an exchange with the world, which eye and ear half-create and half-perceive. In this process, as words guide attention, they acquire qualities of meaning from the qualities of the world known, and how it is known.

Since the 1600s, scientists have attempted to restrict their word use to bare denotations. But it is connotations—"margin of infinite allusions through which imagination and emotion can wander," in the words of the poet Ungaretti—that resonate with embodied autobiographical experience.[33] Chapter 1 suggested (echoing Wordsworth) that strong connotations often go back to childhood when the world was known with particular sensory immediacy and excitement. As much as the poets studied here, psychologists' choice of language reflects implicit relations with nature. By restricting

practice to denotative language and behavioral observations, empiricist psychology has implied that felt qualities of nature, including
childhood feeling, are not significant subjects for study. To give importance to nature's qualities, and qualities of human experience, requires a broadened use of words.

Developmental psychology has extensively investigated how
children learn language structure and vocabulary. It is equally important to understand the genesis of connotations and their context
in life narratives. By encouraging people to describe the "margin of
allusions" that environmental words of strong personal meaning acquire, as well as life events associated with these meanings, memory
researchers can free themselves from their current limited focus on
pragmatic behaviors like way-finding or locating objects. This margin of connotations provides a means to not only understand how
people use their past in meeting their present and their future, but to
also understand how memory's layering of time contributes to the
construction of feelings for place.

At the same time as science began to purge words of their connotations, it began to apply mechanistic and mercantile metaphors
to mind and nature. As chapter 1 illustrated, psychology still com-
monly uses metaphors that compare the mind and nature to a machine—with the updating that seventeenth-century clocks have
turned into twentieth-century computers and filing cabinets. According to Elizabeth Sewell, environmental metaphors that note
likenesses between human experience and external things are one of
language's primary means of attaching people to the physical world
of which they are a part; and whether words relate people to machines or to elements of the natural world matters.[34] An emphasis on
mechanistic metaphors corresponds to a reliance on technological
ingenuity to solve global problems. In contrast, environmental
philosophers have noted, process philosophy observes that the
world's quality is constituted through cooperative relations among
people and between people and their place.[35] This new foundation involves organic metaphors for mind and nature that emphasize interdependence and regeneration.

Identification through Empathy

To understand and affirm relationships with nature, another
form of identification that will be required is empathy, when boundaries between the self and another thing dissolve in an intense act of
perception. In the case of the poets studied here, it is exemplified by
Bronk's loss of self on the canal bridge in April twilight, and by Pon-

sot's responsiveness to a tern's flight. According to many Romantic and modern poets, this form of identification is an essential aspect of creativity, which animates their use of words.

Keats, for example, termed imaginative identification with something outside the self "negative capability." He claimed that a poet "has no identity—he is continually in for—and filling some other Body."[36] The German poet Rilke termed it "inseeing." He said that in this process of closely observing bird or dog or tree, "If I am to tell you where my all-greatest feeling, my world-feeling, my earthly bliss was to be found, I must confess to you: it was to be found time and again . . . in such inseeing, in the indescribably swift, deep, timeless moments of this divine inseeing."[37] According to poets' accounts, whenever this form of identification happens, it is a process that is an event.

The second chapter of this book noted that modern science has relegated this empathic fusion of the self with the surrounding world to women, children, poets, and the insane, and trivialized it as irrational. The physicist Evelyn Fox Keller observes that in rejecting empathic ways of knowing, science has suppressed aspects of its own practice.[38] She suggests that there are two approaches to research, each effective for its own purpose. One way professes detached objectivity, separation between the knower and the thing known, and a search for universal laws of causation. Another way works by intimate familiarity with the thing studied, and even sometimes by a temporary loss of self in the act of observation. The first approach, she observes, tends to discover mechanical laws; the second, patterns of interdependence.

Keller argues that great scientists always alternate between detachment and self-forgetfulness. But in the history of modern science, detachment has been emphasized almost to the denial of identification. This commitment to detached objectivity, she notes, is itself a subjective choice. As science moves from a mechanicist to an organicist view of nature, a corresponding new concern for patterns of interdependence should encourage it to admit empathy within its practice, and to notice how childhood experience may lay a foundation for this way of knowing nature.

Identification through Models of Care

In considering childhood roots of adult ways of knowing nature, this book suggests that identification with role models is generative. The psychologist Martin Hoffman, who has explored how empathy and sympathy develop, begins with the principle assumed since Freud: that young children have difficulty neatly distinguishing their own body and emotions from their environment, and that differentiation and separation proceed gradually.[39] Older children and adults reexperience this fusion with external things in moments of deep empathy. Hoffman adds, however, that the transformation of visceral empathy into articulate sympathy depends upon identification with role models who encourage the growing child to understand and respect other things' feelings and to accept connection and responsibility.

Hoffman sought to explain the development of social sympathy; but given that children animate the world and invest it with responsiveness, it is reasonable to expect that a similar process unfolds with respect to sympathy for natural things. Certainly, in this book's examples, Audre Lorde's and Marie Ponsot's mothers led them to identify with nature and gave them reasons to affirm the connection that they felt. As the daughters learned sympathy with nature, their role model identification was compounded by gender identification.

According to Fox Keller, for science to admit empathy and sympathy with nature, it will need new role models and gender models of its own. Fox Keller and the historian Carolyn Merchant present evidence that, as mechanistic models of nature prevailed over the androgynous imagery of Platonism and alchemy, science came to be identified in theory as well as practice as a solely masculine activity, and scientific knowing came to be described through aggressive sexual metaphors that set nature apart from the observer and made it something to expose, to penetrate, to subdue.[40]

As science responds to feminist critiques that it needs to allow more feminine forms of language and practice, as well as more women, into its profession, it will gain new methods and new subjects for study in terms of human relations with nature. Psychology, in particular, can play an important part by identifying new role models. An empiricist psychology, based as it is upon the passive registering of sensations, corresponds to a society that views the natural world as a passive inventory of materials for consumption. As this book suggests, there are more hopeful relationships with nature, open to both men and women, that psychology can identify and describe.

Qualities of Practice

In the last decade of the twentieth century, there are many signs of shift in the preceding directions. There is now a large literature on women in science; and programs in physics, chemistry, biology, and math seek to recruit women into these disciplines in which they have been underrepresented. At the Earth Summit in Rio de Janeiro in 1992, one of the major issues debated was how to provide support for the stewardship of natural resources by those historically excluded from power—women, children, and native people. Many observers commented that the very fact that the Earth Summit happened signaled the sudden new salience of the natural world in world affairs.

As for the needed shift from an emphasis on quantification to qualities of time, immediate policy responses to this new salience of ecological issues are divided. On the one side, there is increased use of environmental risk assessments and cost-benefit analyses, which translate all human relations with the environment into technical, quantified terms. On the other side, there is increasing discussion about "quality of life" in daily affairs. In the planning profession, the current catchword is "visioning," which brings planners and officials together with local community members to identify the qualities of places that determine the quality of life that residents want to preserve. If we accept that time is life, then this public participation in planning, motivated by a general restiveness that qualities of life cannot be reduced to quantified risk levels and economic output statistics, signals a cultural shift to attention to qualities of time.

In public meetings and official rhetoric, concern for environmental quality is repeatedly justified through expressions of concern for children: for the immediate protection of children, who are most at risk as the environment degrades, and for the future quality of life of the present younger generation and generations yet unborn. In this respect, the "generative time" that Audre Lorde and Marie Ponsot describe—the sense that one's own life is a productive link in the ongoing cycle of generations—is becoming a new measure of quality of life and time.

In the social sciences, one consequence of the preceding shifts is that governments are committing new funds for environmental research, including research into people's environmental behaviors, attitudes, and knowledge. One evidence of recognition that this research must be qualitative as well as quantitative is the publication of this series on environmental and architectural phenomenology to which this book belongs. This series, in turn, is part of a larger effort described by the geographer David Seamon as a "phenomenological ecology" that "explores and describes the ways that things, living forms, people, events, situations and worlds come together environmentally," with a focus on "how all these entities *belong* together in place, why they might not belong, and how they might better belong through more sensitive understanding, design, and policy-making."[41]

All the preceding signs of cultural change are examples of *praxis*, of practice. One of the features of the Cartesian and Comtean program for science that this book has challenged is the privileging of abstract knowledge at the expense of the qualitative connections of daily life. According to the philosophical hermeneutics of Gadamer, one of the essential errors of this scientism is that it distorts the proper relation between theory and practice.[42]

In the classical view of Aristotle, *epistémé*, or scientific knowledge, concerns what is universal, what happens by necessity. *Phronésis*, the knowledge characteristic of practice, involves ethical deliberation and choice, mediating between the universal and particular in concrete situations, and determining how to apply insight into universal necessities for the greatest possible good for oneself and others with whom one is bound up in community.[43] The great error of the modern age, Gadamer charged, is that theory has been uncoupled from the direction of practical wisdom.

According to these definitions, all sciences involve practice as much as theory. They are activities pursued by communities of people and defined by shared rules and goals. The human sciences, in particular, are not only embedded in communities of practice, but they are defined by goals of understanding *and* human well-being. In the case of this book's overlapping disciplines, developmental psychology is constituted by the goal of life-span well-being: environmental psychology, by the goal of encouraging secure and positive relations between people and their place.

The new attention that the environment is receiving in global and local affairs signifies a growing awareness that the interdependent communities of human practice exist within the encompassing communities of the natural world. Therefore *phronésis*, or practical wisdom, which combines understanding of universal necessity and particular circumstances in order to seek the greatest possible good for oneself and one's community, must include attention to the good of the larger community of life.

This book has argued that people's feelings for nature—whether they be separation, alienation, or collaborative trust—are ultimately leaps of faith in an uncertain world. Psychology itself, however, is a practice, not a person. As such, it inherits a predetermined commitment to human well-being, and therefore to the well-being of the encompassing community of life. Considering where the failing mechanistic paradigm of nature has taken us, this commitment to well-being requires that psychology entertain the new paradigm of productive collaboration between mind and nature, and that it attend to qualities of human experience. As psychology gives the qualitative value of people's relations with nature increased attention, it should assume new forms of practice ample enough to care for the quality of the world.

Epilogue

The preceding chapter suggested that in evaluating childhood memory and relationships to nature, all people are as subject to the influences of cultural context and autobiographical experience as any of the poets presented here. According to the history that this book has reviewed, psychology as a discipline and the popular psychologies that it promotes have typically judged childhood ways of knowing nature to be fancifully emotional and animated. To proceed beyond this history and reevaluate memories on more open terms, this book has proposed, psychology must become more phenomenological, more hermeneutic, and observe how different qualities of memory contribute to adult self-understanding under different conditions. It needs to acknowledge that sometimes adult reason and childhood memories conflict, sometimes conform.

The philosopher Martin Heidegger advised that when thinking assumes rigid patterns that are no longer productive—as this book has suggested that hierarchic models of development that distance adulthood from childhood no longer are—then it can be freeing to examine the words in which thinking is conducted.[1] Because language always exceeds any one interpretation, words contain clues to fresh possibilities of thought, and words' histories often contain an intrinsic wisdom of their own. This book has evolved within the discipline of environmental psychology. If readers are willing to trust Heidegger's counsel and hazard his method, it may be fruitful to conclude by scrutinizing the name of this discipline to see what history and possibilities its words suggest.

Environmental. The first source of clues for direction is the word *environmental.* On a literal level, according to the canon of the dictionary, *environmental* is the adjectival form for "all the physical, social, and cultural factors and conditions influencing the existence or development of an organism or assemblage of organisms; .... that which surrounds, surroundings."[2] By itself, when applied to psychology, this definition requires that work be hermeneutic to study social and cultural factors, ecological to include physical factors, and developmental, and that it employ organic paradigms.

Looked at twice, *environmental* contains a puzzle. Environ | mental: as the ecologist Paul Shepard observed, does the word refer to the environs around the mind, or environs constituted in the mind, or both at once?[3] Does the mind look out and discover the world outside it, or, in the world outside it, does the mind discover itself?

Looked at three times, the word is familiar. Environ | mental: it is the same world | self, the same Cartesian division, which this book began by reviewing. No wonder that the issues in environmental psychology that this book has confronted have turned out to be basic issues in the philosophy of science. The basic quandaries of epistemology are implicated by this discipline's name.

If Heidegger is correct in insisting that language has a wisdom of its own, then if we turn to the word one more time, we find that it contains an answer as well as a puzzle. *Environmental . . . .* as it is, the word has no partitions. World and mind combine. As Husserl argued, consciousness is always consciousness *of* something. Therefore the distinctive contribution of environmental psychology to psychology at large is to draw attention to the quality of exchanges between the physical world and the mind. This resolution, however, poses a new question: *"How* are the world and mind related?"

Psychology. The question "How?" brings us to the word *psychology,* which by lexical definition studies "mental and behavioral qualities."[4] Can this word throw any light on how to describe relationships between the mind and its surroundings?

If we go back to beginnings, this book opened with five passages that represented five different means for exploring memory. The first means illustrated was myth. In keeping with the principles of the hermeneutic circle, this point of beginning makes a good point of final return. This point of conclusion also illustrates Gebser's suggestion that an integral intelligence uses myth productively, as well as discursive reason. Psychology, by the one slight respectful gesture of capitalizing the *p,* reveals whom it is discourse about: the mythical maiden Psyche.

Her story is told in Apuleius's *Metamorphoses.*[5] A mortal renowned for her beauty, Psyche incurred the jealousy of Aphrodite, who dispatched her son Eros to inflict punishment. Eros fell in love with the maiden at first sight, however, and had the west wind waft her to his palace. There Eros promised her that she would be mistress of all she surveyed on the condition that he would come only in the dark and she must never look upon his form. After she was visited by her sisters, who turned green with envy and suggested that her husband was a monstrous dragon fattening her for the kill, she held a lamp above him as he slept, knife in hand to stab him, only to discover the god Eros. Oil from her lamp fell upon him, burning him, and he awoke and flew away. Desperate, Psyche flung herself into a river, but its currents carried her to shore. There Pan, the great god of nature, counseled and consoled her. To find her husband again, she had to suffer hard trials. Aphrodite set her to sort a mountain of peas, beans, wheat, millet, and barley into separate piles (the ants helped); to gather golden fleece from violent rams (a reed and trees and bushes helped); to collect an urn of water from the River Styx (an eagle helped); and to run an errand down to dread Persephone, the queen of Hades (Eros had to directly intervene). With the benefit of this aid from nonhuman friends, Psyche triumphed over adversity. She was rewarded by the return of her husband, immortality, lawful matrimony—celebrated to the tune of Pan's pipes—and the birth of a daughter named Pleasure.

In coming to this myth, this book has made progress. Chapter 1 opened with the myth of Mnemosyne, an ancient Titaness. Psyche is the latest born of the Olympians. In keeping with up-to-date modern methods, she is, in fact, a self-conscious literary fabrication. In the second century A.D., the Platonist Apuleius borrowed from old folk legends and characters to compose this allegory.[6]

Contemporary psychologists may be embarrassed to admit a Neoplatonic patroness. Empiricists among them may be more embarrassed if they reflect that Apuleius intended Psyche's story as a rebuke to anyone who seeks to kill love through reductive material curiosity. Psychology cannot expunge her from its name, however, without losing its identity. To avoid giving her unwonted honor, it may try keeping the *p* to lower case and—if we are still willing to trust Heidegger's method—see how *psychology* fares then.

Granted, *psyche* is an ancient word; and back in their own stage of primal unity, the early Greeks did not distinguish psyche and soma. In its oldest recorded uses, the word meant "breath," from the verb "to breathe, to blow."[7] Psychology has taken this approach of identifying body, mind, and soul before, and will surely continue to try it. Beyond this point of innocent nondifferentiation, however, the issue becomes delicate. From the breath of the body, the breath of life, *psyche* came to mean the invisible animating principle in all things. (In this etymology, this sequence of transformations exactly parallels that of the Latin cognate *inspiration*—the aspect of memory that this book set out to explore.) Platonists extended the word's meaning until they made it synonomous with *anima mundi*, the animating and ordering principle of the universe, which sustains the universe just as the individual soul sustains the organism.

Psychologists who accept the constructive postmodernist position that the universe is best described in the responsive terms of an organism may be able to accommodate this etymology. Those uncomfortable with this history may prefer to define themselves via entomology, and choose the second early meaning of the word *psyche*: a butterfly. It is to no avail. Greek artists found the butterfly the perfect symbol for the soul, and attached butterfly wings to Psyche's shoulders to identify her. In keeping with hermeneutic wisdom, attempts to move forward bring inquirers back to the beginning again.

Considered objectively, Psyche is not such an inappropriate patroness for psychologists. She was well acquainted with the problems and pleasures of the body and with personal vicissitudes. Sometimes she engaged in absurd tasks. She even performed some heavy classification and quantification. It was all excusable in her case, however, because she did everything in the name of love. From environmental psychologists' special point of view, the nonhuman environment brought her sustenance.

In one essential, Psyche's character remains problematic. Exactly who she is must somehow relate to the identity of her husband, as she is, from a modern perspective, an old-fashioned wife who keeps him at the center of her devoted attention. Whereas her name consistently refers to union or harmony between body and spirit and preservative attunement to the powers of nature, *his* identity is murky in story, and in this book's account. He could be any one of the following figures to which this book has alluded:

1. According to Socrates' fable in Plato's *Symposium*, he is the begging, scheming offspring of Poverty and Plenty, a great *daimon* who serves as intermediary between gods and mortals, and who provokes philosophy.
2. According to the Renaissance Neoplatonists, whom the Metaphysical poets and Wordsworth took to heart, he is the universal "tye of bodyes" whose power sustains creation by descending through the ranks of all things to draw all things back to God.
3. According to Freud's analysis, he is the mischievous and dangerous figure of Hellenic myth, child of Aphrodite and Ares, lust and

aggression, who shows characteristics of both parents and who hides under deceptive fickle forms.

4. According to Audre Lorde, he is like the Eros of Hesiod's *Theogony*, the youth born of an egg when earth and sky emerged from the void of chaos, imposing form upon chaos through his creative power.
5. According to Marie Ponsot, he is like the redeeming child born in the course of the celebration of the mysteries of Demeter, who signifies connections between mother and daughter, earthly and human fertility.
6. According to William Bronk, he is a name for the nameless god, the one of whom he can only say, "Always, in all the calling, I had thought to call you."
7. According to those, like the sisters, who crave wealth and power at the expense of harmony between Psyche and her surroundings, he is a dragon.

Psychology, like Psyche, is faced with a dilemma. If it is to hold up a lamp, which figure will it light? Psyche herself confronted this question in uncertainty. Her first impulse, which led to difficulties, was empiricist dissection. When she thought to remove all doubts by this method alone, the answer proved fugitive.

The final resolution to this book's questions hangs upon this problem of identity. Its questions were prompted by Wordsworth, whose own answers were Neoplatonic. He believed that people find beauty in nature and in the "simple produce of the common day," and inspiration in their memory, when the intellect is "wedded to this universe / in love and holy passion."[8] The contemporary poets presented here have also explained their relationships to memory and nature according to their individual understandings of the character of love and desire.

Psychology, struggling to evolve new methods, cannot content itself with the answers of old myths. It must work out for itself just whom it is that Psyche wedded. It is a hard problem, which puts everyone to the test; but there is no escape from it. For better or for worse, according to classic myth or modern psychoanalytic theory, she *is* wedded. On the one side, there lurks the possibility of the dragon. Many people claim to have sighted it; and psychologists have sometimes joined their company, anxious to detach themselves from concern for human qualities and values, and ignoring human dependence upon nature's concinnity. If psychology is to form a better union, whom will it choose? How will it conduct itself? Before these unsettled questions, this book must stop. To relate mind and memory to nature in either love or fear is to take a risk, unavoidable as it may be. Therefore the answers to this book's questions, in the end, are left to the reader. At this point of choice, this book can go no further.

Notes

PREFACE

1. Edith Cobb, "The Ecology of Imagination in Childhood," *Daedalus* 88 (1959):539.

2. In order of discipline, selected citations of her work have been: Margaret Mead, "Children, Culture, and Edith Cobb," USDA Forest Service General Technical Report NE-30 (1977), 19–24; Paul Shepard, *Man in the Landscape* (New York: Alfred A. Knopf, 1967), 34–37; Roger Hart, *Children's Experience of Place* (New York: Irvington, 1979); Gary Moore, "State of the Art in Play Environment Research and Applications," *When Children Play*, ed. J. L. Frost and S. Sunderlin (Washington, D.C.: Association for Childhood Education International, 1985); Robin Moore and Donald Young, "Childhood Outdoors: Toward a Social Ecology of the Landscape," *Children and the Environment*, ed. Irwin Altman and Joachim Wohlwill (New York: Plenum Press, 1978), 84; Gary Nabhan and Stephen Trimble, *The Geography of Childhood* (Boston: Beacon Press, 1994), 22–23, 175; David Sobel, *Children's Special Places* (Tucson: Zephyr Press, 1992); Robin Blaser, "The Fire," *Poetics of the New American Poetry*, ed. D. Allen and W. Tallman (New York: Grove Press, 1973), 239.

3. Edith Cobb, *The Ecology of Imagination in Childhood* (New York: Columbia University Press, 1977).

4. Louise Chawla, "Ecstatic Places," *Children's Environments Quarterly* 7(4) (1990):18–23; "The Ecology of Environmental Memory," *Children's Environments Quarterly* (Winter 1986):34–42.

5. Arvid Bengtsson, *Environmental Planning for Children's Play* (New York: Praeger, 1970); Grady Clay, "Remembered Landscapes," *The Subversive Science*, ed. P. Shepard and D. McKinley (Boston: Houghton Mifflin, 1969); Roger Hart, "The Changing City of Childhood," Annual Catherine Maloney Memorial Lecture, City College of New York, 1987; Robin Moore, *Childhood's Domain* (London: Croom Helm, 1986); A. E. Parr, "The Child in the City: Urbanity and the Urban Scene," *Landscape* 16 (1967):3–5; Colin Ward, *The Child in the City* (New York: Pantheon Books, 1978).

CHAPTER ONE: PLACING THE PAST

1. Edith Cobb, "The Ecology of Imagination in Childhood," *Daedalus* 88 (1959):537–48.

2. Gary W. Shannon and Ellen Cromley, "Settlement and Density Patterns: Toward the 21st Century," *Habitats for Children*, ed. J. F. Wohlwill and W. van Vliet (Hillsdale, N.J.: Lawrence Erlbaum, 1985), 111.

3. Denise Levertov, *The Poet in the World* (New York: New Directions, 1973), 92–97.

4. Hesiod, "Theogony," *The Homeric Hymns and Homerica*, trans. H. G. Evelyn-White, Loeb Classical Library (Cambridge, Mass.: Harvard University Press, 1967), 81, 83.

5. Reported in Ernest Schachtel, *Metamorphosis* (New York: Basic Books, 1959), 281–82.

6. William Carlos Williams, *Paterson*, Book 2, part 3 (New York: New Directions, 1963), 96.

7. Barrett Mandel, "Full of Life Now," *Autobiography*, ed. James Olney (Princeton: Princeton University Press, 1980), 240.

8. John Locke, *An Essay Concerning Human Understanding*, ed. Peter Nidditch (Oxford: Clarendon Press, 1975), chapter 10, section 2.

9. Henry C. Ellis, *Fundamentals of Human Learning, Memory, and Cognition* (Dubuque: William C. Brown, 1978), 5.

10. Barrett Mandel, "Autobiography—Reflection Trained On Mystery," *Prairie Schooner* 46 (1972/73):327.

11. Frederic Bartlett, *Remembering* (Cambridge: Cambridge University Press, 1964). (Original edition 1932.)

12. The dependence of memory on language development is argued by G. J. Dudycha and M. M. Dudycha, "Some Factors and Characteristics of Childhood Memories," *Child Development* 4 (1933):265–78; Ulric Neisser, "Cultural and Cognitive Discontinuity," *Anthropology and Human Behavior*, ed. T. E. Gladwin and W. Sturtevant (Washington, D.C.: Anthropological Society of Washington, 1962); Schachtel, *Metamorphosis* (New York: Basic Books, 1959). Neisser has come to emphasize the importance of retrieval contexts and the social learning of what constitutes significant memories for communication, in "Time Present and Time Past," *Practical Aspects of Memory*, vol. 2, ed. M. M. Gruneberg, P. E. Morris, and R. N. Sykes (New York: Wiley, 1988). Katherine Nelson argues the need for established scripts of everyday routines as a background for the extraordinary and memorable, in "The Ontogeny of Memory for Real Events,"

Remembering Reconsidered, ed. U. Neisser and E. Winograd (Cambridge: Cambridge University Press, 1988).

13. D. C. Rubin, S. E. Wetzler, and R. D. Nebes, "Autobiographical Memory Across the Lifespan," *Autobiographical Memory,* ed. D. C. Rubin (Cambridge: Cambridge University Press, 1986).

14. Douglas Herrmann and Ulric Neisser, "An Inventory of Everyday Memory Experiences," *Practical Aspects of Memory,* ed. M. M. Gruneberg, P. E. Morris, and R. N. Sykes (London: Academic Press, 1978), 35–51.

15. Thomas Hobbes, *The English Works of Thomas Hobbes of Malmesbury,* ed. W. Molesworth, 11 vols. (London: John Bohn, 1840; reproduced by Scientia Verlag Aalen, 1966), vol. 4: *Tripos; in Three Discourses,* discourse 1, sections 5.4, 6.1.

16. Ulric Neisser, "Memory: What Are the Important Questions?," *Practical Aspects of Memory* (1978), 4, 12.

17. Gillian Cohen, *Memory in the Real World* (Hillsdale, N.J.: Lawrence Erlbaum, 1989); Henry C. Ellis and R. Reed Hunt, *Fundamentals of Human Memory and Cognition,* 4th ed. (Dubuque: William C. Brown, 1989); ed. M. M. Gruneberg, P. E. Morris, and R. N. Sykes, *Practical Aspects of Memory;* ed. Ulric Neisser and Eugene Winograd, *Remembering Reconsidered;* ed. Ulric Neisser, *Memory Observed* (San Francisco: W. H. Freeman, 1982); ed. David C. Rubin, *Autobiographical Memory.*

18. Steven Smith, "Environmental context-dependent memory," *Memory in Context: Context in Memory,* ed. G. M. Davies and Donald Thomson (New York: Wiley, 1988), 13–34.

19. Elizabeth Sewell, *The Human Metaphor* (Notre Dame, Ind.: University of Notre Dame Press, 1964).

20. Giuseppe Ungaretti, *Innocence et Mémoire,* trans. P. Jacottet (Paris: Gallimard, 1969), 297. English translation by this author.

21. Ibid., 316.

22. William Carlos Williams, *The Autobiography of William Carlos Williams* (New York: Random House, 1951), 13.

23. Howard Nemerov, "The First Country of Places," *Images and Ideas in American Culture,* ed. A. Edelstein (Hanover, N.H.: Brandeis University Press, 1979).

24. For a succinct review of Husserl's ideas, see David Stewart and Algis Mickunas, *Exploring Phenomenology,* 2nd ed. (Athens: Ohio University Press, 1990). For phenomenologies of memory, see Edward S. Casey, *Remembering* (Bloomington: Indiana University Press, 1987); eds. Erwin

Straus and R. M. Griffith, *Phenomenology of Memory* (Pittsburgh: Duquesne University Press, 1970).

25. Edmund Husserl, *The Phenomenology of Internal Time Consciousness*, ed. Martin Heidegger, trans. James Churchill (Bloomington: Indiana University Press, 1964).

26. Thomas Hobbes, *Leviathan*, ed. Richard Tuck (Cambridge: Cambridge University Press, 1991), chap. 2.

27. Heidegger's phenomenological foundation for his hermeneutics is *Being and Time*, trans. J. Macquarrie and E. Robinson (New York: Harper & Row, 1962). He developed the concept of *aletheia* and creating a clearing in "On the Essence of Truth" in *Existence and Being*, trans. R. F. C. Hull and A. Crick (Chicago: Henry Regnery, 1949). For a history of hermeneutics, see Richard E. Palmer, *Hermeneutics* (Evanston, Ill.: Northwestern University Press, 1969).

28. Martin Heidegger, "What Are Poets For?," *Poetry, Language, Thought*, trans. A. Hofstadter (New York: Harper & Row, 1971).

29. See, for example, Heidegger, "What Are Poets For?," 112; and *What Is Called Thinking?*, trans. J. G. Gray (New York: Harper & Row, 1968), 8.

30. Hans-Georg Gadamer, *Truth and Method* (New York: Seabury Press, 1975). A helpful discussion of the application of hermeneutics in social research is found in Joseph Kockelmans, "Toward an Interpretive or Hermeneutic Social Science," *Graduate Faculty Philosophy Journal* 5 (1975):73–96.

31. Hans-Georg Gadamer, *Reason in the Age of Science*, trans. F. G. Lawrence (Cambridge: M.I.T. Press, 1981), 159. Stephen Strasser, in *Phenomenology and the Human Sciences* (Pittsburgh: Duquesne University Press, 1963), 256–59, observes that dialogue, or dialectic, is the necessary method to achieve intersubjective truth. He defines dialectic as "any orderly change in perspectives which enables human beings in search of meaning to overcome the limitations of one-sided perspectives and limited horizons in a systematic manner."

32. Husserl describes the process of *Wesensschau*, or "intuition of essences," which freely varies a phenomenon in imagination in order to intuitively grasp its essential essence, in *Phenomenological Psychology*, trans. J. Scanlon (The Hague: Martinus Nijhoff, 1977). For a review of this concept, see Joseph Kockelman, *Edmund Husserl's Phenomenological Psychology* (Pittsburgh: Duquesne University Press, 1967), 154–61.

33. Gadamer, *Truth and Method*, 333–41. Gadamer's analysis of the dialectic of dialogue and the spiraling search for truth owe a debt to Hegel, which he acknowledges in "The Language of Metaphysics," *Philosophical*

Hermeneutics, ed. David Linge (Berkeley: University of California Press, 1976).

34. Louise Chawla, "Kentucky Conservationists" (1989) and "Childhood in Kentucky" (1991), oral history collections, Special Collections, University of Kentucky, Lexington.

35. Edmund Husserl, *Ideas*, trans. W. R. Boyce-Gibson (New York: Collier Books, 1962).

36. Heidegger, "What Are Poets For?," *Poetry, Language, Thought.*

CHAPTER TWO: CHILDHOOD AND NATURE

1. Edith Cobb, "The Ecology of Imagination in Childhood," *Daedalus* 88 (1959):539.

2. René Descartes, *Discourse on Method*, Book 4. Translation by Joseph Kockelmans in *Edmund Husserl's Phenomenological Psychology* (Atlantic Highlands, N.J.: Humanities Press, 1978), 37–38.

3. John Locke, *Some Thoughts Concerning Education*, paragraph 174. The Harvard Classics, vol. 37, ed. Charles Eliot (New York: Collier, 1910), 159–60.

4. John Locke, *An Essay Concerning Human Understanding*, ed. John Yolton, 2 vols., Everyman's Library (New York: E. P. Dutton, 1974), vol. 2, book 4.

5. Auguste Comte, *The Essential Comte: Selected from Cours de Philosophie Positive*, ed. Stanislav Andreski (London: Croom Helm, 1974), 21.

6. Stephen Jay Gould, *Ontogeny and Phylogeny* (Cambridge: Belknap Press, Harvard University Press, 1977).

7. Arthur Schopenhauer, "On Women," from *Studies in Pessimism*, trans. T. B. Saunders. Reprinted in M. B. Mahowald, *Philosophy of Woman* (Indianapolis: Hackett, 1983), 229.

8. Herbert Spencer, "Moral Education," *Education: Intellectual, Moral and Physical* (New York: Appleton & Company, 1888).

9. Lucien Lévy-Bruhl, *How Natives Think*, trans. Lillian Clare (London: George Allen & Unwin, 1926), 29.

10. Idem, *Primitive Mentality*, trans. Lillian Clare (New York: Macmillan, 1923), 60.

11. Idem, *How Natives Think*, 13, 26.

12. Jean Piaget, *The Child's Conception of the World*, trans. Joan and Andrew Tomlinson (London: Routledge and Kegan Paul, 1929).

13. Ibid. Piaget's comparisons of realism, artificialism, animism, and ancient science come respectively from 34, 253, 275, 250.

14. For a balanced review of criticisms of Piaget, see David Cohen, *Piaget: Critique and Reassessment* (New York: St. Martin's Press, 1983). For radical criticisms of Piaget's system on cultural, logical, and philosophical grounds, respectively, see Susan Buck-Morss, "Socio-Economic Bias in Piaget's Theory and Its Implications for Cross-Culture Studies," *Human Development* 18 (1975):35–49; Susan Sugarman, *Piaget's Construction of the Child's Reality* (New York: Cambridge University Press, 1987); and Gareth B. Matthews, *Philosophy and the Young Child* (Cambridge: Harvard University Press, 1980). Of particular relevance to the present book, Matthews claims that Piaget's simplistic notion of animism, in the light of the philosophical complexities of the notion of life, has had a pernicious effect on psychology and education. See G. Matthews, "Conceiving Childhood: Childhood Animism," *Nous* 14 (1982):29–37.

15. Auguste Comte, *A General View of Positivism*, trans. J. H. Bridges (Dubuque, Iowa: Brown Reprints, 1971), 15. (Original edition 1865.)

16. Lucien Lévy-Bruhl, *The Notebooks on Primitive Mentality*, trans. Peter Riviere (New York: Harper & Row, 1975), 101.

17. Sigmund Freud to Wilhelm Fleiss, 22 September 1898, in *The Origins of Psycho-analysis*, ed. M. Bonaparte, A. Freud, and E. Kris (New York: Basic Books, 1954), 264.

18. Reviewed in Bruno Bettelheim, *Freud and Man's Soul* (New York: Alfred A. Knopf, 1981).

19. An unreferenced quotation from Freud used as epigraph for *Growing Young* by Ashley Montagu (New York: McGraw-Hill, 1981), iii.

20. Sigmund Freud, "Childhood Memories and Screen Memories," *The Standard Edition of the Complete Works of Sigmund Freud*, ed. and trans. under the supervision of James Strachey, 24 vols. (London: Hogarth Press and the Institute of Psychoanalysis, 1960), 6:43–52. (German edition 1905.)

21. Sigmund Freud, "Symbolism in Dreams," *A General Introduction to Psychoanalysis*, trans. Joan Riviere (New York: Liveright Publishing Corp., 1920; rev. ed. 1935), 133–50.

22. Sigmund Freud, "Analysis of a Phobia in a Five-year-old Boy," *Standard Edition*, 10:5–149. (German edition 1909.)

23. Sigmund Freud, *The Future of an Illusion*, trans. James Strachey (New York: W. W. Norton, 1961), 15–17. (German edition 1927.)

24. Sigmund Freud, "The Theme of the Three Caskets," *Standard Edition*, 1958, 12:291–301. (German edition 1913.) Quotation from 301.

25. Sigmund Freud, *Civilization and Its Discontents*, trans. and ed. James Strachey (New York: W. W. Norton, 1961), 12–15. (German edition 1920.)

26. Sigmund Freud, "Formulations on the Two Principles of Mental Functioning," *Standard Edition*, 1958, 12:215–26. (German edition 1911.)

27. Linda Pollock, in a review of parents' diaries entitled *Forgotten Children* (Cambridge: Cambridge University Press, 1984), found references to small children's special qualities from the beginning of diary keeping. Therefore she challenges the notion that childhood was not "discovered" until the eighteenth century. What she found in eighteenth-century entries were increasing references to childhood as an abstract state and first references to its innocence. She has suggested that this idealization reflects nostalgia over the loss of a seemingly simpler agrarian age, as have Peter Coveney in *Image of Childhood* (Harmondsworth: Penguin Books, 1967); David Lowenthal in *The Past is a Foreign Country* (Cambridge: Cambridge University Press, 1985); and Raymond Williams in *The Country and the City* (New York: Oxford University Press, 1973) and *Culture and Society* (London: Chatto & Windus, 1958). Philippe Aries, in *Centuries of Childhood*, trans. R. Baldick (New York: Alfred A. Knopf, 1962) (who initiated the idea of the "discovery of childhood," which Pollock has challenged), has related the idealization of childhood to the formation of the bourgeois family.

28. Owen Barfield, *What Coleridge Thought* (Middletown, Conn.: Wesleyan University Press, 1971), chap. 12.

29. Karl Weintraub argues that the cultural pluralism and political instability of the Renaissance and Reformation encouraged autobiographical reflection (*The Value of the Individual* [Chicago: University of Chicago Press, 1978]).

30. Coleridge to Wordsworth, May 1815, cited in M. H. Abrams, *Natural Supernaturalism* (New York: W. W. Norton, 1971), 145.

31. This analysis of Platonic circle imagery draws upon Abrams, *Natural Supernaturalism*, 46–56.

32. Frances A. Yates, *The Art of Memory* (Chicago: University of Chicago Press, 1966).

33. *The Confessions of St. Augustine*, Book 10, trans. Edward Pusey (New York: Modern Library, Random House, 1949).

34. Bonaventure, *The Mind's Road to God*, trans. George Boas (Indianapolis: Library of Liberal Arts, Bobbs-Merrill, 1953).

35. Augustine, *Confessions*, Book 1, 9.

36. John Purkis, *A Preface to Wordsworth* (New York: Charles Scribners, 1970), 109.

37. "The Retreate," lines 1–20, *The Works of Henry Vaughan*, ed. L. C. Martin (Oxford: Clarendon Press, 1914), vol. 2.

38. Thomas Traherne, "Third Century," section 3.1, *Centuries, Poems, and Thanksgivings*, ed. H. M. Margoliouth, 2 vols. (Oxford: Clarendon Press, 1958).

39. Vaughan, "Childe-hood," lines 35–36, *Works*, vol. 2.

40. Idem, "The Retreate," lines 29–32, *Works*, vol. 2.

41. William Wordsworth, "Ode: Intimations of Immortality from Recollections of Early Childhood," 1.1–5, *The Poetical Works of Wordsworth*, Cambridge edition, revised Paul D. Sheats (Boston: Houghton Mifflin, 1982).

42. Josephine Miles, *Pathetic Fallacy in the Nineteenth Century* (New York: Octagon Books, 1965). In moving from Vaughan to Traherne, there is already a noticeable shift from standard symbol to autobiographical particular. See Sharon C. Seelig, *The Shadow of Eternity* (Lexington: University Press of Kentucky, 1981).

43. Raymond Williams, *The Country and the City, Culture and Society*.

44. John Locke, *Reasonableness of Christianity*, discussed in Basil Willey, *The Seventeenth Century Background* (New York: Columbia University Press, 1950), 283–87.

45. Preface to the *Lyrical Ballads* of 1800, *The Poetical Works of Wordsworth*, 794–95.

46. Plotinus, *Enneads*, 5, tractate 8, section 1. Quoted in I. A. Richards, *Coleridge on Imagination* (Bloomington: Indiana University Press, 1960), 26–27. In this passage Plotinus refers to *techné*, which has been translated here and—according to Richards—interpreted by Wordsworth and Coleridge, as the operation of the informed imagination.

47. David Hartley, *Observations on Man, His Frame, His Duty, and His Expectations* (New York: Garland Publishing, 1971). (Facsimile of 1749 edition.)

48. Wordsworth, "Personal Talk," 2.13–14, *Poetical Works*.

49. Wordsworth, Letter to Landor, cited in Josephine Miles, *Wordsworth and the Vocabulary of the Emotion* (New York: Octagon Books, 1965), 51.

50. Cited in Miles, *Vocabulary of the Emotion*, 43.

51. Samuel Taylor Coleridge, *Biographia Literaria*, 2 vols., ed. G. Watson, Everyman's Library (New York: E. P. Dutton, 1956), 1:59–60.

52. Cited in Miles, *Vocabulary of the Emotion*, 44.

53. Wordsworth, "Lines Composed a Few Miles Above Tintern Abbey," lines 93–102, *Poetical Works*.

54. Henry Weinfield, personal communication, notes that "Tintern Abbey" serves as a mnemonic for the process it encourages.

55. Wordsworth, "Tintern Abbey," lines 43–49, *Poetical Works*.

56. Coleridge, *Biographia Literaria*, 2:6.

57. Abrams, *Natural Supernaturalism*, 46–56, 377–84. Abrams has been criticized for applying one pattern of thought to all Romantic authors. It can be argued, however, that his model does fit Wordsworth, one of the principal authors whom he reviews, and, with qualifications, many other authors.

58. Friedrich von Schiller, "On Naive and Sentimental Poetry." Cited in Abrams, *Natural Supernaturalism*, 215, 214.

59. Ralph Waldo Emerson, "The Transcendentalist," *The Selected Writings of Ralph Waldo Emerson* (New York: Modern Library, 1950), 93.

60. Josephine Miles, *Eras and Modes in English Poetry* (Westport, Conn.: Greenwood Press, 1976).

61. Cecilia Tichi, *New World, New Earth* (New Haven: Yale University Press, 1979).

62. "Contemplations," *The Works of Anne Bradstreet*, ed. J. Hensley (Cambridge: Harvard University Press, 1967).

63. Emerson, "Nature," *Selected Writings*, 6.

64. Ibid.

65. *The Letters of Emily Dickinson*, ed. T. H. Johnson and T. Ward, 3 vols. (Cambridge: Harvard University Press, 1958). Dickinson describes childhood in letters to Abiah Root (1:104), to Dr. and Mrs. J. G. Holland (2:354), and to T. W. Higginson (1:481).

66. Martin Heidegger, "What Are Poets For?," *Poetry, Language, Thought*, trans. and ed. A. Hofstadter (New York: Harper & Row, 1971); Wordsworth, Preface to the *Lyrical Ballads* of 1800, *Poetical Works*.

67. Martin Heidegger, "On the Essence of Truth," *Existence and Being*, trans. R. F. C. Hull and A. Crick (Chicago: Henry Regnery, 1949), 300–303.

CHAPTER THREE: CONFRONTATIONS: WILLIAM BRONK AND HENRY WEINFIELD

1. Robert Bertholf, ed., "A Conversation with William Bronk," *Credences* 1(3) (May 1976):12.

2. William L. Stone, *Washington County, New York: Its History at the Close of the Nineteenth Century* (n.p.: New York History Co., 1901), 380.

3. The description of Bronk's place and family background is taken from a personal interview with him on July 23, 1983.

4. William Bronk, "Where It Ends," *Life Supports* (San Francisco: North Point Press, 1982), 171.

5. Anne Bradstreet, "Contemplations," *The Works of Anne Bradstreet*, ed. J. Hensley (Cambridge: Harvard University Press, 1967), 205.

6. William Bronk, "Herman Melville; or, The Ambiguities," *The Brother in Elysium* (New Rochelle, N.Y.: Elizabeth Press, 1980). Reprinted in *Vectors and Smoothable Curves* (San Francisco: North Point Press, 1985), 163–221.

7. William Bronk to Cid Corman, 18 January 1967, quoted in Cid Corman, *William Bronk* (Carrboro, N.C.: Truck Press, 1976), 36–37.

8. Bronk, "Local Landscapes," lines 13–18, *Life Supports*, 218.

9. Henry Weinfield, ed., "A Conversation with William Bronk," *Sagetrieb* 7(3) (Winter 1988):22.

10. Bronk, "The Greeks, the Chinese, or Say the Mayans," lines 3–6, *Life Supports*, 76.

11. Bronk, "The Bach Trombones at Bethlehem, Pennsylvania," lines 13–15, *Life Supports*, 32.

12. Bronk, "The Arts and Death: A Fugue for Sidney Cox," lines 49–54, *Life Supports*, 35.

13. Bertholf, *Credences*, 26.

14. William Bronk, "Antibiograph," *Careless Love and Its Apostrophes* (New York: Red Ozier Press, 1985), 7.

15. Bronk, "Questions for Eros," lines 11–15, *Life Supports*, 214.

16. Bronk, "Yes: I Mean So OK—Love," lines 1–4, *Life Supports*, 33. Bronk discusses the background to this poem in *Credences*, 27.

17. William Bronk, "Desire and Denial," *A Partial Glossary* (New Rochelle, N.Y.: Elizabeth Press, 1974). Reprinted in *Vectors and Smoothable Curves*, 50–51.

18. Bronk, "At Tikal," lines 17–18, *Life Supports*, 39.

19. Bronk, "We Want the Mark of Time," line 21, *Life Supports*, 38–39.

20. Bronk, "The Real World," lines 13–14, *Life Supports*, 145.

21. Bertholf, *Credences*, 20.

22. Bronk, "The Real Surrounding: On Canaletto's Venice," lines 23–24, *Life Supports*, 112.

23. William Bronk, *The New World* (New Rochelle, N.Y.: Elizabeth Press, 1974), 55. Reprinted in *Vectors and Smoothable Curves*, 39.

24. Bertholf, *Credences*, 22.

25. Bronk, "Of the All with Which We Coexist," lines 9–10, *Life Supports*, 78.

26. Bronk, "The Lover as Not the Loved," *Life Supports*, 167.

27. Bronk, "The Annihilation of Matter," lines 12–16, *Life Supports*, 42.

28. Bronk, "Virgin and Child with Music and Numbers," lines 19–20, *Life Supports*, 53.

29. Bertholf, *Credences*, 24.

30. "Virgin and Child with Music and Numbers," "Poem for the Nineteenth of March, St. Joseph's Day," *Life Supports*, 52–53, 216; "Having Come a Long Way, the Wise Men Wait a Minute," *Light in a Dark Sky* (Concord, N.H.: William B. Ewert, Publisher, 1982), n.p.

31. Bronk, "Out of Context," lines 15–16, *Life Supports*, 86.

32. The quotations in this paragraph come successively from "Some Musicians Play Chamber Music for Us," "My Young Nephew Sends Me His Picture for a Present," *Life Supports*, 26, 37; "Later," *Death is the Place* (San Francisco: North Point Press, 1989), 5.

33. Bronk, "Home Address," lines 15–19, *Life Supports*, 16.

34. Bronk, "My House New-Painted," *Life Supports*, 46–47.

35. Bronk, "The Strong Room of the House," lines 15–20, *Life Supports*, 222.

36. This history of Bronk's fortunes as a writer come from a personal interview with him on July 23, 1983.

37. Bronk described his writing method in *Credences*, 32. His statement that a writer should avoid theory is from his interview of July 23, 1983.

38. Weinfield, *Sagetrieb*, 37.

39. Bertholf, *Credences*, 25.

40. Weinfield, *Sagetrieb*, 38–39.

41. Ernest Bernbaum, *Guide Through the Romantic Movement* (New York: Ronald Press, 1949), 323.

42. Bronk's statements about the universal come from his interviews in *Sagetrieb*, 37, and *Credences*, 25, respectively. The Romantic claims about nature and infinity come from Wordsworth's letter to Landor, cited by Josephine Miles, *Wordsworth and the Vocabulary of the Emotion* (New York: Octagon Books, 1965), 51.

43. Bronk, "The World as a Thieving Woman," *Life Supports*, 20.

44. Bronk, "Walt Whitman's Marine Democracy," *The Brother in Elysium*. Reprinted in *Vectors and Smoothable Curves*, 131–62.

45. Ralph Waldo Emerson, *Nature* (Boston: Beacon Press, 1985), 13.

46. Samuel Taylor Coleridge, *Biographia Literaria*, 2 vols., ed. G. Watson, Everyman's Library (New York: E. P. Dutton, 1956), 2:168–69.

47. Clarence Thorpe, *The Mind of John Keats* (Oxford: Oxford University Press, 1926), 126.

48. All biographical information in this section is drawn from personal interviews with Henry Weinfield on April 15, 1983, and May 9, 1983.

49. Henry Weinfield, revised couplet of "Sonnet VIII," *Sonnets Elegiac and Satirical* (Cincinnati: House of Keys, 1982). Revision in personal letter, March 1984.

50. Henry Weinfield, *The Poet Without a Name* (Carbondale: Southern Illinois University Press, 1991), 48.

51. Henry Weinfield, "The Carnival Cantata," lines 5–12, *The Carnival Cantata* (Santa Barbara: Unicorn Press, 1971), 18.

52. Weinfield, personal interview, April 15, 1983.

53. Henry Weinfield, "The Lives of the Poets," *In the Sweetness of the New Time* (Atlanta: House of Keys, 1980), 43. Weinfield's statement about loving poetry is from his April 15, 1983 interview.

54. Weinfield, interview, April 15, 1983.

55. Henry Weinfield, "Sonnet X," *Sonnets Elegiac and Satirical*, n.p.

56. The following discussion of desire, reality, and language is based upon a personal conversation with Weinfield in April 1984.

57. G. W. F. Hegel, *Phenomenology of Spirit*, trans. A.V. Miller (Oxford: Clarendon Press, 1977), 66.

58. Henry Weinfield, "The Spirit of Utopia," line 17, unpublished manuscript.

59. William Wordsworth, Preface to the *Lyrical Ballads* of 1800, *The Poetical Works of William Wordsworth*, Cambridge edition, ed. Paul D. Sheats (Boston: Houghton Mifflin, 1982).

60. Walt Whitman, "An American Primer," reviewed in F. O. Matthiessen, "Only a Language Experiment," *Whitman: A Collection of Critical Essays*, ed. Roy H. Pearce (Englewood Cliffs, N.J.: Prentice-Hall, 1962). That poetic language should be responsive to local speech is Williams's recurrent theme in *The Selected Letters of William Carlos Williams*, ed. J. C. Thirlwall (New York: McDowell, Obolensky, 1957).

61. Coleridge, *Biographia Literaria*, chap. 17.

62. Henry Weinfield, "Introduction," *The Collected Poetry of Stéphane Mallarmé* (Berkeley: University of California Press, forthcoming).

63. Weinfield, "Slow Steps / The Muddy Shore," *In the Sweetness of the New Time*, 16.

64. Weinfield, personal interview, June 7, 1989. The reference is to William Butler Yeats, *A Vision* (New York: Macmillan, 1965).

65. Weinfield, interview, May 9, 1983.

66. Jacques Derrida, *Writing and Difference*, trans. Alan Bass (Chicago: University of Chicago Press, 1978).

67. Weinfield, interview, April 15, 1983.

68. Weinfield, "Wordsworth and the Reconstitution of the Pastoral," *The Poet Without a Name*, 164–92.

69. Weinfield, interview, June 7, 1989, and personal letter of January 11, 1988.

70. Weinfield, "A Song of Destiny," lines 187–204, part 4 of "The Old Man at the Dump," unpublished manuscript.

71. Weinfield gave reasons for rejecting nostalgia for childhood in his interview of May 9, 1983.

72. Friedrich von Schiller, "On Naive and Sentimental Poetry." Cited in M. H. Abrams, *Natural Supernaturalism* (New York: W. W. Norton, 1971), 214–15.

73. Weinfield, interview, May 9, 1983.

74. Weinfield, "Adam and Eve," *In the Sweetness of the New Time*, 45–46.

75. Homer, *The Iliad*, trans. Robert Fitzgerald (Garden City, N.Y.: Anchor Press/Doubleday, 1974), 3.180, 6.357–8.

CHAPTER FOUR: RECONCILIATION: DAVID IGNATOW

1. William Wordsworth, "The Recluse," lines 93–99. In *The Poetical Works of Wordsworth*, ed. Paul D. Sheats (Boston: Houghton Mifflin, 1982).

2. David Ignatow, *Open Between Us* (Ann Arbor: University of Michigan Press, 1980), 62–63.

3. Information about Ignatow's early years is taken from his autobiographical essays "The Formative Years" and "As Long as Life Matters" in *The One in the Many* (Middletown, Conn.: Wesleyan University Press, 1988), 3–29, 179–87.

4. Ignatow's early job history is reviewed by Ralph J. Mills, Jr. in his Introduction to *The Notebooks of David Ignatow* (Chicago: Swallow Press, 1973), xvii-xviii.

5. David Ignatow, *The Notebooks* (1940 entry), 9–10.

6. Ignatow recounts the incident of the bird in "The Formative Years," 10, and in *Open Between Us*, 269.

7. Ignatow, "As Long as Life Matters," *The One in the Many*, 186.

8. David Ignatow, "Here It Is," *Whisper to the Earth* (Boston: Little Brown, 1981), 16.

9. Ignatow, *The Notebooks* (1961 entry), 237.

10. Ignatow, "Growing Up," *Whisper to the Earth*, 23.

11. Ignatow, *The Notebooks* (1961 entry), 238. The same sentiment is reaffirmed in the poem "In My Childhood," *New and Collected Poems, 1970–1985* (Middletown, Conn.: Wesleyan University Press, 1986), 318.

12. David Ignatow, personal interview, April 18, 1983.

13. David Ignatow, personal interview, April 11, 1983. See also Ignatow's essay, "My Life with Whitman," *The One in the Many*, 69–81.

14. David Ignatow, "From the Notebooks (1972–1974)," *Ironwood 21* (1983), 104–5.

15. David Ignatow, "In the Beginning," *American Poets in 1976*, William Heyen, ed. (Indianapolis: Bobbs-Merrill Company, 1976), 130–42.

16. Ralph J. Mills, Jr., relates Ignatow's early job history and W.P.A. work in his Introduction to *The Notebooks*, xiii.

17. Ignatow, *The Notebooks* (1961 entry), 237.

18. Ignatow, interview of April 11, 1983. Ignatow discussed Williams's encouragement in the same interview.

19. Ignatow, *The Notebooks* (1964 entry), 258.

20. Ibid. (1962 entry), 248.

21. Ignatow, *Open Between Us*, 62–63, 90–91.

22. Ibid., 90.

23. Ibid., 91.

24. Ignatow, "Get the Gasworks," lines 1–5, *Poems 1934–1969* (Middletown, Conn.: Wesleyan University Press, 1970), 51.

25. Ignatow, *The Notebooks* (1961 entry), 235.

26. Ignatow, *Open Between Us*, 89.

27. Ignatow, *The Notebooks* (1960 entry), 209.

28. Ignatow, *Open Between Us*, 105.

29. Ignatow, "Turnings," lines 66–71, *Poems*, 79.

30. Ignatow, *Open Between Us*, 288.

31. David Ignatow, "Brightness as a Poignant Light," lines 1–7, *Tread the Dark* (Boston: Little, Brown, 1978), 3.

32. Ignatow, "Growing Up," *Whisper to the Earth*, 23.

33. Ignatow chronicles the changes in his life between 1955 and 1965 in *The Notebooks*.

34. Ignatow, *The Notebooks* (1961 entry), 239.

35. Ignatow, "Above Everything," *Whisper to the Earth*, 48.

36. The sequence of transitions from the Guggenheim Fellowship through college teaching positions is taken from Ralph Mills, Jr., Introduction to *The Notebooks*, xix. Ignatow described his mugging in his Queens apartment lobby in his interview on April 11, 1983.

37. Ignatow, interview of April 11, 1983.

38. David Ignatow, "Living with Change," *Literature and the Urban Experience*, M. C. Jaye and A. C. Watts, eds. (New Brunswick: Rutgers University Press, 1981), 203.

39. Ignatow, *The Notebooks* (1970 entry), 332.

40. Ignatow, *Open Between Us*, 58.

41. Ignatow, interview of April 18, 1983.

42. Ignatow, "My Life with Whitman," *The One in the Many*, 80.

43. Ignatow, "From the Notebooks," *Ironwood*, 98.

44. Ibid.

45. Ignatow, interview of April 11, 1983.

46. David Ignatow, *Shadowing the Ground* (Hanover: Wesleyan University Press, 1991).

CHAPTER FIVE: CONNECTIONS: AUDRE LORDE AND MARIE PONSOT

1. Basic material regarding Lorde's early childhood and grade school years comes from *Zami: A New Spelling of My Name* (Watertown, Mass.: Persephone Press, 1982), 15–71.

2. Audre Lorde, personal interview, January 5, 1984.

3. The quotations in this paragraph come from "An Interview with Audre Lorde," *American Poetry Review* (March/April 1980), 19.

4. Lorde, *Zami*, 43.

5. Audre Lorde, "An Interview with Audre Lorde: Audre Lorde and Adrienne Rich," *Signs*, 6(4) (1981):714.

6. Regarding Lorde's rediscovery of the world through glasses, see *Zami*, 31–32. Regarding learning to read at the library and first poems, see *Signs*, 714–15. (These two accounts differ as to whether she was three or four when she acquired glasses.)

7. Lorde, personal interview. For an interpretation of the theme of "home" in the work of Lorde, Ponsot, Bronk, and Ignatow, see Louise

Chawla, "Home Is Where You Start From," *The Meaning and Use of Housing*, ed. Ernesto G. Arias (London: Gower, 1992), 479–95.

8. The mother's stories about Carriacou are described in *Zami*, 9–14. The detail about the water buckets comes from this author's personal interview with Lorde on January 5, 1984.

9. Lorde, personal interview.

10. Ibid.

11. Ibid.

12. The line of poetry by Lorde is from "Relevant Is Different Points on the Circle," *Chosen Poems Old and New* (New York: W. W. Norton, 1982), 55. Lorde's memories of being a sojourner and having a standard of comparison come from this author's personal interview with her.

13. Lorde, *Zami*, 32.

14. Lorde, *Signs*, 715.

15. Ibid., 714–15.

16. Lorde, *Zami*, 58–65.

17. Ibid., 68–71.

18. Lorde, personal interview.

19. Audre Lorde, "Outside," lines 1–14, *The Black Unicorn* (New York: W. W. Norton, 1978), 61.

20. Lorde describes her relationship with Genevieve in *Zami*, 85–103. She discussed the relationship between this friendship and her ties to Manhattan in her personal interview.

21. Lorde, "Memorial I," *Chosen Poems*, 3. Lorde made minor revisions in this poem and selected others in *Undersong* (New York: W. W. Norton, 1992). Because this account is chronological, it keeps to the original published versions.

22. Lorde, *Zami*, 104.

23. Lorde, personal interview.

24. Lorde, *Zami*, 169–70.

25. Lorde, *Signs*, 716–17.

26. Lorde, personal interview.

27. Lorde, *Signs*, 714.

28. Ibid., 730.

29. Lorde, personal interview.

30. Lorde, "New York City," lines 23–36, *Chosen Poems*, 73–75.

31. Lorde, personal interview. Lorde discusses the Amazons and Seboulisa in *The Black Unicorn*, 119–21. For a discussion of the influence of Pan-Africanism upon black poetry, which places Lorde's work in context, see Stephen Henderson, *Understanding the New Black Poetry* (New York: William Morrow, 1973), 14–16.

32. Lorde, personal interview.

33. Lorde, "125th Street and Abomey," lines 32–33, *The Black Unicorn*, 12.

34. Audre Lorde, *The Cancer Journals* (Argyle, N.Y.: Spinsters, Ink, 1980), 40.

35. Audre Lorde, *A Burst of Light* (Ithaca, N.Y.: Firebrand Books, 1988), 111, 110.

36. Lorde, *Zami*, 7.

37. Lorde, "Poetry Is Not A Luxury," *Sister Outsider* (Trumansburg, N.Y.: 1984), 36–39.

38. Lorde, "Now," lines 1–5, *Chosen Poems*, 88. Lorde also discusses her particular ties to black women, and through them to children and all sympathetic people, in an interview in *Black Women Writers at Work*, ed. Claudia Tate (New York: Continuum, 1983), 104–5.

39. Lorde, "Coal," *Chosen Poems*, 10–11.

40. Lorde, *American Poetry Review*, 20.

41. Lorde, personal interview.

42. Lorde, "Coping," *The Black Unicorn*, 45.

43. Lorde, "Poetry Is Not A Luxury," 37.

44. Lorde, *American Poetry Review*, 20. Lorde also identifies Afro-American literature with an African tradition that teaches that people must live in correspondence with nature's life force in "My Words Will Be There," *Black Women Writers (1950–1980)*, ed. Mari Evans (Garden City, N.Y.: Anchor Press/Doubleday, 1984), 261–68. For a review of African ontology and the tradition of song and poetry that Lorde draws upon, see *The Concept of Négritude in the Poetry of Leopold Sedar Senghor* by Sylvia Washington Ba (Princeton: Princeton University Press, 1973), 44–73.

45. Lorde, personal interview.

46. The quotations in this paragraph are from Lorde's interview in *Signs*, 729.

47. Lorde, "Poetry Is Not A Luxury," 36–39.

48. Audre Lorde, "Uses of the Erotic," *Sister Outsider*, 53–59.

49. Lorde, "Prologue," lines 15–27, *Chosen Poems*, 58.

50. Lorde, *The Cancer Journals*, 17.

51. Lorde, personal interview.

52. Audre Lorde, "On My Way Out I Passed Over You and the Verrazano Bridge," lines 103–16, *Our Dead Behind Us* (New York: W. W. Norton, 1986), 57.

53. Janheinz Jahn, *Muntu* (New York: Grove Press, 1961).

54. Unless otherwise noted, all biographical information in this chapter comes from personal interviews with Marie Ponsot on November 3 and November 28, 1983.

55. Marie Ponsot, "Interview with Marie Ponsot," *Woman Poet: The East* (Reno, Nevada: Women-in-Literature, 1980), 48.

56. Marie Ponsot, "Advice: Ad Haereditates, II," 3.19, *Admit Impediment* (New York: Alfred A. Knopf, 1981), 117.

57. The quotations regarding city and country identities come from Ponsot's poem "Field of Vision," *Admit Impediment*, 106 and 101, respectively.

58. Ponsot, *Woman Poet*, 48.

59. Ponsot, personal interview of November 3, 1983. Ponsot recalls her eventual mastery of sonnets, villanelles, and other "mean" forms in *Woman Poet*, 48.

60. Ponsot, "A Third Thank-You Letter," lines 66–69, *Admit Impediment*, 96. Ponsot discussed the Vert-Galant in the interview of November 28, 1983.

61. Ponsot, "Downtown," *True Minds*, the Pocket Poet Series: Number Five (San Francisco: City Lights Pocket Bookshop, 1956), 25.

62. Ponsot, *Woman Poet*, 49.

63. Marie Ponsot, "Interview with Marie Ponsot," *Dialog* 1 (2) (April 1983):3.

64. Ponsot, "Unabashed," *Admit Impediment*, p. 64.

65. Northrop Frye, "Charms and Riddles," *Spiritus Mundi* (Bloomington: Indiana University Press, 1976), 123–47. Quotations are from p. 126.

66. Ponsot, personal interview of November 3, 1983.

67. Ponsot, *Dialog,* 3.

68. Ibid.

69. Ponsot, personal interview of November 28, 1983.

70. Adrienne Rich, *Of Woman Born* (New York: Norton, 1976), 15.

71. Ponsot, *Dialog,* 4.

72. Ponsot, "Late," *Admit Impediment,* 70–73.

73. Ponsot, "Take Time, Take Place," 3.85–98, *The Green Dark* (New York: Alfred A. Knopf, 1988), 69–70.

74. Ponsot, "Field of Vision," 1.28–31, *Admit Impediment,* 101–2.

75. In this paragraph and the paragraphs that follow, the discussion regarding publishing, silence, and the need for fluid and unconstrained memory come from the interview with Marie Ponsot on November 3, 1983.

76. Ponsot, interview of November 28, 1983.

77. This quotation and Ponsot's following discussion of the usefulness of things as sources for metaphor comes from her interview on November 3, 1983.

78. Ponsot, "Advice: Ad Haereditates, I," lines 1–14, 120–25, *Admit Impediment,* 109, 113.

79. Ponsot, interview of November 3, 1983.

CHAPTER SIX: CHILDHOOD AND NATURE RECONSIDERED

1. M. Bullock, "Animism in Childhood Thinking," *Developmental Psychology* 21 (1985):217–25.

2. William Bronk, "Music That Sees Beyond The World," line 22, *Life Supports* (San Francisco: North Point Press, 1982), 34.

3. Louise Chawla, "The Ecology of Environmental Memory," *Children's Environments Quarterly* 3(4) 1986:34–42; Clare Cooper, "Remembrance of Landscapes Past," *Landscape* 22(3) (1978):35–43; Alvin Lukashok and Kevin Lynch, "Some Childhood Memories of the City," *Journal of the American Institute of Planners* 22(3) (1956):142–52.

4. M. H. Abrams, *Natural Supernaturalism* (New York: W. W. Norton, 1971); Ernst Cassirer, *The Platonic Renaissance in England*, trans. J. P. Pettegrove (New York: Gordian Press, 1970); W. H. Coates, H. V. White, and J. S. Schapiro, *The Emergence of Liberal Humanism* (New York: McGraw-Hill, 1966); Arthur O. Lovejoy, *The Great Chain of Being* (New York: Harper & Row, 1936); Marjorie H. Nicholson, *The Breaking of the Circle* (New York: Columbia University Press, 1960); Stephen Prickett, ed., *The Romantics* (New York: Holmes & Meier, 1981); John H. Randall, Jr., *The Making of the Modern Mind* (New York: Columbia University Press, 1976; rev. ed.).

5. The quotations in this paragraph come from Abrams, *Natural Supernaturalism*, 75 and 268–69, respectively.

6. David Ignatow, *Open Between Us* (Ann Arbor: Michigan University Press, 1980), 91.

7. All quotations of Marie Ponsot on the subject of men's and women's relationship to nature are from interviews with her on November 3 and 28, 1983.

8. Marie Ponsot, "Skambha, Guess-Worker, Both Within and Beyond," lines 18–26, *Thirteenth Moon* 6(1 & 2) (1983): 107. The myth the poem incorporates is adapted from *Hamlet's Mill* by Giorgio De Santillana and Hertha von Dechend (Boston: Gambit, 1969). The interpretation of the poem is Marie Ponsot's own, from her interview on November 28, 1983.

9. All quotations of Audre Lorde regarding men, women, and nature are from a January 5, 1984 interview with her.

10. Bronk, "The Outer Becoming Inner," lines 1–2, *Life Supports*, 53.

11. *The Prelude*, 2.232–44. All quotations from *The Prelude* in this chapter are from the 1850 edition in *The Poetical Works of Wordsworth*, Cambridge edition, ed. Paul D. Sheats (Boston: Houghton Mifflin, 1982).

12. *The Prelude*, 2.245–51.

13. William Wordsworth to Mrs. Clarkson, December 1814, *Letters: The Middle Years*, ed. Ernest de Selincourt, 2 vols. (Oxford: Clarendon Press, 1937), 2:619.

14. Marie Ponsot, "The Great Dead, Why Not, May Know," lines 7–12, *Admit Impediment* (New York: Alfred A. Knopf, 1981), 141.

15. Janheinz Jahn, *Muntu* (New York: Grove Press, 1961); John S. Mbiti, *Introduction to African Religion* (New York: Praeger, 1975). It is interesting that in stressing the beneficence of the dead, Lorde, Mbiti, and Jahn contradict the view of African religion that Freud culled from colonial accounts. In *Totem and Taboo* (New York: W. W. Norton, 1950), Freud

described the African dead as vengeful ghosts, whom he diagnosed to be projections of the living's suppressed hostilities and fears. Lorde and the above scholars find dead and living joined by a common aspiration to see life prosper.

16. *The Prelude*, 14.446–50.

17. Edith Cobb, "The Ecology of Imagination in Childhood," *Daedalus* 88 (1959): 539.

18. Carl G. Jung, "The Psychological Aspects of the Kore." In *Essays on a Science of Mythology*, ed. C. G. Jung and C. Kerenyi, trans. R. F. C. Hull, Bollingen Series 22 (Princeton: Princeton University Press, rev. ed., 1969), 162. The Eleusinian mysteries are described by Carl Kerenyi in *Eleusis*, trans. R. Manheim, Bollingen Series 65 (New York: Pantheon Books, 1967). This sense of memory has also been identified by Stephanie A. Demetrakopoulos, "The Metaphysics of Matrilinearism in Women's Autobiography," *Women's Autobiography*, ed. Estelle Jelinek (Bloomington: Indiana University Press, 1980).

19. Jung, "Psychological Aspects of the Kore," 162–63. For an examination of how Jungian psychology both affirms and subverts women's experience, see Demaris Wehr, *Jung and Feminism* (Boston: Beacon Press, 1987).

20. That women record more memories is reported by Ulric Neisser, "Memory: What are the Important Questions?," in *Memory Observed*, ed. U. Neisser (San Francisco: W. H. Freeman, 1982). The finding that they rate childhood memories higher is reported by Douglas Herrmann and Ulric Neisser, "An Inventory of Everyday Memory Experiences," *Practical Aspects of Memory* (London: Academic Press, 1978), 35–51.

21. Harvey Peskin and Norman Livson, "Uses of the Past in Adult Psychological Health," *Present and Past in Middle Life*, ed. D. H. Eichorn et al. (New York: Academic Press, 1981), 153–81. Their suggestion that the approach of old age signals a life review draws upon the theory of Erik Erikson in *Life History and the Historical Moment* (New York: W. W. Norton, 1975).

22. David Ignatow, "From the Notebooks (1972–1974)," *Ironwood 21* (1983), 98.

23. David Ignatow, personal interview, April 11, 1983.

24. Ibid.

25. David Ignatow, "Invocation," lines 3, 8–10, *Facing the Tree* (Boston: Little Brown, 1975), 17.

26. Nancy Chodorow, *The Reproduction of Mothering* (Berkeley: University of California Press, 1978); Dorothy Dinnerstein, *The Mermaid and the Minotaur* (New York: Harper & Row, 1977); Jane Flax, "The conflict

between nurturance and autonomy in mother-daughter relationships and within feminism," *Feminist Studies*, 4 (1978):171–89.

27. Catherine Keller, *From a Broken Web* (Boston: Beacon Press, 1986).

28. This term is taken from the essay "Child-watching" by Ann Fosnocht Miller, *Bryn Mawr Alumnae Bulletin* (Fall 1988): 9–10. Miller begins the essay with an episode of pulling up to a stop sign on a winter afternoon, to be riveted by the sight of a young woman watching preschoolers playing in the snow. The sight set off a chain reaction of memories as she recalls herself watching her own children discover snow, and herself as a child in it.

29. The phrase "redoing time" appears in the essay "Stillness Within" by Celia Coates Slocombe, in a special issue on time and relationships between the generations, *Bryn Mawr Alumnae Bulletin* (Fall 1988):20.

30. Ponsot, "Sois Sage O Ma Douleur," lines 24–30, *Admit Impediment*, 31–32.

31. Katherine Nelson, "The Ontogeny of Memory for Real Events," *Remembering Reconsidered*, ed. U. Neisser and E. Winograd (New York: Cambridge University Press, 1988).

32. Sara Ruddick, *Maternal Thinking* (Boston: Beacon Press, 1989).

33. Louise Chawla, "Kentucky Conservationists," 1989; "Childhood in Kentucky," 1991: oral history collections, Special Collections, University of Kentucky, Lexington.

CHAPTER SEVEN: A RECOLLECTIVE PSYCHOLOGY

1. Ulric Neisser, "Memory: What Are the Important Questions?," *Practical Aspects of Memory*, ed. M. M. Gruneberg, P. E. Morris, and R. N. Sykes (London: Academic Press, 1978), 12.

2. B. F. Skinner, *Particulars of My Life* (New York: New York Universities Press, 1985).

3. For a review of the implications of object relations theory for environmental feeling, see Louise Chawla, "Childhood Place Attachments," *Place Attachment*, ed. Irwin Altman and Setha Low (New York: Plenum Press, 1992), 63–86.

4. William Wordsworth, *The Prelude*, 2.392–94, 1850 edition, *The Poetical Works of Wordsworth*, Cambridge edition, ed. Paul D. Sheats (Boston: Houghton Mifflin, 1982).

5. Ibid., 2.419–25.

6. Edmund Husserl, *Ideas*, trans. W. R. Boyce Gibson (New York: Collier Books, 1962); *The Crisis of European Sciences and Transcendental Phenomenology*, trans. David Carr (Evanston, Ill.: Northwestern University Press, 1970), part 3–A.

7. Hannah Arendt, *Thinking* (New York: Harcourt Brace Jovanovich, 1978). Aristotle describes contemplation as the fulfillment of human beings' highest potential in the *Nicomachean Ethics*, Book 10, and *Politics*, Book 7.

8. Jonathan Bate, *Romantic Ecology* (London: Routledge, 1991).

9. Ian G. Barbour, *Western Man and Environmental Ethics* (Menlo Park, Calif.: Addison-Wesley, 1973); Morris Berman, *The Reenchantment of the World* (Ithaca: Cornell University Press, 1981); Elizabeth Dodson Gray, *Green Paradise Lost* (Wellesley, Mass.: Roundtable Press, 1981); William Leiss, *The Domination of Nature* (Boston: Beacon Press, 1974); Theodore Roszak, *Person/Planet* (Garden City, N.Y.: Anchor Press/Doubleday,1978).

10. Richard Brandt, *The Philosophy of Schleiermacher* (New York: Greenwood Press, 1968); Friedrich Schleiermacher, "Academy Addresses, 1829," *Hermeneutical Inquiry*, vol. 1, *The Interpretation of Texts*, ed. David E. Klemm (Atlanta: Scholars Press, 1986), 61–88.

11. Richard Popkin, *The History of Skepticism from Erasmus to Darwin* (Assen, Netherlands: Van Gorcum, 1960).

12. Hans-Georg Gadamer, *Truth and Method* (New York: Seabury Press, 1975).

13. Biographical information on Gebser is taken from Jean Keckeis, "In Memoriam Jean Gebser," in Jean Gebser, *The Ever-Present Origin*, trans. Noel Barstad with Algis Mickunas (Athens: Ohio University Press, 1985), xviii-xxii; and from Georg Feuerstein, *Structures of Consciousness* (Lower Lake, Calif.: Integral Publishing, 1987), 21–34.

14. J. Baird Callicott, "Intrinsic Value, Quantum Theory, and Environmental Ethics," *In Defense of the Land Ethic* (New York: State University of New York Press, 1989), 157–74.

15. Ilya Prigogine and Isabelle Stengers, *Order Out of Chaos* (Toronto: Bantam Books, 1984).

16. Gregory Bateson, *Mind and Nature* (New York: Bantam Books, 1988); Rupert Sheldrake, *The Presence of the Past* (New York: Times Books/Random House, 1988). A collection that summarizes the constructive postmodern position in different disciplines is *The Reenchantment of Science*, ed. David Ray Griffin (Albany: State University of New York Press, 1988).

17. Alfred North Whitehead, *Process and Reality*. Corrected edition edited by David Ray Griffin and Donald W. Sherburne (New York: Free Press, 1978).

18. Kenneth Olwig, "Designs Upon Children's Special Places?," *Children's Environments Quarterly* 7(4) (1990):47–53; *Sexual Cosmology*, Working Paper No. 5, Humanities Research Center, Odense University, 1992.

19. Gareth Matthews, "Conceiving Childhood: Childhood Animism," *Nous* 14: (1982):29–37.

20. Gebser, *The Ever-Present Origin*, xxvii.

21. Edith Cobb, "The Ecology of Imagination in Childhood," *Daedalus* 88 (1959):539.

22. Jean Gebser, *Anxiety: A Condition of Modern Man*, trans. Peter Heller (New York: Dell, 1962), 9.

23. Ibid., 11.

24. Keckeis, "In Memoriam Jean Gebser," *The Ever-Present Origin*, xviii.

25. Gebser, *The Ever-Present Origin*, 51.

26. Hesiod, "Theogony," *The Homeric Hymns and Homerica*, trans. H. G. Evelyn-White, Loeb Classical Library (Cambridge: Harvard University Press, 1967), 81. Also see chapter 1 of this book.

27. Henry C. Ellis, *Fundamentals of Human Learning, Memory, and Cognition* (Dubuque: William C. Brown, 1978), 5.

28. Barrett Mandel, "Full of Life Now," *Autobiography*, ed. James Olney (Princeton: Princeton University Press, 1980), 240.

29. Georg Feuerstein discusses historical and developmental parallels to Gebser's categories of consciousness in *Structures of Consciousness* (Lower Lake, Calif.: Integral Publishing, 1987).

30. Extemporaneous speech by Goethe, reported in Ernest Schachtel, *Metamorphosis* (New York: Basic Books, 1959), 281.

31. Gebser, *The Ever-Present Origin*, 289.

32. William Carlos Williams, *Paterson*, Books 1–5 (New York: New Directions, 1963), 96.

33. Giuseppe Ungaretti, *Innocence et Mémoire*, trans. P. Jacottet (Paris: Gallimard, 1969), 316. English translation by this author.

34. Elizabeth Sewell, *The Human Metaphor* (Notre Dame: University of Notre Dame Press, 1964).

35. Herman Daly and John Cobb, Jr., *For the Common Good* (Boston: Beacon Press, 1989).

36. John Keats to George and Thomas Keats, 21 December 1817, *Letters*, ed. M. B. Forman (London: Oxford University press, 1952), 71.

37. Rainier Maria Rilke, quoted in Denise Levertov, *Light Up the Cave* (New York: New Directions, 1981), 287.

38. Evelyn Fox Keller, *Reflections on Gender and Science* (New Haven: Yale University Press, 1985).

39. Martin L. Hoffman, "Empathy, Role-taking, Guilt, and the Development of Altruistic Motives," *Moral Development and Behavior*, ed. Thomas Lickona (New York: Holt, Rinehart, & Winston, 1976). For further elaboration of the suggestion that Hoffman's theory can be extended to explain sympathy for nonhuman things, see Roger Hart and Louise Chawla, "The Roots of Environmental Concern," *People Needs/Planet Management: Paths to Coexistence*, ed. D. Lawrence, R. Habe, A. Hacker, and D. Sherrod (Washington, D.C.: Environmental Design Research Association, 1988).

40. Keller, *Reflections on Gender and Science*; Carolyn Merchant, *The Death of Nature* (San Francisco: Harper & Row, 1980).

41. David Seamon, ed., *Dwelling, Seeing, and Designing* (New York: State University of New York Press, 1993), 16.

42. Hans-Georg Gadamer, *Reason in the Age of Science*, trans. F. G. Lawrence (Cambridge: M.I.T. Press, 1982).

43. "Nicomachean Ethics," Book 6, *The Basic Works of Aristotle*, ed. Richard McKeon (New York: Random House, 1941). For a discussion of the prerequisites for practice in Aristotle's and Gadamer's sense, see Richard Bernstein, "From Hermeneutics to Praxis," *Hermeneutics and Praxis*, ed. Robert Hollinger (Notre Dame: University of Notre Dame Press, 1985), 272–96.

EPILOGUE

1. Martin Heidegger, *On the Way to Language*, trans. by Peter Hartz [except for "Words," trans. by Joan Stambaugh] (New York: Harper & Row, 1971).

2. *The Living Webster Encyclopedic Dictionary*, 1975, 329.

3. Paul Shepard, *Environ / Mental* (Boston: Houghton Mifflin, 1971).

4. *Encyclopedic Dictionary*, 771.

5. This summary is based on Erich Neumann's retelling of Apuleius's story in *Amor and Psyche* (New York: Bollingen Library, Harper & Row, 1956), 3–53.

6. Pierre Grimal, "Greece: Myth and Logic," *Larousse World Mythology* (London: Paul Hamlyn, 1965), 173–75. Historic and psychoanalytic parallels to the legend of Eros and Psyche are explored by the Jungian psychoanalyst Marie-Louise von Franz, *An Interpretation of Apuleius' Golden Ass* (Irving, Tex.: Spring Publications, 1980).

7. James A. Murray, ed., *A New English Dictionary on Historical Principles* (Oxford: Clarendon Press, 1888), 7:1549–50.

8. William Wordsworth, "The Recluse," *The Poetical Works of Wordsworth*, Cambridge edition, revised Paul D. Sheats (Boston: Houghton Mifflin, 1982).

Index

Abrams, M. H., 45, 147

African philosophy, 118–21, 126, 152–53, 159, 185

Anamnesis, 35–36, 45

Anima mundi, 26, 35, 198

Animism, 3, 25–26, 49, 121, 145, 158

Apuleius, 196–97

Arendt, H., 172

Aristotle, 172, 192

Ashbery, J., 95

Augustine, Saint, 36–38, 60

Autobiography, 46, 49, 146; Bronk on, 55–56, 58, 63, 83, 134; and environmental memory, viii–x; Ignatow on, 86–87, 105, 148; reviewed by Cobb, ix, 21–22; Weinfield on, 69, 76, 83, 134; Wordsworth on, 86–87, 105

B

Bartlett, F., 11

Bate, J., 173

Bateson, G., 176

Behaviorism, 170–71

Blake, W., 46

Bloom, H., 71

Bonaventure, Saint, 36–37

Bradstreet, A., 47–48, 53–54

Brentano, F., 16

Bronk, W., 4–5, 70, 85–87, 171; on autobiography, 55–56, 58, 63, 83, 134; on childhood, 52, 61–62, 161; on death, 157; early background, 52–53, 56, 62–63; on desire, 56–57, 199; on imagination, 65; on language, 55, 58, 82; on memory, 61–62, 148, 184; on nature, 51–54, 57, 59, 62, 64–66, 147–48, 150–51, 157, 167, 188; on poetry, 59, 63–65, 82–83, 161; on place, 55; on reason, 54, 58; on the sacred, 60–61; on the self, 58–60, 63, 65; on time, 55, 58; on Transcendentalism, 52–53, 66

C

Callicott, J. B., 176

Catholicism, 126, 131, 140, 159

Childhood: concept of, 33–34, 145, 172; in Christianity, 22, 33–35, 38; in empiricist science, 23–24, 27–28, 41, 169–71; and language, 14–15, 79–80; and nature, 20, 41, 49–50, 145–46, 163–65, 167, 171, 175, 177–78, 191, 197

Childhood memory, 164; in empiricist psychology, 169–71; of men, 6, 11, 155–56, 161–62, 165; and nature, vii–x, 19, 22, 145–46, 174, 177–78, 185, 195; in poetry, x–xi, 21, 33–50; in psychoanalytic theory, 28–33, 169–71; of women, 6, 11, 106, 155–56, 159, 161–65. *See also* Metaphysical poetry, Roman-